Lecture Notes in Artificial Intelligence 3275

Edited by J. G. Carbonell and J. Siekmann

Subseries of Lecture Notes in Computer Science

Petra Perner (Ed.)

Advances in Data Mining

Applications in Image Mining, Medicine and
Biotechnology, Management and Environmental
Control, and Telecommunications

4th Industrial Conference on Data Mining, ICDM 2004
Leipzig, Germany, July 4-7, 2004
Revised Selected Papers

 Springer

Series Editors

Jaime G. Carbonell, Carnegie Mellon University, Pittsburgh, PA, USA
Jörg Siekmann, University of Saarland, Saarbrücken, Germany

Volume Editor

Petra Perner
Institute of Computer Vision and Applied Computer Sciences
Körnerstr. 10, 04107 Leipzig, Germany
E-mail: ibaiperner@aol.com

Library of Congress Control Number: 2004116339

CR Subject Classification (1998): I.2.6, I.2, H.2.8, K.4.4, J.3, I.4, J.6, J.1

ISSN 0302-9743
ISBN 3-540-24054-3 Springer Berlin Heidelberg New York

Springer is a part of Springer Science+Business Media

springeronline.com

© Springer-Verlag Berlin Heidelberg 2004
Printed in Germany

Typesetting: Camera-ready by author, data conversion by Scientific Publishing Services, Chennai, India
Printed on acid-free paper   SPIN: 11365860   06/3142   5 4 3 2 1 0

Preface

The Industrial Conference on Data Mining ICDM-Leipzig was the fourth meeting in a series of annual events which started in 2000, organized by the Institute of Computer Vision and Applied Computer Sciences (IBaI) in Leipzig.

The mission of the conference is to bring together researchers and people from industry in order to discuss together new trends and applications in data mining. This year a broad spectrum of work of different applications was presented ranging from image mining, medicine and biotechnology, management and environmental control, to telecommunications. Besides that an industrial exhibition showed the successful application of data mining methods by industries in different areas such as medical devices, mass data management systems, data mining tools, etc.

During the discussion many projects were inspired leading to new and joint work. The fruitful discussions, the exchange of ideas and the spirit of the conference made it a remarkable event for both sides, industry and research.

We would like to express our appreciation to the reviewers for their precise and highly professional work. We appreciate the help and understanding of the editorial staff at Springer and in particular Alfred Hofmann, who supported the publication of these proceedings in the LNAI series.

Last, but not least, we wish to thank all speakers, participants and industrial exhibitors who contributed to the success of the conference.

We are looking forward to welcoming you to ICDM 2005 (www.data-mining-forum.de) and to the new work you will present there.

July 2004   Petra Perner

**Industrial Conference
on Data Mining 2004**

04. 07. - 05. 07. 2004
Leipzig/Germany

Program Committee

Co-Chairs:

P. Perner   Germany
A. Ahlemeyer   Germany
Stubbe

Committee

K.-D. Althoff   Germany
C. Apte   USA
P. Cunningham   Irland
D. Deng   New Zealand
R. S. Kenett   Israel
E. Pauwels   Netherlands

4th Industrial Conference on Data Mining ICDM´2004

The Aim of the Conference

This conference is the fourth conference in a series of industrial conferences on Data Mining that will be held on yearly basis. Experts from different fields will present their applications and the results obtained by applying data mining. Besides that, newcomers in the field can get a fast introduction to Data Mining by taking the tutorial running in connection with the conference. In a problem/solution hour you will have the opportunity to present your application and ask for support by others or for cooperation in solving the problem.

Paper submission

Paper submissions should be related but not limited to any of the following topics: Applications of Data Mining in ...

- Marketing
- Medicine
- E-Commerce
- Biotechnology
- Quality Management
- Knowledge extraction from text, video, signals and images.

Potentials speakers should submit an abstract of their talk (not more than 2 pages long) to the e-mail address: ibai@aol.com at the:

> **Institut für Bildverarbeitung
> und angewandte Informatik**
> Koernerstraße 10
> 04107 Leipzig/Germany
>
> Telephone: +49 (0) 341 86 12 273
> FAX: +49 (0) 341 86 12 275
> Homepage: www.ibai-institut.de

For the latest news as well as for the program of the previous ICDM and the publications within ICDM look at:

> http://www.data-mining-forum.de

The abstracts will be reviewed by the program committee. The abstract of accepted talks will be published in a special edition of an international journal by Springer Verlag. Extended versions of selected papers will be published after the workshop.

Former proceedings from ICDM have been published by Springer Verlag in Advances in Data Mining, P. Perner (Ed.).

Table of Contents

Case-Based Reasoning

Neuro-symbolic System for Business Internal Control
  Juan M. Corchado, M. Lourdes Borrajo, María A. Pellicer,
  J. Carlos Yáñez.. 1

Applying Case Based Reasoning Approach in Analyzing Organization
Change Management Data
  Orit Raphaeli, Jacob Zahavi, Ron Kenett............................... 11

Improving the K-NN Classification with the Euclidean Distance Through
Linear Data Transformations
  Leon Bobrowski, Magdalena Topczewska............................... 23

An IBR System to Quantify the Ocean's Carbon Dioxide Budget
  Juan M. Corchado, Emilio S. Corchado, Jim Aiken.................... 33

A Beta-Cooperative CBR System for Constructing a Business
Management Model
  Emilio S. Corchado, Juan M. Corchado, Lourdes Sáiz, Ana Lara.............. 42

Image Mining

Braving the Semantic Gap: Mapping Visual Concepts from Images and Videos
  Da Deng.. 50

Mining Images to Find General Forms of Biological Objects
  Petra Perner, Horst Perner, Angela Bühring, Silke Jänichen.................... 60

Applications in Process Control and Insurance

The Main Steps to Data Quality
  Joachim Schmid.. 69

Cost-Sensitive Design of Claim Fraud Screens
  Stijn Viaene, Dirk Van Gheel, Mercedes Ayuso, Montserrat Guillén........... 78

An Early Warning System for Vehicle Related Quality Data
  Matthias Grabert, Markus Prechtel, Tomas Hrycej, Winfried Günther......... 88

Clustering and Association Rules

Shape-Invariant Cluster Validity Indices
  Greet Frederix, Eric J. Pauwels.. 96

Mining Indirect Association Rules
  Shinichi Hamano, Masako Sato.. 106

An Association Mining Method for Time Series and Its Application in the
Stock Prices of TFT-LCD Industry
  Chiung-Fen Huang, Yen-Chu Chen, An-Pin Chen................................ 117

Clustering of Web Sessions Using Levenstein Metric
  Andrei Scherbina, Sergey Kuznetsov.. 127

Telecommunication

A Data Mining Approach for Call Admission Control and Resource
Reservation in Wireless Mobile Networks
  Sherif Rashad, Mehmed Kantardzic, Anup Kumar............................... 134

Mining of an Alarm Log to Improve the Discovery of Frequent Patterns
  Françoise Fessant, Fabrice Clérot, Christophe Dousson...................... 144

Medicine and Biotechnology

Feature Selection and Classification Model Construction on Type 2
Diabetic Patient's Data
  Yue Huang, Paul McCullagh, Norman Black, Roy Harper.................... 153

Knowledge Based Phylogenetic Classification Mining
  Isabelle Bichindaritz, Stephen Potter, Société Française de Systématique.... 163

Author Index... 173

Neuro-symbolic System for Business Internal Control

Juan M. Corchado[1], M. Lourdes Borrajo[2], María A. Pellicer[1], and J. Carlos Yáñez[3]

[1] Deparatamento de Informática y Automática,
University of Salamanca, Plaza de la Merced s/n, 37008 Salamanca, Spain
corchado@usal.es
[2] Department of Computer Science,
University of Vigo, Campus As Lagoas, s/n, 32004 Ourense, Spain
[3] Department of Financial Accounting,
University of Vigo, Campus As Lagoas, s/n, 32004 Ourense, Spain
{lborrajo, jcyanez}@uvigo.es

Abstract. The complexity of current organization systems, and the increase in importance of the realization of internal controls in firms, make it necessary to construct models that automate and facilitate the work of auditors. An intelligent system has been developed to automate the internal control process. This system is composed of two case-based reasoning systems. The objective of the system is to facilitate the process of internal auditing in small and medium firms from the textile sector. The system, analyses the data that characterises each one of the activities carried out by the firm, then determines the state of each activity, calculates the associated risk, detects the erroneous processes, and generates recommendations to improve these processes. As such, the system is a useful tool for the internal auditor in order to make decisions based on the risk generated. Each one of the case-based reasoning systems that integrates the system uses a different problem solving method in each of the steps of the reasoning cycle: fuzzy clustering during the retrieval phase, a radial basis function network and a multi-criterion discreet method during the reuse phase and a rule based system for recommendation generation. The system has been proven successfully in several small and medium companies in the textile sector, located in the northwest of Spain. The accuracy of the technologies employed in the system has been demonstrated by the results obtained over the last two years.

1 Introduction

Nowadays, organization systems employed in enterprises are increasing in complexity. Moreover, in recent years, the number of regulatory norms has increased considerably. As a consequence of this, the need has arisen for periodic internal audits. But the evaluation and the prediction of the evolution of these types of systems, characterized by their great dynamism, are, in general, complicated. It is necessary to construct models that facilitate analysis work carried out in changing environments, such as finance.

P. Perner (Ed.): ICDM 2004, LNAI 3275, pp. 1–10, 2004.

The processes carried out inside a firm can be included in functional areas [19]. Each one of these areas is denominated a "Function". A Function is a group of coordinated and related activities, which are necessary to reach the objectives of the firm and are carried out in a systematic and reiterated way [11]. Functions are divided into activities, which are associated to well defined objectives. The functions that are usually carried out within a firm are: Purchases, Cash Management, Sales, Information Technology, Fixed Assets Management, Compliance to Legal Norms and Human Resources.

In turn, each one of these functions is broken down into a series of activities. For example, the function Information Technology is divided in the following areas: Computer Plan Development, Study of Systems, Installation of Systems, Treatment of Information Flows and Security Management.

Each activity is composed of a number of tasks, for example: register, authorise, approve, harmonise, separate obligations, operate, etc. Control procedures are established in the tasks to assure that the established objectives are achieved. Rule-based systems (RBS) have traditionally been used with the purpose of delimiting the audit decision-making tasks [6]. However, Messier and Hansen [13] found many situations in which auditors resolved problems by referring to previous situations. This contrasts with the very nature of RBS systems, since they have very little capacity for extracting information from past experience and present problems in order to adapt to changes in the environment.

In contrast, case based reasoning systems (CBR) are able to relate past experiences or cases to current observations, solving new problems through the memorization and adaptation of previously tested solutions. This is an effective way of learning, similar to the general structure of human thought. CBR systems are especially suitable when the rules that define a knowledge system are difficult to obtain, or the number and complexity of the rules is too large to create an expert system. Moreover, CBR systems have the capacity to update their memory dynamically, based on new information (new cases), as well as, improving the resolution of problems [14].

However, in problems like those presented in this study, standard techniques of monitoring and prediction cannot be applied due to the complexity of the problem, the existence of certain preliminary knowledge, the great dynamism of the system, etc. In these types of systems it is necessary to use models that combine the advantages of several mechanisms of problem-solving capable to of resolving specific parts of the general problem and attending other parts.

In this sense, an adaptive system has been developed. The system possesses the flexibility to behave in different ways and to evolve, depending on the environment in which it operates. The developed system is composed of two fundamental subsystems:

- Subsystem IEA (Identification of the State of the Activity) whose objectives are:
    1. to identify the state or situation of each one of activities of the company.
    2. to calculate the risk associated with this state.
- Subsystem GR (Generation of Recommendations), whose goal is:
    1. generation of recommendations from the detection of inconsistent processes. These recommendations will allow the positive evolution of the internal processes of the company.

Both subsystems are implemented with the use of two CBR systems (one for each subsystem). Each one of the CBR systems is used as a basis for the integration of symbolic and connectionist models, used in different steps of the reasoning cycle.

The rest of this article is structured as follows: firstly, to explain the concept of internal control (IC) and describe its importance within the modern company; secondly, the basic concepts that characterize case based reasoning are presented, an explanation given of how the system has been constructed; finally, the initial results will be presented.

2 Internal Control

Small to medium enterprises require an internal control mechanism in order to monitor their modus operandi and to analyse whether they are achieving their goals. Such mechanisms are constructed around a series of organizational policies and specific procedures dedicated to giving reasonable guarantees to their executive bodies. This group of policies and procedures are named "controls", and they all conform to the structure of internal control of the company. The establishment of objectives (which is not a function of the Internal Control) is a previous condition for control risk evaluation, which is the main goal of the Internal Control.

In a wide sense, the administration of a firm has three large categories of objectives when designing a structure for internal control [2]:

1. Reliability of financial information.
2. Efficiency and effectiveness of operations.
3. Fulfillment of the applicable rules and regulations.

The internal auditor must monitor the internal controls directly and recommend improvements on them. Therefore, all the activities carried out inside the organization can be included, potentially, within the internal auditors' remit. Essentially, the activities of the auditor related to IC can be summarised as follows:

- To be familiar with and possess the appropriate documentation related to the different components of the system that could affect financial aspects.
- To assess the quality of internal controls in order to facilitate the planning of the audit process with the aim of obtaining necessary indicators.
- To assess internal controls in order to estimate the level of error and reach a decision on the final opinion to be issued in the memorandum on the system under consideration.

As a consequence of the great changes in firms brought about by current technological advances, considerable modifications have taken place in the area of auditing, basically characterized by the following features [16]:

- Progressive increase in the number and level of complexity of audit rules and procedures.
- Changes in the norms of professional ethics, which demand greater control and quality in auditing.

- Greater competitiveness between auditing firms, consequently resulting in lower fees; the offer of new services to clients (e.g. financial or computing assessment...).
- Development of new types of auditing (e.g. operative management auditing, computer auditing, environmental auditing...).

Together, these circumstances have made the audit profession increasingly competitive. Consequently, the need has arisen for new techniques and tools, which can be provided by information technology and artificial intelligence. The aim is to achieve more relevant, more suitable information, in order to help auditors make decisions faster and thereby increase the efficiency and quality of auditing.

3 Case Based Reasoning Systems: An Overview

A case based reasoning system (CBR) solves a given problem by means of the adaptation of previous solutions to similar problems [1]. The CBR memory stores a certain number of cases. A case includes a problem and the solution to this problem. The solution of a new problem is obtained recovering similar cases stored in the CBR memory.

A CBR is a dynamic system in which new problems are added continuously to its memory, the similar problems are eliminated and gradually new ones are created by combination of other several existent ones. This methodology is based on the fact that human use the knowledge learned in previous experiences to solve present problems.

CBR systems record past problem solving experiences and, by means of indexing algorithms, retrieve previously stored problems with their solutions (cases), and match and adapt them to a given situation. This means that the set of cases stored in the memory of CBR systems represents the knowledge concerning the domain of the CBR. As discussed below, this knowledge is updated constantly.

A typical CBR system is composed of four sequential steps which are recalled every time a problem needs to be solved [9, 1, 17]:

1. *Retrieve* the most relevant case(s).
2. *Reuse* the case(s) in order to solve the problem.
3. *Revise* the proposed solution if necessary.
4. *Retain* the new solution as a part of a new case.

Like other mechanisms of problem solving, the objective of a CBR is to find the solution for a certain problem. A CBR is a system of incremental learning, because each time a problem is solved, a new experience is retained, thereby making it available for future reuse.

CBR systems have proven to be an effective method for problem solving in multiple domains, for example, prediction, diagnosis, control and planning [10]. This technology has been successfully used in several disciplines: law, medicine, diagnosis systems etc. [17].

The case based reasoning can be used by itself, or as part of another conventional or intelligent system [12]. Although there are many successful applications based on CBR methods alone, CBR systems can be improved by combining them with other technologies [8]. Their suitability to integration with other technologies, creating a global hybrid reasoning system, stems from the fact that CBR systems are very flexible algorithms, capable of absorbing the beneficial properties of other technologies.

4 Hybrid Neuro-symbolic System for Internal Control

This section describes the intelligent system in detail. The objective of the system is to facilitate the internal control process in small to medium sized enterprises. After analyzing the data relative to each activity that is developed within the firm, this system determines the state of each activity and calculates the associated risk. It also detects any erroneous processes and generates recommendations for improving these processes.

In this way, the system helps the internal auditor make decisions based on the risk associated to the current state of each one of the activities in the firm.

The cycle of operations of the developed case based reasoning system is based on the classic life cycle of a CBR system [1, 18]. This cycle is executed twice, since the system bases its operation on two CBR subsystems (subsystem IEA-Identification of the State of the Activity and subsystem GR-Generation of Recommendations). Both subsystems share the same case base (Table 1 shows the attributes of a case) and a case represents the "shape" of a given activity developed in the company.

Table 1. Case structure

IDENTIFICATION	DESCRIPCTION
Case number	Unique identification: positive integer number.
Input vector	Information about the tasks (n sub-vectors) that compose an industrial activity: $(GI_1,V_1),(GI_2,V_2),...,(GI_n,V_n))$ for n tasks. Each task sub-vector has the following structure (GI_i,V_i): • GI_i: importance rate for this task inside the activity. Can only take one of the following values: ▪ VHI (Very high importance). ▪ HI (High Importance). ▪ AI (Average Importance) ▪ LI (Low Importance) ▪ VLI (Very low importance) • V_i: Value of the realization state of a given task. Positive integer number (between 1 and 10).
Function number	Unique identification number for each function
Activity number	Unique identification number for each activity
Reliability	Percentage of probability of success. It represents the obtained percentage of success using the case as a reference to generate recommendations.
Degree of membership	$((n_1,\mu_1), (n_2,\mu_2), ..., (n_k,\mu_k))$ • n_i represent the ith cluster • μ_i represent the membership value of the case to the cluster n_i
Activity State	Degree of perfection of the development of the activity, expressed by percentage.

(Rows "Case number" through "Degree of membership" are grouped under PROBLEM; "Activity State" is grouped under SOLUTION.)

In the subsystem IEA the state or situation of each company activity is predicted, in real time, and the associated risk to this state is calculated, as can be seen in Table 2 and Figure 1. First, the more similar cases of the case base are grouped, using fuzzy clustering [3, 5]. When a new problem case is presented, the cluster to which it belongs is identified, than all k cases from this cluster which present a high degree of ownership to the case problem are retrieved.

The retrieved cases are used in the reuse phase to train an RBF network (Radial Basis Function) [7, 4]. The goal of the network is to build a generic solution from the k retrieved cases. The network determines the company state.

If the internal auditor, in the analyzed company, thinks the initial solution is coherent, the problem, together with his solution (the state of the activity identified by the system) is stored in the case base, as it is a new case, a new piece of knowledge. The addition of a new case to the case base causes the redistribution of the clusters. Also, from this solution, the level of risk inherent to the state of the activity is calculated. The subsystem GR generates the recommendations for improving the state of the analyzed activity, as represented in Figure 1 and Table 3. In order to recommend changes in the execution of the processes in the firm, the subsystem compares the obtained state of the activity to the cases belonging to the cluster used in the initial phase of subsystem IEA, which reflect a better situation for this activity in the firm. Therefore, in the retrieval phase, a selection is made of those cases whose solution or state of activity is higher (in an interval between 15% and 20%) than the

Table 2. Summary of technologies employed in the IEA subsystem

CBR's Phases	Technology	Input	Output
Retrieve	Fuzzy Clustering	Problem case	K similar cases
Reuse	RBF network	Problem case K similar cases	Initial solution: state of the activity
Revise	RBS	Problem case Initial solution: state of the activity	Revised solution: state of the activity level of risk inherent to the state of the activity
Retain	RBF network	Problem case Final solution	New Case

Table 3. Summary of technologies employed in the GR subsystem

CBR's Phases	Technology	Input	Output
Retrieve	Fuzzy Clustering	Problem case	K similar cases
Reuse	method ELECTRE	K similar cases	Most favourable case(s)
Retain	Manual	Most favourable case(s) (used to generate recommendations)	Modified case(s)

solution generated as output in the subsystem IEA. In the reuse phase, the multicriteria decision-making method Electre [15] is used to obtain the most favorable case of all, depending on the degree of relevance of the tasks.

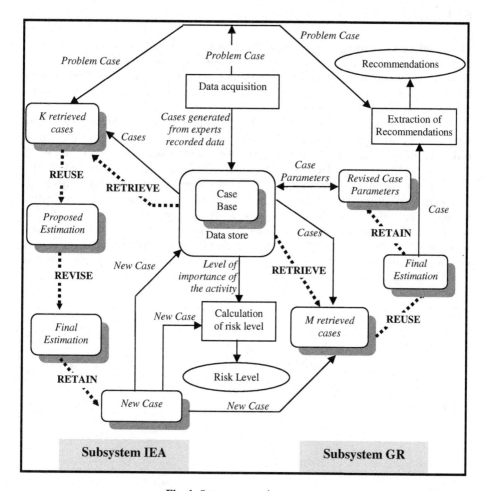

Fig. 1. System reasoning process

The selected case is compared with the initial case problem, using a simple rule based system to determine the order in which the recommendation should be taken to minimize or eliminate the erroneous processes.

This is a decision support system that facilitates the auditing process for internal auditors. After the time necessary for correcting the errors detected, the firm is evaluated again. Auditing experts consider that three months are enough to evolve the company towards a more favourable state. If it is verified that the erroneous processes and the level of risk have diminished, the retention phase is carried out, modifying the case used to generate the recommendations. The reliability (percentage of successful identifications obtained with this case) of this case is thereby increased. In contrast, when the firm happens not to have evolved to a better state, the reliability of the case is decreased.

5 Results

The developed hybrid system has been tested in several small to medium companies in the textile sector, located in the northwest of Spain. Previously, surveys were carried out by auditors and experts in different functional areas of the firms within the sector. These surveys have provided the necessary prototype cases in order to construct the case bases of the system.

Results obtained demonstrate that the application of the recommendations generated by the system causes a positive evolution in firms. This evolution is reflected in the reduction of erroneous processes. The system has been tested in 22 companies (12 medium-sized and 10 small). The best results occurred in the companies of a smaller size. Figure 2 presents a graphical representation of the companies evolution. This is due to the fact that these firms have a greater facility to adapt and adopt the changes suggested by the system's recommendations., because of their smallest size. 15 of them evolved successfully, 5 of them did not improve their results and 2 of them reduced their business. These results demonstrate the suitability of the techniques used for their integration in the developed intelligent control system.

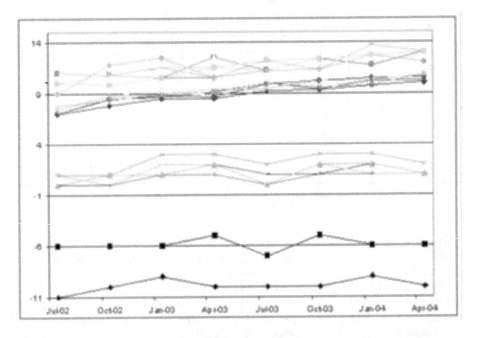

Fig. 2. Firms' evolution

6 Conclusions

This article presents a neuro-symbolic system that uses two CBR systems employed as a basis for hybridization of a multicriteria decision-making method, a fuzzy clustering method, and an RBF net. Therefore, the developed model combines the complementary properties of the connectionist methods with the symbolic methods of Artificial Intelligence.

The used reasoning model can be applied in situations that satisfy the following conditions:

1. Each problem can be represented in the form of a vector of quantified values.
2. The case base should be representative of the totality of the spectrum of the problem.
3. Cases must be updated periodically.
4. Enough cases should exist to train the net.

The system is able to estimate or identify the state of the activities of the firm and their associated risk. Furthermore the system generates recommendations that will guide the internal auditor in the elaboration of action plans to improve the processes in the firm.

The estimation in the environment of firms is difficult due to the complexity of the environment from where the prediction should be obtained and the great dynamism of this environment. However, the developed model is able to produce a prediction with enough precision, and within the limitations of time, imposed by the nature of the problem.

Nevertheless, the system will produce better results with data from firms belonging to the same sector. This is due to the dependence that exists between the processes in the firms and the sector where the company is located.

Although we haven't had the opportunity to test these techniques in big firms, we think that they would be satisfactorily applicable, although changes would take place more slowly than in small and medium firms.

References

1. Aamodt A. and Plaza E. (1994). Case-Based Reasoning: foundational Issues, Methodological Variations, and System Approaches. AICOM. Vol. 7. N° 1, Marzo 1994.
2. American Institute of Certified Public Accountants (AICPA), Statements on Auditing Standards No. 78 (SAS No. 78) (1996). Consideraciones de la Estructura del Control Interno en una Auditoría de Estados Financieros. (Amendment to SAS núm. 55), The Auditing Standards Executive Committee, New York.
3. Bezdek J. C. (1981). Pattern Recognition with Fuzzy Objective Function Algorithms. Plenum Press, New York.
4. Corchado, J.M., Díaz, F., Borrajo, L. and Fdez-Riverola F. (2000). Redes Neuronales Artificiales: Un enfoque práctico. Departamento de publicaciones de la Universidad de Vigo.
5. Dave, R.N. (1992). Generalized fuzzy C-shells clustering and detection of circular and elliptic boundaries. Pattern Recogn. 25, 713-722.
6. Denna, E.L., Hansen, J.V. and Meservy, R. (1991). Development and application of expert systems in audit services. Transactions on Knowledge and Data Engineering.

7. Fritzke, B. (1994). Fast Learning with Incremental RBF Networks. Neural Processing Letters. Vol. 1. No. 1. pp. 2-5.
8. Hunt, J. and Miles, R. (1994). Hybrid case-based reasoning. The Knowledge Engineering Review. Vol. 9:4. pp. 383-397.
9. Kolodner J. (1993). Case-Based Reasoning. San Mateo. CA, Morgan Kaufmann. 1993.
10. Lenz M., Bartsch-Spörl B., Burkhard D. and Wees S. (eds.) 1998. Case-based Reasoning Technology: From Fundations to Applications, Springer Verlag, LNAI 1400.
11. Mas, J. and Ramió, C. (1997). La Auditoría Operativa en la Práctica. Ed. Marcombo, Barcelona.
12. Medsker L. R. (1995). Hybrid Intelligent Systems. Kluwer Academic Publishers.
13. Messier, W.F. and Hansen, J.V. (1988). Inducing rules for expert systems development: an example using default and bankruptcy data. Management Science, 34, No. 12, December, 1403-15.
14. Riesbeck, C.K. and Schank, R.C. (1989). Inside case-based reasoning. Lawrence Erlbaum Associates. Hillsdale, NJ.
15. Romero, C. (1993) Teoría de la decisión multicriterio: Conceptos, técnicas y aplicaciones. Alianza Editorial. ISBN: 84-206-8144-X
16. Sánchez, A (1995): "Los Sistemas Expertos en la Contabilidad", Biblioteca Electrónica de Contabilidad, Vol. 1, N. 2.
17. Watson I. (1997). Applying Case-Based Reasoning: Techniques for Enterprise Systems. Morgan Kaufmann.
18. Watson, I. and Marir, F. (1994). Case-Based Reasoning: A Review. The Knowledge Engineering Review. Vol. 9. No. 4. pp. 355-381.
19. Yáñez, J.C., Borrajo, L. and Corchado, J.M. (2001). A Case-based Reasoning System for Business Internal Control. Fourth International ICSC Symposium. Soft Computing and Intelligent Systems For Industry. Paisley, Scotland, United Kingdom, June 26-29, 2001.

Applying Case Based Reasoning Approach in Analyzing Organizational Change Management Data

Orit Raphaeli[1], Jacob Zahavi[2], and Ron Kenett[3]

[1] Faculty of Management, Tel-Aviv University & KPA Ltd., Israel
oritishi@inter.net.il
[2] The Wharton School, University of Pennsylvania
zahavi@wharton.upenn.edu
[3] KPA Ltd., Raanana, Israel
ron@kpa.co.il

Abstract. This work is a first step towards the application of a Case Based Reasoning (CBR) model to support the management of Enterprise System Implementation (ESI) related organizational change processes. Those processes are characterized by the occurrences of unplanned problems and events, which may lead to major restructuring of the process. We rely on ESI theory developed by the BEST project. The paper's focus is the matching process within the retrieval phase. We propose a procedure for similarity assessment between current experiences and past experiences. We enhance the applicability of CBR to ESI by encoding domain knowledge, according to BEST approach. The similarity measures are based on nearest-neighbor approach and Tversky's Contrast model. The proposed method assesses the similarity between events, while accounting their context similarity. Plans for future work are outlined.

1 Introduction

Enterprise System (ES) are software packages that offer integrated solutions to companies' information needs [1]. Enterprise Systems like ERP (Enterprise Resource Planning), CRM (Customer Requirement Management), and PDM (Product Data Management) have gained great significance for most companies on an operational as well as a strategic level. An ES implementation (ESI) process, as other system development processes, is a complex and dynamic process that cannot be fixed from the start. The process is characterized by the occurrences of unplanned problems and events [2]. These situations may lead to major restructuring of the process with severe implications to the whole company.

Given the growing significance and high risk of ESI projects, much research has been undertaken to develop better understanding of such processes, in various disciplines. Yet, the literature on ESI, information technology and organizational change management do not give substantial and reliable generalizations about the process dynamics and the relationships between information technology and organizational change.

P. Perner (Ed.): ICDM 2004, LNAI 3275, pp. 11–22, 2004.
© Springer-Verlag Berlin Heidelberg 2004

In order to fill this gap, a European FP5 project, **B**etter **E**nterprise **S**ys**T**em implementation (BEST) was launched in 2002 [7]. The aim of the BEST project is to understand the dynamics of ESI processes, and help improve organization readiness to deal with such issues by acquiring knowledge of process dynamic from existing ESI projects. The BEST project developed a general construct that can be used to capture the knowledge accumulated in existing implementation processes. This includes identification of events that occur within the implementation process, and the mapping of these events in terms of chains called Cause-Event-Action-Outcome (CEAO). Knowledge on what happens in an implementation project is documented using CEAOs and, in that way, the capability of analysts and consultants to identify and act upon unexpected or unintended events and problems is enhanced (see [9],[12]).

In this work we apply quantitative analysis to CEAO chains in order to improve ESI management by combining the ESI theory developed in BEST with a Case Based Reasoning framework.

Case Based Reasoning (CBR) is a problem-solving approach that relies on past similar cases to find solutions to problems [3]. Case-based Reasoning means to use previous experience represented as cases to understand and solve new problems. A case based reasoner remembers former cases to fit for the current problem.

In this paper we focus on the matching process within the retrieval phase and propose a procedure for similarity assessment between current experiences and past experiences. We enhance the applicability of CBR to ESI by encoding domain knowledge into several similarity measures. We propose a method to assess the similarity between events, while accounting their context similarity and outline plans for future research [21].

2   Why Case Based Reasoning to Support Organizational Change Management?

ESI related organizational change is a complex and dynamic process, with high uncertainty accompanied by unexpected problems. These potential events are related to a large number of variables that belong to organizational, human and technological aspects. In addition, the relationship among these variables is unclear. Knowledge acquisition in such an ill structured domain is very complex, so that applying Rule Based models, with problem solving algorithms expressed as rules, is highly unsuitable. In addition, even if the necessary knowledge is elicited, the representation of this knowledge would generate a multitude of rules and modeling all its interactions would be infeasible. Unlike Rule Based models, CBR models deal with case specific knowledge and do not require that the domain knowledge is modeled by rules.

The management of the ESI process is highly dependent on the ability of the people involved in the process (e.g. project manager, ES vendor, consultant, etc) to identify and solve problems. In general the solutions that are given to such problems rely on experiential knowledge and intuitive appreciation rather than on a systematic methodology. The solutions often have qualitative and subjective argumentations and sometimes cannot be characterized as effective or not. ESI experience is difficult to formulate using rules, but easier to be viewed as distinct cases. For these reasons, we find the CBR approach a suitable paradigm for supporting the ESI process management.

3 Case Based Reasoning Background

3.1 CBR Cycle

The CBR principle is based on an analogy to the human task of "mentally searching for similar situations which happened in the past and reusing the experience gained in those situations" [4]. The underlying idea is the assumption that similar problems have similar solutions. Though this assumption is not always true, it holds in many practical domains [5]. CBR works on a set of cases derived from experience and stored in a CEAO data base. When faced with a new specific problem, CBR retrieves a case that is similar to it from a CEAO data base, and if necessary, will adapt it to provide the desired solution [6].

Although the full CBR cycle is a retrieve–evaluate–adapt-learn process, many CBR systems implement only the retrieve step, thus applying the concept of reuse of experience. Retrieval-only CBR is useful when the differences between two cases are complex, and the main request from the system is to visualize current and similar cases, and point out the important differences between them. Such systems are common in the medical domain, e.g. [8].

3.2 The Matching Process in the Retrieval Phase

The measure of success of a CBR system depends on its ability to retrieve the most relevant previous cases to support the handling of a target case, and ignore irrelevant previous cases [6]. The retrieval of more similar cases to a new problem reduces the load of adaptation and leads to more precise solution.

Thus, one of the key issues of CBR is to define how a previous case (a source case) is selected given a current case (a target case). The retrieval step is based on creating a searching mechanism to estimate the similarity between source and target case. The searching mechanism is differentiating between CBR retrieval and a simple database search. CBR retrieval is based mainly on two methods, both can be found in most commercial CBR tools [10]: Inductive methods which use an induction algorithm to produce decision trees that classifies the cases, and similarity classification methods that assess the similarity between cases by aggregation of pair-wise similarity along case's descriptors, using predefined similarity measures [11]. Combinations between the two are common, sometimes accompanied by knowledge-guided approach applies existing domain knowledge to locate relevant cases [17].

"Matching" assesses the degree of similarity of a candidate previous case with a current case. Since the formulation of a similarity function that approximates directly the degree of similarity is usually unattainable, one tries to decompose the problem so that matching involves establishing the similarity of the representation of the current case with the representation of the previous case. The procedure usually employed to define similarity measure is a "bottom up" approach that can be characterized as a "Divide and Conquer" strategy [14]. It assumes an attribute-value based case representation.

Two procedures that have been widely used to determine overall similarity are nearest-neighbor approach and Tversky's contrast model [16]. Both methods assume that objects are represented as collections of attributes, so that similarity becomes an attribute matching process. A comprehensive investigation of similarity indices in the context of comparing frequency distributions of genetic characteristics of various populations is presented in [18]. Statistical properties of such indices can be derived using cross-validation and bootstrapping techniques [25], [26].

Nearest Neighbor Approach

The nearest neighbor technique is a nonparametric classification algorithm in which the similarity is based on matching a weighted sum of attributes between stored cases and the current problem case.

The feature weighting algorithms alleviate the problem of the presence of irrelevant features in the case representation. Usually, the number of attributes and the weighting coefficient of each attribute are invariant for all cases [19]. The overall similarity (SIM) determined by nearest-neighbor matching function is mathematically represented as follows [3]:

$$SIM(T, C_k) = \frac{\sum_{i=1}^{n} w_i \cdot sim(a_i^T, a_i^{C_k})}{\sum_{i=1}^{n} w_i} \qquad (1)$$

where, a_i^T is the ith descriptor of the target case, $a_i^{C_k}$ is the ith descriptor of the kth candidate source case, the superscripts T and C_k refer to the target case and the source case respectively, sim(.) is a function, rule, or heuristic that determines the pair-wise similarity along a descriptor; and w_i is the weight representing degree of importance of the ith descriptor towards the problem.

Tversky's Contrast Model

Tversky's Contrast model is one of the most influential models in the psychology research [20]. The similarity between objects A and B is based on the ratio between their common and distinctive features [16]. Specifically as in [22]:

$$S(A, B) = \frac{|D_i|}{\alpha|D_i| + \beta|E_i| + \gamma|F_i|} \qquad \alpha = 1, \beta, \gamma = 0.5 \qquad (2)$$

with D_i the features that are common to both A and B; E_i the features that belong to A but not to B ; and F_i the features belong to B but not to A.

4 Domain Knowledge – The BEST Approach

This section presents some of the BEST project outcomes [9], which serves as a basis to the knowledge we utilize in the model.

Reference Framework
The reference framework addresses the view of the overall enterprise characteristics and constitutive elements, which influence the implementation of an ES. The framework identifies important technical as well as organizational and human aspects that play a role in several processes. These processes are called dimensions and include the Business process, the Project Management process and the ES process. In addition it defines six organizational aspects: Strategy & Goals, Management, Structure, Process, Knowledge & Skills and Social dynamics. The 18 cells created by the intersection of dimension and aspect are called focus cells [12], [13].

CEAO Chains Database
CEAO chain is a mapping of a problem and solution, contains of the following items: *Event* is defined as a problem created by decisions, actions, or by events outside the control of the organization. A *cause* is an underlying reason or action, leading to the event. For each event it is possible to specify one or several causes, which are linked to the event through a parent-child relationship. An *Action* is the solution taken to resolve the event; it includes method of performing or means used. Each action is connected to *outcomes*.

The CEAO chains identified through the case studies and were captured and perceived by actors with different roles involved in an ESI-process. The mapping of causes of the CEAO chains into reference framework has led to different clusters of CEAO chains. Each cluster belongs to a focus cell in the framework.

Context of the ES Implementation
Context data provide a view of the company and ES, such as company size, type of ES, cultural region etc. It is expected that ES implementation process execution is influenced by those characteristics. Context sensitivity analysis was done in an attempt to distinguish between local pattern (occur only in specific situations due to the context characteristic), and generic pattern that can be generalized across ES implementation processes. For example, if we compare two different size companies: SME (less then 250 employees) and Large (more then 250 employees), it is expected that there are size-dependent patterns, such as greater project resources and higher complexity adoption process in a large company, that cause major differences in the ESI processes.

Readiness Scoring
The readiness scoring provides a measure of readiness according to the BEST Reference Framework. This step consists of answering the questions related to the aspects of the reference framework. Each answer is scored according to predefined scores. The scores are summed in the aspect level and create an aspect score indicating the status of the company in each aspect.

5   Knowledge-Based CBR Retrieval to Support Organizational Change Management

5.1   Domain Knowledge Utilized

We combine the knowledge gathered in BEST ESI theory to improve the matching process. The proposed matching process is based on the following constructs:

1. The problem is defined in terms of the event's causes and not in terms of the event. The underlying assumption is that the solutions (actions in the CEAO chains) are suited to handle the origin of the problem, i.e. the cause, since the same event may stem from totally different causes.
2. The search for similar events is focused by inferred local /generic patterns of the context properties, due to their considerable influence on ESI processes.
3. The company profile score in each of the six aspects is a risk indicator to the company status in this aspect. Similar scores between cases implies similar environment, and similar influence on the problem solution process.

   Figure 1 describes the knowledge-based matching. It is assumed that if cases are similar, effective solution strategies adopted in past case is expected to be effective on the target case as well.

   In this work we do not include the solution component (chain's actions and out-comes) in the case representation since it is relevant to the adaptation stage which is out of scope of this paper.

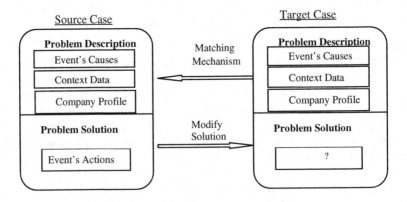

Fig. 1. Knowledge-based Matching Mechanism

5.2   Case Representation

An ordered vector of four components represents each case (C). Each element (E_i) of this vector describes a property, this property's importance (weight), the property's value and the property's group $C = \{E_1,..., E_l\}, E_i = (P_i, W_i, X_i, G_i)$ where P_i is the property's name, W_i is its weight , X_i is the value assigned to this property , and Gi is the property group.

The constructs of the model, distinguishes between three properties' groups (see equation (3)). The G_1 properties are the event's causes' clusters. Each event may have several causes' clusters. We compute the marginal distribution of each event causes clusters in the CEAO chain by summing the reference framework rows, resulting in the definition of event's aspect. The G_2 properties are the context data and the G_3 are the company profile scores. The property's weight (W_i) is used, in this paper, only by G_3 properties and denotes the importance of the company profile score in each aspect, with respect to event's aspects. The weights are assigned by a domain expert who estimates this importance level.

$$X_i = \begin{cases} n_{event\_aspect_i} & P_i \in G_1 \quad i=1,..,6 \quad n=1,..,r \\ Context\_attribute\_value & P_i \in G_2 \quad i=1,..,m \\ Score_{profile\_aspect_i} & P_i \in G_3 \quad i=1,..,6 \end{cases} \tag{3}$$

5.3 The Retrieval Phase

5.3.1 Overview
The retrieval process is described in figure 2. Based on the context properties of the target case, the case-base is searched for candidate previous cases that match the context attributes of the target case. This is done according to the existence of generic and local patterns. This search increases the efficiency of the retrieval because only a subset of the case-base is examined. However, appropriate cases may not be retrieved. This is followed by a matching process, presented in the following section, that combines similarity between the events and similarity between the company profiles [21].

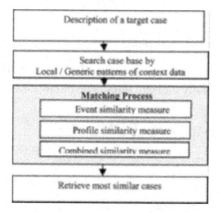

Fig. 2. The retrieval phase

5.3.2 Matching Process

Step 1 - Event Similarity Assessment

The overall event similarity measure $SIM_{event}(T, C_k)$ is based on Tversky's contrast model (equation 4):

$$SIM_{event}(T, C_k) = \frac{\alpha |D_i|}{\alpha |D_i| + \beta |E_i| + \gamma |F_i|} \qquad \alpha = 1, \beta, \gamma = 0.5 \qquad (4)$$

where D_i is the number of the common aspects in both events, E_i and F_i are the number of contradicting aspects. The local similarity measure between each event's aspects (cause's clusters) of a target event and a source event is defined in equation (5):

$$sim_{event\_aspect_i}(T, C_k) = \begin{cases} D_i & n^T_{event\_aspect_i} \geq 1, n^{C_k}_{event\_aspect_i} \geq 1 \\ E_i & n^T_{event\_aspect_i} \geq 1, n^{C_k}_{event\_aspect_i} = 0 \\ F_i & n^T_{event\_aspect_i} = 0, n^{C_k}_{event\_aspect_i} \geq 1 \\ N_i & n^T_{event\_aspect_i} = 0, n^{C_k}_{event\_aspect_i} = 0 \end{cases} \qquad (5)$$

Step 2 – Profile Similarity Assessment

The overall profile similarity measure $SIM_{profile}(T, C_K)$ is based on nearest-neighbor approach, a weighted sum of the profile similarity measures, over all six profile aspects (equation 6).

$$SIM_{profile}(T, C_K) = \frac{\sum_{i=1}^{6} sim_{profile\_aspect_i}(T, C_k) \cdot w_{profile\_aspect_i}}{\sum_{i=1}^{6} w_{profile\_aspect_i}} \qquad (6)$$

where $sim_{profile\_aspect_i}$ is the local similarity measure between the profiles in each of the six aspects (equation 7), and $w_{profile\_aspect_i}$ is its weight (equation 8).

The local profile similarity measure is a simple distance-based function [27]:

$$sim_{profile\_aspect_i}(T, C_k) = 1 - \frac{\left| score^T_{profile\_aspect_i} - score^{C_k}_{profile\_aspect_i} \right|}{score^{max}_{profile\_aspect_i} - score^{min}_{profile\_aspect_i}} \qquad (7)$$

in which $score^{max}_{profile\_aspect_i}$ and $score^{min}_{profile\_aspect_i}$ are the maximal and minimal values among all cases (including the target case), respectively.

The profile similarity measure weight $w_{profile\_aspect_i}$ is a combination of the two compared case's weights (W_i), as in equation (8):

$$w_{profile\_aspect_i} = weight\_combination(W^T_{profile\_aspect_i}, W^{c_k}_{profile\_aspect_i}) \qquad (8)$$

The weight combination is the method used to designate the importance of the local profile similarity in the overall profile similarity calculation, as induces by the weights of the corresponding company profile aspects in the compared cases. This method enables the assignment of an independent weight to each company and then combines it by a method such as "minimum", "maximum", "mean" or "1-power"[31]. The different choices of weight combination will place more or less emphasis on company profile aspects affecting strongly only one of the cases. For example, the "minimum" combination, which takes the lesser of the two cases weights, tends to give less importance to properties affecting strongly only one of the cases.

Step 3 – Combined Similarity Assessment
Based on Tversky's Contrast Model, under the assumption proposed in [28], a function f(object) can be defined as an interval scale of each of the objects (D,E,F).The function reflects the salience or prominence of the various objects, thus measuring the contribution of each feature to the overall similarity.

The scale values f(D), f(E) and f(F) associated with objects (D,E,F) are therefore measures of the overall salience of D,E,F which might depend, for instance, on intensity, frequency, familiarity or informational content [29].

We apply this logic, and define the overall salience of D, E and F to be the sum of the local profile similarity measure in this aspect. In this way the relevant profile aspect similarity is combined into the event causes similarity, expressing the "amount" of similarity between the events in a 'wider environmental context'. This is expressed in equation (9):

$$SIM\ (T,C_K) = \frac{\alpha \sum_{i \in D} ws_{profile\_aspect_i}(T,C_k) \cdot}{\alpha \sum_{i \in D} ws_{profile\_aspect_i}(T,C_k) + \beta \sum_{i \in E \cup F} ws_{profile\_aspect_i}(T,C_k)} \qquad (9)$$

where, $ws_{profile\_aspect_i}(T,C_k) = sim_{profile\_aspect_i}(T,C_k) \cdot w_{profile\_aspect_i}$ is the weighted similarity between target and source case in aspect i, and $\alpha = 1, \beta = 0.5$.

An alternative to this method is to combine between the overall event similarity-measure $SIM_{event}(T,C_k)$ (equation (4)) and the overall profile similarity measure $SIM_{profile}(T,C_K)$ (equation (6)) by ranking into order of similarity, calculating a Rank Score (RS), in the following manner [23]:

1. Ranking all the matching candidate cases in ascending order by the overall event similarity measure $SIM_{event}(T,C_k)$.
2. Ranking all the matching candidate cases in ascending order by the overall profile similarity measure $SIM_{profile}(T,C_K)$.
3. Taking an average of the two rankings, as shown in Equation (10).

$$RS = round(\frac{R_{SIM_{event}}(T,C_k) + R_{SIM_{profile}}(T,C_k)}{2})$$ (10)

where: $R_{SIM_{event}}(T,C_k)$ and $R_{SIM_{profile}}(T,C_k)$ is the ascending overall event and profile similarity case's ranks, respectively.

6 Concluding Remark and Future Work

This work is a first step towards a CBR model to support the management of ESI related organizational change processes. We have used domain knowledge in order to represent an event in its wider environmental context, i.e. the characteristics of the company and the ESI process. We propose a matching process in which a linear weighting model provides a company's profile similarity measure that is combined with the events' similarity measure through Tversky's Contrast model [21]. The proposed matching approach is more of a demonstrative and confirmatory proof to the capability of CBR model, however it may not well address all problem's components. The presumed linear effect of the profile similarity measure on each aspect may be not realistic. Moreover, profile scores are taken as deterministic, and the weights assessment is a highly subjective process. This implies that more robustness evaluation methods are needed. The evaluation of methods applied to the BEST database, can rely on bootstrapping and cross-validation techniques [25, 26].

Below, we detail some planned directions to enhance the ESI CBR model. Fuzzy set theory was proved to model reality more naturally and adequately [30]. Since the ESI CBR model is connected with human judgment, evaluation and reasoning, a hybrid approach with fuzzy methods may make it more powerful.

In order to reduce the sensitivity of the nearest neighbor approach to the profile weight an Analytic Hierarchy Process (AHP) methodology can be incorporated in the CBR model [24]. AHP is an effective methodology in obtaining domain knowledge from numerous experts. It can be used for assigning relative importance of profile weighting. The sensitivity to the distance function can be handled through the use of various distance functions as demonstrated in [18].

In this work we focus on the CBR retrieval phase. The CBR adaptation phase, in which the solutions of former similar cases are modified to fit the current event will be presented in future work. A catalogue of ESI Improvement tools [9] was developed by BEST project and forms a basis for tailoring improvement actions according to a specific situation. The catalogue may enhance the expert knowledge in formulating the adaptation method.

Acknowledgment

This work was partially supported by BEST (Better Enterprise SysTems implementation) project, IST-2001-35385 www.best-project.com.

References

1. Davenport, T.: Mission Critical: Realizing the promise of Enterprise Systems; Harvard Business School Press, Boston,(2000).
2. Lanzara , G., Mathiassen, L.: Mapping situations within a systems development project, Information and Management, 8(1) (1985).
3. Kolonder, J. L. : Case-based reasoning; San Mateo, CA : Morgan Kaufmann, (1993).
4. Leake, D.: Case Based Reasoning: Experiences, Lessons, and Future Directions. Morgan Kaufmann, (1996).
5. Shmidt, R., Montani, S., Bellazzi, R.: Case-based reasoning for medical knowledge-based systems. : International Journal of Medical Informatics 64 (2001), 355-367.
6. Aamodt, A., Plaza, E.: Case-based reasoning: foundational issues, methodological variations, and system approaches.: AI Communications (1994) 39–59.
7. While D.: The BEST solution, IT Buyers Guide,(2004).
8. Macura, R., Macura, K.: MacRad: radiology image resource with a Cased-Based retrieval system. in: M. Veloso, A. Aamodt (Eds.), Proceedings of 1st International Conference on CBR, Springer, Berlin(1995),43–54.
9. BEST (Better Enterprise SysTems implementation) project, IST-2001-35385 www.best-project.com
10. Watson, I.: Applying Case-Based Reasoning. Morgan Kaufman (1997).
11. McKenzie, D. P.: Classification by Similarity: An Overview of Statistical Methods of Case-Based Reasoning,: Computers in Human Behavior, 11- 2 (1995) 273-288.
12. Fan, I., Wognum, N., Buhl, H.: Getting Organization and Human Ready for Information System eChallenges, Vienna (2004).
13. Kenett,R,, Raphaeli,O., Methods to Collect and Analyze Organizational Change Management Data: The BEST Approach, Colloquium of the Haifa University research Center of Organizational Behavior HR Management, 24/3/2004
14. Stahl, A.: Defining Similarity Measures: Top-Down vs. Bottom-Up.: in: Craw, Preece (Eds.), ECCBR2002, (2002) 406-420.
15. Duda, D., Hart, P.: Pattern Classification and Scene Analysis, Wiley, New-York, (1973).
16. Tversky, A.: Features of Similarity, Psychological Review 84 (4), (1977), 327-352.
17. Gupta K.M. ,. Montazemi A.R: A connectionist approach for similarity assessment in case-based reasoning systems, Decision Support Systems 19, (1997), 237-253.
18. Karlin S., Kenett, R, Bonne-Tamir, B.: Analysis of Biochemical Genetic Data on Jewish Populations: II. Results and Interpretations Heterogeneity Indices and Distance Measures with Respect to Standards. American Journal of Human Genetics 31,(1979) 341-365.
19. Lee, R., Barcia, R. Khator, S.: Case based reasoning for cash Flow forecasting using fuzzy retrieval. In Proc of First International Conference, ICCBR-95 (1995) 510- 519.
20. Hann, U., Chater, N.: Understanding Similarity: A Joint Project for Psychology, Case-Based Reasoning, and Law, Artificial Intelligence Review 12(1998) 393–427.
21. Raphaeli, O.: Applying Case Based Reasoning in Analyzing Organizational Change Management Data, Working Paper, Tel-Aviv University, 2004.
22. Perner, P.: Data Mining on Multimedia Data, Springer-Verlag, Berlin Heidelberg New York (1998) LNCS 2558.
23. Bradburn, C., Zeleznikow, J.: The application of Case-Based reasoning to the tasks of health care planning, in: S. Wess et al , Proceedings of European Workshop on CBR, Springer, Berlin(1993)365-378.

24. Park,C., Han, I.: A case-based reasoning with the feature weights derived by analytic hierarchy process for bankruptcy prediction, Expert Systems with Applications 23(3) (2002) 255-264.
25. Efron B., and Tibshiriani R., An Introduction to the Bootstrap , Chapman and Hall, New York(1993).
26. Kenett R. , Zacks S. :Modern Industrial Statistics: Design and Control of Quality and Reliability, Duxbury Press, San Francisco(1998).
27. Cheng, C. B.: A Fuzzy Inference System for Similarity Assessment in Case-Based Reasoning systems: An Application to Product Design, Mathematical and Computer Modeling 38 (2003) 385-394.
28. Vargas, J., Bourne, J., Hoffman, M. Collins, G.: Similarity-based Reasoning about Diagnosis of Analog Circuits, ACM 1988.
29. Tversky, A., Gati, I.: Similarity, Separability and the triangle inequality. Psychological Review 89 (1982) 123–154.
30. Liao, T., Zhang, Z.: Similarity Retrieval in Case-Based Reasoning Systems, Applied Artificial Intelligence 12 (1998), 267- 288.
31. Slonim, T., Schneider, M.: Design issues in fuzzy case-based reasoning, Fuzzy Sets and Systems 117 (2001) 251-267.

Improving the K-NN Classification with the Euclidean Distance Through Linear Data Transformations[1]

Leon Bobrowski[1,2] and Magdalena Topczewska[1]

[1]Faculty of Computer Science, Bialystok Technical University
[2]Institute of Biocybernetics and Biomedical Engineering, PAS, Warsaw

Abstract. One of the most popular techniques in pattern recognition applications is the nearest neighbours (K-NN) classification rule based on the Euclidean distance function. This rule can be modified by data transformations. Variety of distance functions can be induced from data sets in this way. We take into considerations inducing distance functions by linear data transformations. The results of our experiments show the possibility of improving K-NN rules through such transformations.

Keywords: classification rules, the nearest neighbours technique, Euclidean distance, Mahalanobis distance.

1 Introduction

Classification can be seen as the decision making process that aims at correct allocation of a given object or a situation into one of the predefined categories or classes ω_k ($k = 1,....,K$) [1], [2]. Classification problems are very often encountered in practice. In particular, many decision making problems in industry can be solved by applying the classification scheme. As an example, we can mention the automatic detection of machine failure on the base of noise measurements, or the computer systems for character recognition.

The classification systems are designed on the base of data sets composed of numerical results from previous experiences (database systems) or by using sets of rules representing theoretical knowledge in a given domain (expert systems). We are paying particular attention to the database systems with the learning sets C_k ($k = 1,....,K$). The learning set C_k contains m_k representatives (precedents) of the category ω_k.

The classification rules based on the nearest neighbours *K-NN* scheme [2] and on the Case Base Reasoning (*CBR*) approach [3] are central to us. In accordance with

[1] This work was partially supported by the W/II/1/2004 and SPB-M (COST 282) grants from the Białystok University of Technology and by the 16/St/2004 grant from the Institute of Biocybernetics and Biomedical Engineering PAS.

P. Perner (Ed.): ICDM 2004, LNAI 3275, pp. 23–32, 2004.

these techniques, a new object is classified to such a category ω_k, which contains the most similar precedents in a related learning set.

The similarity between a new object and its precedents from the database is commonly determined on the base of the Euclidean distance between adequate feature vectors. Applying other types of the similarity measures results sometimes in the improvement of classification rules. Variety of similarity measures modifications can be introduced through data sets transformations. We examine the linear data transformations as a tool for the improving similarity measures.

2 Nearest Neighbours Classification Rules

The similarity between objects is computed on the base of the numerical representation of these objects in the form of the n-dimensional feature vectors $\mathbf{x} = [x_1,.......,x_n]^T$. The vectors $\mathbf{x}$ can be also treated as the points in the n-dimensional feature space. The components x_i of the vector $\mathbf{x}$ are called the *features*. Given feature vector $\mathbf{x}_j$ can contain the numerical results of the fixed set of n measurements x_i on particular object O_j.

Let the symbol $\mathbf{x}_j(k)$ mean the feature vector assigned (labelled) to the k-th class ω_k. The assignment of the feature vectors $\mathbf{x}_j = [x_{j1},.......,x_{jn}]^T$ $(j =1,.....,m)$ from the database to particular categories ω_k is performed by applying some additional (expert) information. The learning set C_k contains m_k feature vectors $\mathbf{x}_j(k)$ labelled to the same class ω_k:

$$C_k = \{\mathbf{x}_j(k)\} \quad (j \in I_k) \tag{1}$$

where I_k is the set of indices j of the feature vectors $\mathbf{x}_j(k)$ belonging to the class ω_k.

In accordance with the *K-NN* rule a new object is allocated to this category ω_k to which most of the K nearest neighbours $\mathbf{x}_j[k]$ of the vector $\mathbf{x}_0$ belong, where vector $\mathbf{x}_0$ represents a new object. Similar scheme is applied in the *Case Based Reasoning* *(CBR)* scheme [3]. The CBR scheme includes standardised parameterization of the regarded problem and the search for similar problems in the Case Base [4]. The result of the last stage depends strongly on the applied measure of the similarity between the cases.

Let us assume that the labelled feature vectors $\mathbf{x}_j(k)$ from the learning sets C_k (1) can be *ranked* in respect to the distances $\delta(\mathbf{x}_0,\mathbf{x}_j(k))$ between the vectors $\mathbf{x}_0$ and $\mathbf{x}_j(k)$:

$$(\forall i \in \{1,....,m\text{-}1\}) \quad \delta(\mathbf{x}_0,\mathbf{x}_{j(i)}) < \delta(\mathbf{x}_0,\mathbf{x}_{j(i+1)}) \tag{2}$$

The ball $B(\mathbf{x}_0,K)$ centred in $\mathbf{x}_0$ and containing exactly K ranked vectors $\mathbf{x}_{j(i)}(k)$ can be defined as:

$$B(\mathbf{x}_0,K) = \{\mathbf{x}: \ \delta(\mathbf{x}_0,\mathbf{x}) \leq \delta(\mathbf{x}_0,\mathbf{x}_{j(K)}) \tag{3}$$

The set $B_E(\mathbf{x}_0, K)$ defines the Euclidean *neighbourhood* of the point $\mathbf{x}_0$. In accordance with the K-nearest neighbours (K-NN) rule, the object $\mathbf{x}_0$ is allocated into this class ω_k, where most of the labelled feature vectors $\mathbf{x}_j(k)$ from the neighbourhood $B_x(\mathbf{x}_0, K)$ belong [2]:

$$if \ (\forall l \in \{1,...,K\}) \ n_k \geq n_l \ then \ \mathbf{x}_0 \in \omega_k \tag{4}$$

where n_k is the number of the vectors $\mathbf{x}_j(k)$ from the set C_k (1) contained in the ball $B_x(\mathbf{x}_0, K)$.

The K-NN classification rule (5) depends on the number K of the neighbours taken into consideration and on the applied distance function $\delta(\mathbf{x}_0, \mathbf{x}_j[k])$. The Euclidean distance function $\rho_E(\mathbf{x}_0, \mathbf{x}_j[k])$ is most commonly used for the nearest neighbours classifiers

$$\delta_E(\mathbf{x}_0, \mathbf{x}_j[k]) = \{(\mathbf{x}_0 - \mathbf{x}_j[k])^T (\mathbf{x}_0 - \mathbf{x}_j[k])\}^{1/2} \tag{5}$$

Both the K number as well as the distance function $\rho(\mathbf{x}_0, \mathbf{x}_j[k])$ could be optimised by minimisation of the error rate related to the given rule (5) [2].

3   Linear Transformations of the Learning Sets

This Euclidean distance function $\rho_E(\mathbf{x}_0, \mathbf{x}_j[k])$ can be modified by transformations of the feature vectors $\mathbf{x}_j$. We are considering using the linear transformations of the feature vectors for this purpose

$$\mathbf{y}_j = A \ \mathbf{x}_j \quad (j = 0, 1, ..., m) \tag{6}$$

where A is a matrix of dimension $n' \times n$.

The Euclidean distance functions $\delta_E(\mathbf{y}_0, \mathbf{y}_j(k))$ (3) between the transformed vectors $\mathbf{y}_j$ can be expressed as:

$$\delta_E^{\ 2}(\mathbf{y}_0, \mathbf{y}_j) = (\mathbf{y}_0 - \mathbf{y}_j)^T (\mathbf{y}_0 - \mathbf{y}_j) = (\mathbf{x}_0 - \mathbf{x}_j)^T A^T A (\mathbf{x}_0 - \mathbf{x}_j) \tag{7}$$

The Euclidean neighbourhood $B_E(\mathbf{y}_0, K)$ of the point $\mathbf{y}_0$ in the transformed feature space can be defined by using the distances $\delta_E(\mathbf{y}_0, \mathbf{y}_{j(i)})$ (7) in a similar manner to (4).

$$B_E(\mathbf{y}_0, K) = \{\mathbf{y} : \delta_E(\mathbf{y}_0, \mathbf{y}) \leq \delta_E(\mathbf{y}_0, \mathbf{y}_{j(K')})\} \tag{8}$$

The ball $B_E(\mathbf{y}_0, K)$ (8) is centred in the point $\mathbf{y}_0 = A\mathbf{x}_0$ (6) and contains K ranked points $\mathbf{y}_{j(i)}(k)$ (3). Let us assume that the symbol $B_l(\mathbf{x}_0, K)$ stands for such set of the feature vectors $\mathbf{x}$, that there are transformed by $\mathbf{y} = A \ \mathbf{x}$ (6) into the Euclidean ball $B_E(\mathbf{y}_0, K)$ (8):

$$B_l(\mathbf{x}_0, K) = \{\mathbf{x} : \mathbf{y} \in B_E(\mathbf{y}_0, K)\} \tag{9}$$

The set $B_1(\mathbf{x}_0,K)$ is called the neighbourhood of the point $\mathbf{x}_0$ *induced* by the transformation $\mathbf{y} = A\mathbf{x}$ (6). The shape of the induced neighbourhood $B_1(\mathbf{x}_0,K)$ (9) depends on the transformation (6) properties. The K nearest neighbours (K -NN) classification rule (4) of the point $\mathbf{x}_0$ can be based on the set $B_1(\mathbf{x}_0,K)$:

if the most of the labelled vectors $\mathbf{x}_j(k)$ *from the set* $B_1(\mathbf{x}_0,K)$ (9) *belong*

to the class ω_k, $\qquad\qquad\qquad\qquad\qquad\qquad\qquad\qquad$ (10)

$\qquad$ **then** *the object* represented by $\mathbf{x}_0$ *should be also allocated to this class.*

An adequate choice of the linear transformation matrix A (6) could allow for reducing the error rate of the K-NN classification rule (5).

4   The Mahalanobis Distance Function

The Mahalanobis distance function $\delta_M(\mathbf{x}_0,\mathbf{x}_j)$ in the feature space X is defined on the base of the covariance matrix Σ [5]

$$\delta_M^2(\mathbf{x}_0,\mathbf{x}_j) = (\mathbf{x}_0\text{-}\mathbf{x}_j)^T \Sigma^{-1} (\mathbf{x}_0\text{-}\mathbf{x}_j)^{1/2} \qquad (11)$$

The Mahalanobis distance function $\rho_M(\mathbf{x}_0,\mathbf{x}_j)$ takes into account the linear dependencies in the pairs of the features x_k and x_1. When the covariance matrix Σ is equal to the unit matrix I_n, then the Mahalanobis distance function $\rho_M(\mathbf{x}_0,\mathbf{x}_j)$ is reduced to the Euclidean distance functions $\delta_E(\mathbf{x}_0,\mathbf{x}_j)$ (3).

The Mahalanobis neighbourhood $B_M(\mathbf{x}_0,K)$ of the point $\mathbf{x}_0$ in the feature space X is defined through using the distances $\delta_M(\mathbf{y}_0,\mathbf{y}_{j(i)})$ (7) in a manner similar to (11).

$$B_M(\mathbf{x}_0,K) = \{\mathbf{x}:\ \delta_M(\mathbf{x}_0,\mathbf{x}) \le \delta_M(\mathbf{x}_0,\mathbf{x}_{j(K)})\} \qquad (12)$$

An important role in the pattern recognition is played by such linear transformations (6) which reduce correlation or whitening the learning sets C_k (1) [2]. Such transformations can be build on the base of the eigenvectors $\mathbf{k}_i$ and the eigenvalues λ_i of the covariance matrix Σ. Let us take into consideration the covariance matrix Σ_k estimated on the set C_k (1)

$$\Sigma_k = \Sigma_{j \in I_k} (\mathbf{x}_j - \boldsymbol{\mu}_k) (\mathbf{x}_j - \boldsymbol{\mu}_k)^T / (m_k - 1) \qquad (13)$$

where $\boldsymbol{\mu}_k$ is the mean vector in the set C_k

$$\boldsymbol{\mu}_k = \Sigma_{j \in I_k} \mathbf{x}_j / m_k \qquad (14)$$

The eigenvalue problem with the covariance matrix Σ_k is formulated as the search for the eigenvectors $\mathbf{k}_i$ and the eigenvalues λ_i which fulfil the below equation:

$$\Sigma_k \mathbf{k}_i = \lambda_i \mathbf{k}_i \qquad (15)$$

Let us assume that there exists n eigenvalues λ_i greater than zero. Such eigenvalues λ_i and eigenvectors $\mathbf{k}_i$ are ranked in the following manner

$$\lambda_1 \geq \lambda_2 \geq \ldots\ldots\ldots \geq \lambda_n > 0$$
$$\mathbf{k}_1, \quad \mathbf{k}_2, \ldots\ldots\ldots\ldots, \mathbf{k}_n \qquad (16)$$

The eigenvectors $\mathbf{k}_i$ can be chosen as orthogonal ($\mathbf{k}_k^T \mathbf{k}_l = 0$ if $k \neq l$, and $\mathbf{k}_k^T \mathbf{k}_k = 1$). In result, the matrix $K = [\mathbf{k}_1, \ldots\ldots, \mathbf{k}_n]$ is also orthogonal ($K^{-1} = K^T$)

$$K^T K = K^{-1} K = I_n \qquad (17)$$

where I_n is the unit matrix of the dimension ($n \times n$).

We are considering the linear transformation (5) of the following form

$$\mathbf{y}_j(k) = B^T \mathbf{x}_j(k) \quad (j = 1, \ldots\ldots, m) \qquad (18)$$

where matrix B of the dimension ($n \times n$) has the columns constituted by the vectors $\mathbf{k}_i / (\lambda_i)^{1/2}$.

$$B = [\mathbf{k}_1 / (\lambda_1)^{1/2}, \ldots\ldots\ldots, \mathbf{k}_n / (\lambda_n)^{1/2}] \qquad (19)$$

The following relation results from the orthogonality of the eigenvectors $\mathbf{k}_i$ (17)

$$B^T B = \Lambda_n^{-1} \qquad (20)$$

where Λ_n is the diagonal matrix with the eigenvalues λ_i on the diagonal.

The transformed vectors $\mathbf{y}_j(k)$ (18) are constituting (1) the sets $C'_k = \{\mathbf{y}_j(k)\}$ ($j \in I_k$) with the mean vectors $\boldsymbol{\mu}'_k$ (14). The correlation matrix Σ'_k (13) is defined on the transformed vectors $\mathbf{y}_j$ (18) from one set C'_k

$$\Sigma'_k = \sum_{j \in I_k} (\mathbf{y}_j - \boldsymbol{\mu}'_k)(\mathbf{y}_j - \boldsymbol{\mu}'_k)^T / (m_k - 1)$$

$$= B^T \sum_{j \in I_k} (\mathbf{x}_j - \boldsymbol{\mu}_k)(\mathbf{x}_j - \boldsymbol{\mu}_k)^T B / (m_k - 1) = B^T \Sigma_k B = I_n \qquad (21)$$

where I_n is the unit matrix of the dimension ($n \times n$).

The equation (21) shows, that the linear transformation (18) with a special matrix B (19) is linked to changing the correlation matrix Σ_k (13) into the unit matrix $\Sigma'_k = I_n$. It means that the components y_k and y_l of the transformed vector $\mathbf{y} = [y_1, \ldots\ldots, y_n]^T$ (the extracted features) are uncorrelated in the data set C'_k and have the unit variances.

$$(\forall k \neq l;\ k, l \in \{1, \ldots, n\}) \quad \rho'_{kl} = 0 \qquad (22)$$

$$(\forall k \in \{1, \ldots, n\}) \qquad \sigma'_k = 1 \qquad (23)$$

The data sets C'_k which fulfill the above conditions are called sets with "white" structure.

Lemma 1. The linear transformation $\mathbf{y} = \boldsymbol{B}^T\mathbf{x}$ (18) with the matrix $\boldsymbol{B}$ (19) design on the eigenvectors $\mathbf{k}_i$ and the eigenvalues λ_i of the covariance matrix $\boldsymbol{\Sigma}$ induces the Mahalanobis neighbourhood $B_M(\mathbf{x}_0, K)$ (12) from the Euclidean ball $B_E(\mathbf{y}_0, K)$ (8).

Proof: The proof of Lemma can based on the relation (21) which describes changing the correlation matrix $\boldsymbol{\Sigma}$ into the unit matrix I_n. In the result, the Mahalanobis neighbourhood $B_M(\mathbf{x}_0, K)$ (12) of the point $\mathbf{x}_0$ in the feature space X is transformed (17) in the Euclidean neighbourhood $B_E(\mathbf{y}_0, K)$ (7) of the point $\mathbf{y}_0$ in the transformed feature space Y. The transformation diverse to (18) exists and can be determined by the following equations (17):

$$\mathbf{y}_j = \boldsymbol{B}^T\mathbf{x}_j = \boldsymbol{\Lambda}_n^{-1/2}\boldsymbol{K}^T\,\mathbf{x}_j \tag{24}$$

thus (25)

$$\boldsymbol{\Lambda}_n^{1/2}\,\mathbf{y}_j = \boldsymbol{K}^{-1}\,\mathbf{x}_j \tag{25}$$

and

$$\mathbf{x}_j = \boldsymbol{K}\,\boldsymbol{\Lambda}_n^{1/2}\,\mathbf{y}_j \tag{26}$$

The linear transformation (18) with the matrix $\boldsymbol{B}$ (19) allows for changing the correlation matrix $\boldsymbol{\Sigma}_k$ (11) into the unit matrix $\boldsymbol{\Sigma}'_k = I_n$ in one learning set C_k (1) (or in other single set of the vectors $\mathbf{x}_j$). There exists also the designing procedure for such a linear transformation, which gives the correlation matrix $\boldsymbol{\Sigma}'_k$ in one set C_k, which fulfils the equations (22) and (23), and the diagonal correlation matrix $\boldsymbol{\Sigma}'_{k'}$ in another set $C_{k'}$ [2]. In other words, there exists such a linear transformation which decorrelates simultaneously two data sets C_k and $C_{k'}$.

5 Experiments with the Normal Model

To examine the influence of the learning sets C_k (1) structure on the K-nearest neighbours (K-NN) classification rule (4), we hove conducted a series of experiments with the normal model describing two classes ω_1 and ω_2. In accordance with the normal model, each of the two classes ω_k are described by the normal distribution $N(\mu_k, \boldsymbol{\Sigma})$ with the mean vector μ_k and the same covariance matrix $\boldsymbol{\Sigma}$. The symbol $P(\omega_k)$ will mean the a priori probability of each class ω_k.

The optimal, Bayesian classification rule for the normal model has the linear form [5]

$$\textit{if } \mathbf{w}^T\mathbf{x} > \theta, \textit{ then } \mathbf{x} \in \omega_2, \textit{ else } \mathbf{x} \in \omega_1 \tag{27}$$

where

$$w = \Sigma^{-1} (\mu_2 - \mu_1) \tag{28}$$

and

$$\theta = (\mu_2 - \mu_1)^T \Sigma^{-1} (\mu_1 + \mu_2)/2 + ln[P(\omega_1)/P(\omega_2)] \tag{29}$$

If the probabilities a priori $P(\omega_k)$ are equal $(P(\omega_1) = P(\omega_2))$, then the threshold θ is reducing to:

$$\theta = (\mu_2 - \mu_1)^T \Sigma^{-1} (\mu_2 + \mu_1)/2 = w^T(\mu_2 + \mu_1)/2 \tag{30}$$

The linear transformation $y = B^T x$ with the matrix B (19) allows to transform the normal model into two normal distributions $N(\mu'_1, I_n)$ and $N(\mu'_2, I_n)$ with the mean vectors μ'_k and the unit covariance matrix I_n, where:

$$\mu'_k = B^T \mu_k \tag{31}$$

The mean vectors μ'_k can be used in determining the distance d between the normal distributions $N(\mu_1, \Sigma)$ and $N(\mu_2, \Sigma)$.

$$d^2 = (\mu'_2 - \mu'_1)^T (\mu'_2 - \mu'_1) \tag{32}$$

Let us assume, that the probabilities a priori $P(\omega_k)$ are equal $(P(\omega_1) = P(\omega_2) = 1/2)$. In this case, the error probability $e_B(d)$ of the Bayesian classification rule (27) is determined by the below expression:

$$e_B(d) = \int_{d/2}^{\infty} exp\ [-t^2/2]\ dt / (2\pi)^{1/2} \tag{33}$$

where, the parameter d is given by the relation (32). We can remark, that the linear transformation $y = B^T x$ with the matrix B (18) does not change the value of the error rate $e_B(d)$.

The numerical experiments has been done by using the artificial data sets C'_1 and C'_2 generated on the plane $(n = 2)$ in accordance with two normal distributions $N(\mu'_1, I_2)$ and $N(\mu'_2, I_2)$. Each data set C'_k contained 200 points $y_j(k)$ on the plane Y $(m_1 = m_2 = 200)$. The data sets C'_1 and C'_2 has been generated many times for each selected value of the distance d. The reverse transformation (26) allowed to generate the learning sets C_k (1) of the feature vectors $x_j(k)$ from the data sets C'_1 by assuming the eigenvectors k_i and eigenvalues λ_i (18).

The covariance matrix Σ_k (13) can be also computed by using the orthogonal matrix $K = [k_1, \ldots\ldots, k_n]$ (17) of the eigenvectors k_i and the eigenvalues λ_i. As it results from the relations (21) and (24)

$$\Lambda_n^{-1/2} K^T \Sigma_k K \Lambda_n^{-1/2} = I_n \tag{34}$$

thus

$$K^{-1} \, \Sigma_k \, K = \Lambda_n^{1/2} I_n \, \Lambda_n^{1/2} \tag{35}$$

and

$$\Sigma_k = K \, \Lambda_n \, K^T = \lambda_1 \, k_1 \, k_1^T + \ldots\ldots + \lambda_n \, k_n \, k_n^T \quad (\text{spectral decomposition}) \tag{36}$$

The correlation coefficients ρ_{kl} and the variances σ_k of particular features x_k can be extracted from the covariance matrix Σ_k.

The K-NN classification rule (4) has been compared on the base of the evaluated error rate $e(d)$. The error rate $e(d)$ has been evaluated on the learning sets C_k and C'_k by applying the *leave one out* method [2]. In accordance with this method, each element $x_j(k)$ of the learning sets C_k has been classified in accordance with the decision rule (4). The error has been made, if the allocation (4) of the element $x_j(k)$ was different from the class ω_k. The error rate $e(d)$ has been computed as:

$$e(d) = m_e / m \tag{37}$$

where m_e is the number of such elements $x_j(k)$ from the learning sets C_k which have been wrongly classified by the rule (4) and m is the number of the all elements of these sets.

The K-NN classification rule (4) with the fixed number K of the Euclidean nearest neighbours has been applied both to the elements $x_j(k)$ of the learning sets C_1 and C_2 as well as to the elements $y_j(k)$ of the decorellated sets C'_1 and C'_2. Let us remark that the Euclidean K-NN classification rule (4) applied to the elements $y_j(k)$ of the decorellated sets C'_k is equivalent with the Mahalanobis K-NN rule applied to the elements $x_j(k)$ of the learning sets C_k. The below results contain results of the classifiers evaluation and comparison for data sets C_k and C'_k generated in accordance with the normal model for different values of the distance d (32) between the distributions.

The numerical experiments have been performed on two-dimensional data sets C_k and C'_k (points on the plane). The correlation coefficient has had value of $\rho = 0.95$ in the case of the learning sets C_1 and C_2. In accordance with the model assumptions, the transformed data sets C'_1 and C'_2 have been uncorrelated ($\rho = 0$).

We can observe in the above results that the decorrelation of the learning sets Ck (1) can improve the K-NN rule (4) based on the Euclidean distance $\delta E(x0,xj)$ (7). The decorrelation of the learning sets Ck (1) has entailed including the Mahalanobis distance $\delta M(xo,xj)$ (11) from these sets. With such interpretation, we can claim that the replacement of the Euclidean distance $\delta E(x0,xj)$ (7) by Mahalanobis distance $\delta M(xo,xj)$ (11) can lead to the improvement of the K-NN rule (4).

Let us remark also, that the difference between the distance functions $\delta_E(x_0,x_j)$ (7) and $\delta_M(x_0,x_j)$ (11) depends on the distance d (32) between the distributions and is greater for small distances d (greater overlapping of the classes ω_k). The difference between the distance functions $\delta_E(\mathbf{x}_0,\mathbf{x}_j)$ (7) and $\delta_M(\mathbf{x}_0,\mathbf{x}_j)$ (11) could be demonstrated in even stronger manner, if we use a local measure of this difference. The local measure could mean the evaluation of the classifiers quality not by the global error rate $e(d)$ (37) but by the local error rate evaluated only in the area of the strongest overlapping of the classes ω_k. In the case of the normal model, the area of the strongest overlapping is situated near the hyperplane, which separates two classes ω_k. Such local evaluation which is oriented at he most difficult cases in the classification process has important practical meaning.

Distance d	Error_B	Error_1	Error_2
0,2	0,440	0,710	0,515
0,4	0,386	0,538	0,428
0,6	0,330	0,470	0,428
0,8	0,281	0,395	0,350
1,0	0,233	0,330	0,278
1,2	0,189	0,255	0,238
1,4	0,154	0,220	0,218
1,6	0,121	0,175	0,148
1,8	0,093	0,143	0,130
2,0	0,072	0,113	0,100
2,2	0,054	0,088	0,068
2,4	0,040	0,060	0,040
2,6	0,029	0,038	0,040
...	...	...	...
5	0,000	0,000	0,000

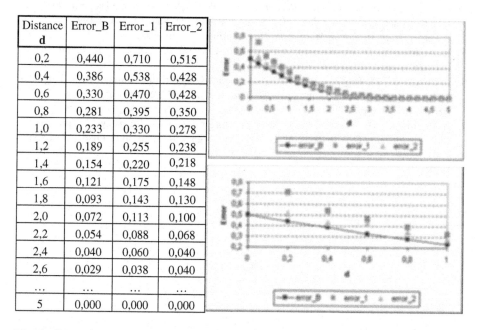

Fig. 1. Comparison of the error rate $e(d)$ (37) for two 3-NN classifiers (K =3) with the error probability $e_B(d)$ (33) of the Bayesian classification rule (27) for different distance d (32) values (**error_B** – the probability $e_B(d)$ (37), **error_1** - the error rate $e(d)$ (37) for correlated learning sets C_k, **error_2** - the error rate $e(d)$ (37) for decorrelated sets C'_k)

6 Conclusions

Modification of the distance functions $\delta(\mathbf{x}_0,\mathbf{x}_j)$ can improve the nearest neighbours K-NN rule (4). We have demonstrated that replacement of the Euclidean distance $\delta_E(\mathbf{x}_0,\mathbf{x}_j)$ (7) by the induced Mahalanobis distance $\rho_M(\mathbf{x}_0,\mathbf{x}_j)$ (11) can lead to improvement of the K-NN rule (4) in the case of the normal model of data sets.

Other procedures for the induction of distance functions and similarity measures from data sets have been proposed and implemented. We are referring here to the methods based on the concept of the mixed and clear dipoles and minimization procedures for convex and piecewise linear criterion functions [6]. The linear transformation of data sets designed on the base of these principles resulted in the improvement of the diagnosis support rules of the *Hepar* system [7].

References

1. O. R. Duda and P. E. Hart, D. G. Stork: *Pattern   Classification,* J. Wiley, New York, 2001.
2. K. Fukunaga: *Statistical Pattern Recognition,* Academic Press, Inc., San Diego, 1990.
3. J. L. Kolodner: *Case-based Reasoning,* Morgan Kaufmann, San Mateo, CA 1993.
4. P. Perner, *Data Mining on Multimedia Data,* Springer, Berlin 2002
5. R. A. Johnson, D. W. Wichern: *Applied Multivariate Statistical Analysis,* Prentice-Hall, Inc., Englewood Cliffs, New York, 1991
6. L. Bobrowski, M. Topczewska: "Tuning of diagnosis support rules through visualizing data transformations", pp. 15-23 in *Medical Data Analysis,* P. Perner et al., Springer-Verlag Berlin , Heidelberg 2003
7. L. Bobrowski, H. Wasyluk, Diagnosis supporting rules of the *Hepar* system, pp. 1309 - 1313 in: *MEDINFO 2001,* Eds: V. L. Petel, R. Rogers, R. Haux, IOS Press, Amsterdam 2001

An IBR System to Quantify the Ocean's Carbon Dioxide Budget

Juan M. Corchado[1], Emilio S. Corchado[2], and Jim Aiken[3]

[1] Departamento Informática y Automática,
Universidad de Salamanca, Plaza de la Merced s/n,
37008, Salamanca, Spain
corchado@usal.es

[2] Departamento de Ingeniería Civil, Escuela Politécnica Superior,
Universidad de Burgos, C/ Francisco de Vitoria s/n,
09006, Burgos, Spain
escorchado@ubu.es

[3] Centre for Air-Sea Interactions and fluxes (CASIX),
Plymouth Marine Laboratory, Prospect Place,
Plymouth, PL1 3 DH, U.K.
ja@mail.pml.ac.uk

Abstract. The interaction of the atmosphere and the ocean has a profound effect on climate, while the uptake by the oceans of a major fraction of atmospheric carbon dioxide has a moderating influence. By improving accuracy in the quantification of the ocean's carbon dioxide budget, a more precise estimation can be made of the terrestrial fraction of global carbon dioxide budget and its subsequent effect on climate change. First steps have been taken towards this from an environmental and economic point of view, by using an instance based reasoning system, which incorporates a novel clustering and retrieval method. This paper reviews the problems of measuring the ocean's carbon dioxide budget and presents the model developed to resolve them.

1 Introduction

An instance based reasoning system (IBR) has been developed to estimate the global budgets of carbon dioxide between the atmosphere and the ocean surface. IBR systems have been successfully used in several domains such as diagnosis, prediction, control and planning [5, 9]. However, a major problem with these systems is the difficulty of case retrieval and case matching when the number of cases increases; large case bases are difficult to handle and require efficient indexing mechanisms and optimised retrieval algorithms. Moreover, there are very few standard techniques for automating their construction, since each problem may be represented by a different data set and requires a customised solution. Based on recent successful experiments with connectionist systems an instance based reasoning system has been developed for estimating the partial pressure of carbon dioxide in the ocean [3].

P. Perner (Ed.): ICDM 2004, LNAI 3275, pp. 33–41, 2004.
© Springer-Verlag Berlin Heidelberg 2004

The IBR system developed incorporates a novel Cooperative Maximum Likelihood Hebbian Learning model for the data clustering and retrieval and a radial-bases function neural network for instance adaptation and forecast. A case-based reasoning system solves new problems by adapting solutions that were used to solve old problems. The case base holds a number of problems with their corresponding solutions. Once a new problem arises, the solution to it is obtained by retrieving similar cases from the case base and studying the similarity between them. CBR/IBR systems record past problem solving experiences and, by indexing algorithms, retrieve previously stored cases, along with their solutions, and match them and adapt them to a given situation, in order to generate a solution. A typical CBR system is composed of four sequential steps which are recalled every time a problem needs to be solved: Retrieve the most relevant case(s), reuse the case(s) to attempt to solve the problem, revise the proposed solution if necessary, and retain the new solution as a part of a new case.

CBR is an incremental learning approach because every time a problem is solved, a new experience can be retained and made immediately available for future retrievals. There are five different types of case based reasoning systems, and although they share similar features, each of them is more appropriate for a particular type of problem: exemplar based reasoning, instance based reasoning, memory-based reasoning, analogy-based reasoning and typical case-based reasoning. Instance-based reasoning can be considered to be a type of exemplar-based reasoning in highly syntax-dependent problem areas. This type of CBR system focuses on problems in which there are a large number of instances which are needed to represent the whole range of the domain and where there is a lack of general background knowledge.

This paper outlines the problem first and then presents the IBR system developed to estimate the partial pressure of carbon dioxide and presents some initial results obtained with it.

2 Ocean's Carbon Dioxide Budget

The carbon dioxide concentration in the atmosphere is governed primarily by the exchange of carbon dioxide with the ocean. The atmospheric content of carbon dioxide is increasing at an annual rate of about 3 billion tons which corresponds to one half of the annual emission rate of approximately 6 billion tons from fossil fuel combustion. Whether the missing carbon dioxide is mainly absorbed by the oceans or by the land and their ecosystems have been debated extensively over the past decade. It is important, therefore, to fully understand the nature of the physical, chemical and biological processes which govern the oceanic sink/source conditions for atmospheric carbon dioxide [7].

Satellite-borne instruments provide high-precision, high-resolution data on atmosphere, ocean boundary layer properties and ocean biogeochemical variables, daily, globally, and in the long term. All these new sources of information have changed our approach to oceanography and the data generated needs to be fully exploited. Wind stress, wave breaking and the damping of turbulence and ripples by surface slicks, all affect the air-sea exchange of carbon dioxide. These processes are closely linked to the "roughness" of the sea surface, which can be measured by satellite radars and microwave radiometers. Our aim is to model both the open ocean and shelf seas, and it is believed that by assimilating earth observation data into artificial intelligence models these problems may be solved. Satellite information is very important for the construction of oceanographic models, and in this case, to produce estimates of air-sea fluxes of carbon dioxide with much higher spatial and temporal resolution, using artificial intelligence models than can be achieved realistically by direct in situ sampling of upper ocean carbon dioxide. The systems have been tested in a number of cruises carried out off Chile during the austral summer of 2000. During the cruise, data was obtained in situ from temperature, chlorophyll, fluorescence and salinity sensors, and satellite images were also obtained. This data was used to test the IBR system developed to calculate the ocean's carbon dioxide buget.

3 The Instance-Based Reasoning System

An instance-based reasoning system has been constructed to obtain the value of the surface partial pressure of carbon dioxide in oceanographic waters from biological parameters and satellite information. The main part of the model is an IBR system that incorporates several connectionist techniques in the retrieval, reuse and retain stages. The IBR system uses the Cooperative Maximum Likelihood Hebbian Learning Model for clustering the Instance-base and for the retrieval of the instances most similar to the "problem instance", due to its topology preserving properties [8]. The Cooperative Maximum Likelihood Hebbian Learning method is a novel approach that features both selection, in which the aim is to visualize and extract information from complex, and highly dynamic data. This method is a mixture of factor analysis and exploratory projection pursuit [4] based on a family of cost functions proposed by Fyfe and Corchado [6] which maximizes the likelihood of identifying a specific distribution in the data while minimizing the effect of outliers [11]. It employs cooperative lateral connections derived from the Rectified Gaussian Distribution [1, 10] in order to enforce a more sparse representation in each weight vector. The adaptation step is carried out using a radial basis function network while the revision stage is manually carried out by an oceanographer (since the specific aim of this project is to construct a tool for oceanographers) [2]. Finally, the system is updated continuously with data obtained from satellites and sensors.

The radial function neural network provides the value of the carbon dioxide buget for a given point and the result is evaluated by an oceanographer. The learning (retain stage) is carried out by updating the instance base [2], updating the weights of the radial basis function network and by re-calling the Cooperative Maximum Likelihood

Hebbian Learning Model for the clustering of the data. Figure 1 presents a schema of the problem solving model.

Maximum Likelihood Hebbian Learning algorithm automatically groups the instances into clusters, grouping together those of similar structure. This technique is a classification and visualisation tool for high dimensional data on a low dimensional display. One of the advantages of this technique is that it is an unsupervised method so we do not need to have any information about the data beforehand. When a new instance is presented to the IBR system, it is identified as belonging to a particular cluster. This mechanism may be used as a universal retrieval and indexing mechanism to be applied to any problem similar to the one presented here.

Each stored instance contains information relating to a specific situation. An instance is a numerical vector containing the following information JD (Serial day of the year), LAT (Latitude), LONG (Longitude), SST (Temperature), S (Salinity), WS (Wind strength), WD (Wind direction), Fluo_calibrated (fluorescence calibrated with chlorophyll) and SW (surface partial pressure of carbon dioxide). Where JD, LAT, LONG, SST, S, WS, WD, Fluo_calibrated represent the problem description and where SW is the value that the IBR system has to identify from the problem descriptor. These values for a given point can be obtained from cruises using sensors or from satellite images. This initial system has been tested with data obtained in an area of the Pacific ocean from Latitude 22,6°S to 24°S and Longitude 70°W to 72°W, which corresponds to a water mass situated off the Chile coasts of "Mejillones" and "Antofagasta", in the austral summer of 2000.

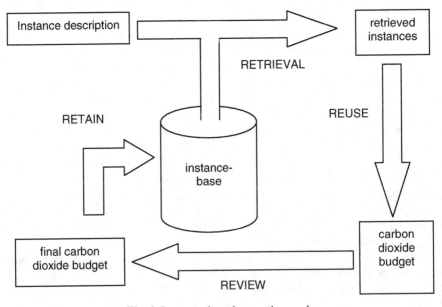

Fig. 1. Instance–based reasoning cycle

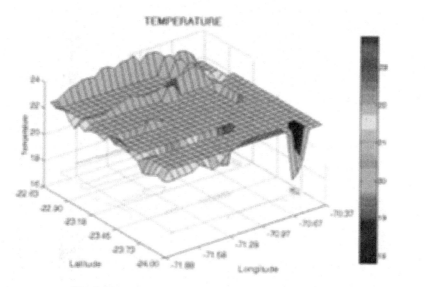

Fig. 2. Temperature values along the cruise track presented

4   Initial Results

The system was tested *in situ* during the cruise carried out in Pacific waters, see Figure 2. The instance-base of the system was fed with 85% of the instances recorded during the cruise (over 15.000 instances). The other 15%, homogeneously spread along the cruise track, was left in order to test the system after the cruse was completed. Figure 2 presents the temperature (averaged) values along the cruise track. It is a three dimensional view of the water temperature, where outside the track, the values that appear are the average value of the water temperature along the track. Figure 3 presents a top view of the temperature values along the cruise track shown in Figure 2. The results obtained were very accurate, with an average error of 7,4%, which is less than the error provided by the other techniques we used to evaluate the IBR system. Table 1 presents the average error obtained with the Instance-based Reasoning System, and other methods such as a Radial-basis Function Neural Network, a Multi-layer Perceptron Neural Network, a Growing Cell Structures Neural Network and a K-nearest neighbour algorithm.

Starting from the error series generated by the different models, the Kruskall-Wallis test has been carried out. Since the P-value is less than 0,01, there is a statistically significant difference between the models at the 99,0% confidence level. Table 2 shows a multiple comparison procedure (Mann-Withney test) used to determine which models are significantly different from the others. The asterisk indicates that these pairs show statistically significant differences at the 99.0% confidence level.

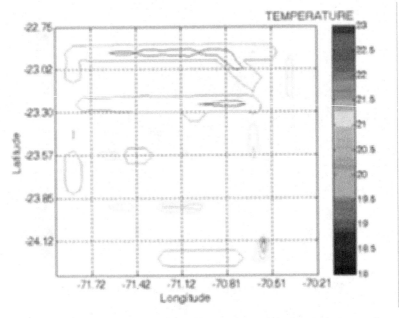

Fig. 3. Top view of the Temperature values along the cruise track presented

Table 1. Average error obtained with the IBR system and other methods

Method	Average Error
Instance-based System	7,7%
Radial-basis Function	10,6%
Multi-layer Perceptron	11,2%
Growing Cell Structures	15,1%
K-nearest neighbour	16,3%

Table 2. Mann-Withney test results

	Instance-based System	Radial-bases Function	Multi-layer Perceptro	Growing Cell Structures	K-nearest neighbor
Instance-based System					
Radial-bases Function	*				
Multi-layer Perceptron	*	=			
Growing Cell Structures	*	*	*		
K-nearest neighbor	*	*	*	=	

Table 2, shows that the IBR system presents statistically significant differences from the other models. The proposed model generates the best results of all the tested techniques. Figure 4 presents the error obtained in 40 instances in with the system was tested. These cases have been randomly obtained from the testing data set (15% of the whole data set), the other 85% of the data set was used to create the model.

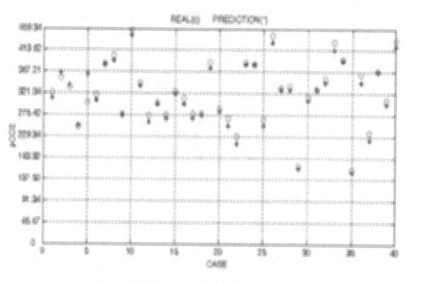

Fig. 4. Error obtained in 40 instances

The final goal of the project is to calculate the value of carbon dioxide from satellite images. Most of the values of the parameters presented that describe the problem can be directly obtained from such photographs and others may be extracted with some simple calculation. For example, there exists a well known correlation between the water temperature and the salinity, as can be seen in Figure 5.

Table 3. Average error obtained with the IBR system and other methods on Satellite data

Method	Average Error
Instance-based System	10,2%
Radial-basis Function	12,51%
Multi-layer Perceptron	16,1%
Growing Cell Structures	16,6%
K-nearest neighbour	19,4%

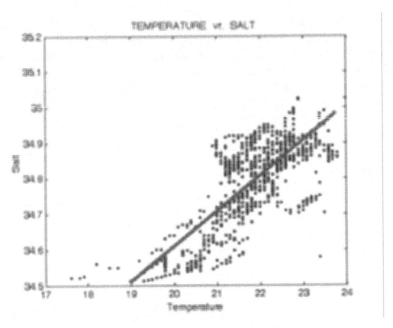

Fig. 5. Salinity/Temperature relationship

In this case, the IBR system was tested with data extracted from satellite images of the area in which the cruise took place. Problem instances (vectors with the values of: JD, LAT, LONG, SST, S, WS, WD, Fluo_calibrated and SW) were constructed, along the cruise track from such images and were fed into the IBR system, in order for it to obtain the value of the pCO2. In this case the average error of the IBR system was slightly higher, but still very accurate compared with the results obtained with the other techniques. Oceanographers have also considered these results to be highly significant.

5 Conclusions

The IBR system presented in this paper is able to produce a forecast with an acceptable degree of accuracy. The final constructed tool constitutes the first system developed for calculating the carbon dioxide budget *in situ* and from satellite images. The IBR system incorporates a novel clustering technique capable of indexing huge instance-bases in an unsupervised way and of successfully retrieving instances with a similar structure, which is vital for constructing a model with a radial basis function neural network.

The Cooperative Maximum Likelihood Hebbian Learning Model has probed its retrieval ability and the radial basis function its modelling capability. With these techniques, the retrieval of the best matching instance is a very simple operation and they do not presents major computational obstacles. The results obtained in the experiments carried out are very encouraging and the model presents great potential. The first experiment has allowed us to determine the efficiency of the model when the data used to create the instance-base and the problem instances is reliable. The second experiment shows the potential of the model to automate the resolution of the problem with the help of satellite photographs. In this second experiment the error may be due to calibration imbalances, lack of definition of the photographs, presence of clouds, errors in the wind measures, etc. These are some of the problems that have to be solved in the framework of this project. Table 3 also shows the generalization capabilities of the proposed model, since it is even able to generate reasonable results in an extended area, when the instance-base has only been constructed with data from one part of the area.

References

1. Corchado E. and Fyfe C. (2003) Orientation Selection Using Maximum Likelihood Hebbian Learning, International Journal of Knowledge-Based Intelligent Engineering Systems Volume 7 Number 2, April 2003. Brighton, United Kingdom.
2. Corchado J. M. and Aiken J. (2002) Hybrid Artificial Intelligence Methods in Oceanographic Forecasting Models. IEEE SMC Transactions Part C. Vol. 32, No.4. pp. 307-313.
3. Corchado J. M., Corchado E. S., Aiken J., Fyfe C., Fdez-Riverola F. and Glez-Bedia M. (2003) Maximum Likelihood Hebbian Learning Based Retrieval Method for CBR Systems. 5th International Conference on Case-Based Reasoning, Trondheim, Norway, June 23 to 26, 2003. Springer-Verlag
4. Freedman J. and Tukey J. (1974) A Projection Pursuit Algorithm for Exploratory Data Analysis. IEEE Transaction on Computers, (23): 881-890, 1974.
5. Fyfe C. and Corchado J. M. (2001) Automating the construction of CBR Systems using Kernel Methods. International Journal of Intelligent Systems. Vol 16, No. 4, April.
6. Fyfe C., and Corchado E. S. (2002) Maximum Likelihood Hebbian Rules. European Symposium on Artificial Neural Networks. 2002.
7. Lefevre N., Aiken J., Rutllant J., Daneri G., Lavender S. and Smyth T. (2002) Observations of pCO2 in the coastal upwelling off Chile: Sapatial and temporal extrapolation using satellite data. Journal of Geophysical research. Vol. 107, no. 0
8. MacDonald D., Corchado E. and Fyfe C. (2004) Analysing Spectroscopic Data Using Hierarchical Cooperative Maximum Likelihood Hebbian Learning. Mexican International Conference on Artificial Intelligence. 2004. Lecture Notes in Computer Science (LNCS), Springer Verlag.
9. Pal S. K., Dillon T. S. and Yeung D. S. (2000) Soft Computing in Case-based Reasoning. (eds.). Springer Verlag, London, U.K.
10. Seung H.S., Socci N.D. and Lee D. (1998) The Rectified Gaussian Distribution, Advances in Neural Information Processing Systems, 10.
11. Smola A.J. and Scholkopf B. (1998) A Tutorial on Support Vector Regression. Technical Report NC2-TR-1998-030, NeuroCOLT2 Technical Report Series.

A Beta-Cooperative CBR System for Constructing a Business Management Model

Emilio S. Corchado[1], Juan M. Corchado[2], Lourdes Sáiz[1], and Ana Lara[1]

[1]Department of Civil Engineering,
University of Burgos, Spain
{escorchardo, lsaiz, amlara}@ubu.es
[2]Departamento Informática y Automática,
Universidad de Salamanca, Plaza de la Merced s/n,
37008, Salamanca, Spain
corchado@usal.es

Abstract. Knowledge has become the most strategic resource in the new business environment. A case-based reasoning system has been developed for identifying critical situations in business processes. The CBR system can be used to categorize the necessities for the Acquisition, Transfer and Updating of Knowledge of the different departments of a firm. This technique is used as a tool to develop a part of a Global and Integral Model of Business Management, which brings about a global improvement in the firm, adding value, flexibility and competitiveness. From this perspective, the data mining model tries to generalize the hypothesis of organizational survival and competitiveness, so that the organization that is able to identify, strengthen, and use key knowledge will reach a pole position. This case-based reasoning system incorporates a novel artificial neural architecture called Beta-Cooperative Learning in order to categorize the necessities for the Acquisition, Transfer and Updating of Knowledge of the different departments of a firm. This architecture is used to retrieve the most similar cases to a given subject.

1 Introduction

In this paper, we have centre our attention specifically on the problem of knowledge management from a pragmatic and managerial point of view that contemplates, first and foremost, the possibility that knowledge can be classified and organised in order to achieve a better understanding. This issue is based, above all, on understanding the distinctions between transformations in forms of knowledge, starting from an inferior level - data and information - and advancing towards higher levels, such as knowledge itself and its management, individual, and even organizational responsibilities. This paper outlines the results obtained with a case-based reasoning system (CBR) developed to identify critical situations that allow firms to take decisions about acquisition, transfer and updating processes in knowledge management. Case-based reasoning (CBR) systems have been successfully used in several domains such as diagnosis, monitoring, prediction, control and planning [1] [2]. CBR systems require adequate

P. Perner (Ed.): ICDM 2004, LNAI 3275, pp. 42–49, 2004.
© Springer-Verlag Berlin Heidelberg 2004

retrieval and reuse mechanisms to provide successful results. Such mechanisms need to be consistent with the problem that has to be solved and with the data used to represent the problem domain. A CBR system is a methodology used to construct software tools to assist experts in the resolution of problems. The CBR system presented in this paper incorporates mechanisms that facilitate the data clustering and indexation and automates the retrieval and adaptation stages of the CBR system.

A novel method which is closely related to exploratory projection pursuit has been used for the clustering and retrieval stages of the developed CBR system. It is a neural model based on the Negative Feedback artificial neural network, which has been extended by the combination of two different techniques. Initially by the selection of a proper cost function from a family of data, to identify the right distribution related to the data problem. This method is called Beta learning (BL). Then, lateral connections derived from the Rectified Gaussian Distribution are added to the Beta architecture [3]. These enforce a greater sparcity in the weight vectors. After presenting the Beta-cooperative network, the case-based reasoning system is employed and finally the results obtained with it are outlined.

2 Beta-Cooperative Learning

The model used in this study is based, as mentioned above, on the Negative Feedback Network [4]. Consider an N-dimensional input vector, $\mathbf{x}$, and a M-dimensional output vector, $\mathbf{y}$, with W_{ij}, being the weight linking input j to output i and let η be the learning rate.

The initial situation is that there is no activation at all in the network. The input data is fed forward via weights from the input neurons (the $\mathbf{x}$ -values) to the output neurons (the $\mathbf{y}$ -values) where a linear summation is performed to give the activation of the output neuron. We can express this as:

$$y_i = \sum_{j=1}^{N} W_{ij} x_j, \forall i \tag{1}$$

The activation is fed back through the same weights and subtracted from the inputs (where the inhibition takes place):

$$e_j = x_j - \sum_{i=1}^{M} W_{ij} y_i, \forall j, \tag{2}$$

After that, simple Hebbian learning is performed between input and outputs:

$$\Delta W_{ij} = \eta e_j y_i \tag{3}$$

This network is capable of finding the principal components of the input data in a manner that is equivalent to Oja's Subspace algorithm [5], and so the weights will not find the actual Principal Components but a basis of the Subspace spanned by these components.

We can start with the probability density function of the Beta distribution and derive rules which will optimally find the distribution. If the residual is drawn from the Beta distribution, $B(v,\omega)$, with the following probability density function:

$$p(e) = \mathbf{e}^{v-1}(1-\mathbf{e})^{\omega-1} = (\mathbf{x} - W\mathbf{y})^{v-1}(1-\mathbf{x}+W\mathbf{y})^{\omega-1} \tag{4}$$

then if we wish to maximise the likelihood of the data with respect to the weights, we will perform gradient ascent using:

$$\frac{\partial p}{\partial W} = \mathbf{e}^{v-2}(1-\mathbf{e})^{\omega-2}\mathbf{y}(-(v-1)(1-\mathbf{e})+\mathbf{e}(\omega-1)) \tag{5}$$

which is a rather cumbersome rule.

So the learning rule is:

$$\Delta W = \eta \mathbf{e}^{v-2}(1-\mathbf{e})^{\omega-2}\mathbf{y}(-(v-1)(1-\mathbf{e})+\mathbf{e}(\omega-1)) \tag{6}$$

However for the case in which $v = \omega = 2$:

$$\frac{\partial p}{\partial W} = \mathbf{y}(-(1-\mathbf{e})+\mathbf{e}) \tag{7}$$

So the learning rule is simplified to:

$$\Delta W = \eta \mathbf{y}(2\mathbf{e}-1) \tag{8}$$

This method has been linked to the standard statistical method of Exploratory Projection Pursuit (EPP) [6].

The Rectified Gaussian Distribution [3] is a modification of the standard Gaussian distribution in which the variables are constrained to be non-negative, enabling the use of non-convex energy functions. The multivariate normal distribution can be defined in terms of an energy or cost function in that, if realised samples are taken far from the distribution's mean, they will be deemed to have high energy and this will be equated to low probability. More formally, we may define the standard Gaussian distribution by:

$$p(\mathbf{y}) = Z^{-1}e^{-\beta E(\mathbf{y})}, \tag{9}$$

$$E(\mathbf{y}) = \frac{1}{2}\mathbf{y}^T \mathbf{A}\mathbf{y} - \mathbf{b}^T \mathbf{y} \tag{10}$$

The quadratic energy function $E(\mathbf{y})$ is defined by the vector $\mathbf{b}$ and the symmetric matrix $\mathbf{A}$. The parameter $\beta = 1/T$ is an inverse temperature. Lowering the temperature concentrates the distribution at the minimum of the energy function.

An example of the Rectified Gaussian distribution is the cooperative distribution. The modes of the cooperative distribution are closely spaced along a non-linear continuous manifold. Our experiments focus on a network based on the use of the cooperative distribution.

Neither distribution can be accurately approximated by a single standard Gaussian. Using the Rectified Gaussian, it is possible to represent both discrete and continuous variability in a way that a standard Gaussian cannot.

The sorts of energy function that can be used are only those where the matrix A has the property:

$$\mathbf{y}^T \mathbf{A} \mathbf{y} > 0 \text{ for all } \mathbf{y}: y_i > 0, i = 1...N \tag{11}$$

where N is the dimensionality of **y**. This property blocks the directions in which the energy diverges to negative infinity.

The cooperative distribution in the case of N variables is defined by:

$$A_{ij} = \delta_{ij} + \frac{1}{N} - \frac{4}{N} \cos\left(\frac{2\pi}{N}(i-j)\right) \text{ and} \tag{12}$$

$$b_i = 1 \tag{13}$$

where δ_{ij} is the Kronecker delta and i and j represent the identifiers of output neuron.

To speed up learning, the matrix **A** can be simplified [7] [8] to:

$$A_{ij} = \left(\delta_{ij} - \cos(2\pi(i-j)/N)\right) \tag{14}$$

The matrix **A** is used to modify the response to the data based on the relation between the distances among the outputs. Note that the modes of the Rectified Gaussian are the minima of the energy function, subject to non-negativity constraints. We use the projected gradient method, consisting of a gradient step followed by a rectification:

$$y_i(t+1) = [y_i(t) + \tau(b - Ay)]^+ \tag{15}$$

where the rectification $[\ ]^+$ is necessary to ensure that the y-values keep to the positive quadrant. If the step size τ is chosen correctly, this algorithm can provably be shown to converge to a stationary point of the energy function [9]. In practice, this stationary point is generally a local minimum.

The mode of the distribution can be approached by gradient descent on the derivative of the energy function with respect to **y**. This is:

$$\Delta \mathbf{y} \propto -\frac{\partial E}{\partial \mathbf{y}} = -(\mathbf{Ay} - \mathbf{b}) = \mathbf{b} - \mathbf{Ay} \tag{16}$$

which is used as in Eq. 15.

Thus we will use this movement towards the mode in the Beta Learning Network before training the weights as previously. The net result will be shown to be a network which can find the independent factors of a data set but do so in a way which captures some type of global ordering in the data set.

We use the Beta Learning Network but now with a lateral connection (which acts after the feed forward but before the feedback). Thus we have:

Feed forward:

$$y_i = \sum_{j=1}^{N} W_{ij} x_j, \ \forall i \tag{17}$$

Lateral Activation Passing:

$$y_i(t+1) = \left[y_i(t) + \tau(b - Ay) \right]^+ \tag{18}$$

Feedback:

$$e_j = x_j - \sum_{i=1}^{M} W_{ij} y_i, \tag{19}$$

Weight change:

$$\Delta W = \eta e^{\nu-2} (1-e)^{\omega-2} \mathbf{y} \left(-(\nu-1)(1-e) + e(\omega-1) \right) \tag{20}$$

Where the parameter τ represents the strength of the lateral connections.

3 Problem Case

In this study we have analysed a multinational group, leader in the design and production of a great variety of components for the automotive industry. The justification of this choice lies in the fact that the characteristics of its management represent a favourable environment and opportune moment for the introduction of Knowledge Management. It is undergoing organisational change and faces great growth and expansion, which requires a rapid adaptation to the demands of the sector, with greater resources, imminent transfers and accurate forecasting of knowledge, together with the immediate demand to capitalise on them, to share and use them within the firm.

The design of the preliminary theoretical model of Knowledge Management is based on three components: the Organisation - Strategy and People - Processes - Acquisition, Transfer and Updating of Knowledge - and Technology – Technological Aids, from which the propositions of the model are defined. The population sample used came to 277 registries (individuals) that correspond with the "necessities of knowledge" showed by the head of eleven departments of the company studied. This knowledge gathers different stages (knowledge levels) that depict the current situation of each department for the tasks or activities assigned to each department to be successfully accomplished. Also, it has been possible to obtain valuable data on the degree of importance for the company of the gathered knowledge. This way, it is possible to identify the lack of the knowledge that it is necessary to perform the activity, so as to make the right decision on its acquisition in terms of how it is acquired, or what is the cost or time needed. In the same way, it is possible to specify the knowledge possessed which is not comprehensively employed, either because the person does not use it in its entirety or because it has additional value and potential use for other departments. Furthermore, it is possible to include the analysis corresponding to the necessary evolution of the present knowledge to detect new knowledge, to eliminate the obsolete knowledge and to validate new needs, among others.

4   The Beta Cooperative Case-Based Reasoning System

The case-based reasoning developed assists experts in the decision processes taken, and helps to improve business processes. Case-based reasoning systems are used to solve new problems by adapting solutions that were used to solve previous similar problems [10]. The operation of a CBR system involves the adaptation of old solutions to match new experiences, using past cases to explain new situations, using previous experience to formulate new solutions, or reasoning from precedents to interpret a similar situation.

The reasoning cycle of a typical CBR system includes four steps that are cyclically carried out and in a sequenced way: retrieve, reuse, revise, and retain [1][2]. During the retrieve phase those cases that are most similar to the problem case are recovered from the case-base. The recovered cases are adapted to generate a possible solution during the reuse stage. Such a solution is reviewed and if it is appropriate, a new case is created and stored, during the retain stage, in the memory. Therefore CBR systems update (with every retain step) their case-bases and evolve with their environment.

CBR systems represent a methodology that requires the use of different techniques in each of the four stages. In this particular problem the case memory is indexed and the cases are classified with the help of the Beta-cooperative learning technique previously presented. The knowledge necessities are classified and once a new one is identified or reviewed the Beta-cooperative learning technique is recalled to identify similar knowledge necessities. During the reuse stage a radial basis function is used to identify the risk level associated with the new knowledge necessity [10]. The revision is manually carried out and the knowledge needs evaluated are added to or updated in the CBR system case base.

5   Results and Conclusions

The system presented above has been applied to the business management problem. The Beta-cooperative learning technique has been applied to classify the knowledge needs and the result obtained is presented in Figure 1. The knowledge needs with the same risk level associated are grouped together. Figure 1 presents the labelled groups.

The Beta-cooperative architecture can be used as a knowledge generation tool and can be used to analyse the business requirements. In terms of firm type, the points of the top right cloud are related to a GOOD SITUATION. The firm is located in this place because the level of knowledge required is low and therefore the acquisition of knowledge is not a priority.

In a contrasting case, in the area occupied by the bottom left clouds, there is a lot of urgency to acquire knowledge at a wide level. This area is called "CHAOS". In a similar way, in the top left area there is a need to acquire knowledge urgently at a half

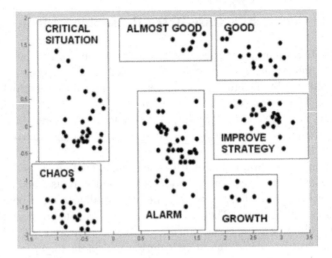

Fig. 1. The result of the application of the Beta-learning algorithm to the data. The projection identifies separate clusters (clouds), each of the groups has been labelled

or basic level. It could be that in these cases there is a holding of knowledge that can put the company in a CRITICAL SITUATION, since it may depend on the concession of new projects, the incorporation of new clients and all those parameters that somehow help to generate activity within the firm.

The area occupied by the right points outlines the possibility to acquire knowledge at a later stage but at half level. This could mean an IMPROVE STRATEGY in the firm, where it needs to improve in what it already possesses.

However, bottom right cloud represents the situation that the firm has to acquire the knowledge later but at a wide level. This means that the company should think about the idea of enlarging and growing, both in terms of new processes and new products. This is: GROWTH STRATEGY.

The points corresponding to top area are related to an ALMOST GOOD area, because the knowledge is needed urgently at a basic level. The centre and bottom cloud identify an ALARM area, because there is no urgency and the level needed is half.

As a final conclusion we could say that we have presented and applied a model called Beta-Cooperative Learning as a novel and robust tool to identify critical situations that allow firms to take decisions about acquisition, transfer and updating processes about knowledge management.

We have applied some other methods such as PCA [5] [6] or MLHL [7], but Beta-Cooperative Learning provides more sparse projections [8] and captures a form of global ordering in the data set.

The initial results show that the system presented is a reliable tool for classifying the different situations (clusters) which the firm may face and to identify whether the firm is at a situation that requires it to take decisions about acquisition, transfer and updating processes about knowledge management. A second prototype of this system is under construction.

References

1. Watson I. and Marir F. (1994) *Case-Based Reasoning: A Review*. Cambridge University Press, 1994. The knowledge Engineering Review. Vol. 9. No. 3.
2. Pal S. K., Dillon T. S. and Yeung D. S. (2000) Soft Computing in Case-based Reasoning. (eds.). Springer Verlag, London, U.K.
3. Seung H. S., Socci N. D., and Lee D. (1998) The Rectified Gaussian Distribution, Advances in Neural Information Processing Systems, 10. 350 (1998).
4. Fyfe C. (1996) A Neural Network for PCA and Beyond, Neural Processing Letters, 6: 33-41.
5. Oja E. (1989) Neural Networks, Principal Components and Subspaces, International Journal of Neural Systems, 1:61-68.
6. Friedman J. and Tukey J. (1974) A Projection Pursuit Algorithm for Exploratory Data Analysis. IEEE Transaction on Computers, (23): 881-890.
7. Charles D. (1999) Unsupervised Artificial Neural Networks for the Identification of Multiple Causes in Data. PhD thesis, University of Paisley.
8. Corchado E., Han Y. and Fyfe C. (2003) Structuring global responses of local filters using lateral connections. J. Exp. Theor. Artif. Intell. 15(4): 473-487.
9. Bertsekas D. P. (1995) Nonlinear Programming. Athena Scientific, Belmont, MA.
10. Corchado J. M. and Aiken J. (2002) Hybrid Artificial Intelligence Methods in Oceanographic Forecasting Models. IEEE SMC Transactions Part C. Vol. 32, No.4. pp. 307-313.

Braving the Semantic Gap: Mapping Visual Concepts from Images and Videos

Da Deng

Department of Information Science, University of Otago, New Zealand
ddeng@infoscience.otago.ac.nz

Abstract. A set of feature descriptors have been proposed and rigorously in the MPEG-7 core experiments. We propose to extend the use of these descriptors onto semantics extraction from images and videos, so as to bridge the semantic gap in content-based image retrieval and enable multimedia data mining on semantics level. A computational framework consisting of a clustering process for feature mapping and a classification process for object extraction is introduced. We also present some preliminary results obtained from the experiments we have conducted.

1 Introduction

Seeing is believing, and vision is understanding. For the research on image processing and computer vision, the importance of image analysis, a process spanning from data pre-processing, feature extraction, towards object detection or even image understanding, has never been overlooked. However, despite the rapid theoretical advances observed in relevant research areas such as artificial intelligence, pattern recognition, and more recently machine learning, no significant breakthrough has been achieved in the modeling, manipulation and understanding of image contents.

In the early 1990s, content-based image retrieval (CBIR) [1] was proposed to overcome the limitation of the traditional annotation-based retrieval systems for images and videos. Aimed at effective multimedia asset management and efficient information retrieval, a typical content-based image retrieval system (e.g., [2]) operates basically on low-level visual features such as color, texture, shape or regions. While CBIR revived the research in image analysis and multimedia representation to some extent, it is generally understood that the problem of effective image retrieval is still far from being solved. The similarity of image contents can vary on different levels - locally or globally, on different characteristics, or on account of different psychological effects. Even though techniques such as joint histograms, image classification and relevance feedback have been investigated to more or less improve the retrieval quality, there is still a persisting gap - on one side is the lack of semantic representation in image and video data, but on the other, our capability in deriving meaningful semantics from the varying and multi-dimensional information in images and videos remains rather

P. Perner (Ed.): ICDM 2004, LNAI 3275, pp. 50–59, 2004.
© Springer-Verlag Berlin Heidelberg 2004

limited. Such a gap implies that significant challenges still exist in areas such as image understanding, image data mining, and image retrieval.

Recently research attempts in bridging the semantic gap are becoming a trend. In [3], color semantics of art works are used for image retrieval, investigating into perceptual concepts on as color qualities and sensation, such as warmth, harmony, and anguish. In [4] support vector machines are used to match image feature clusters onto visual concepts.

On the other hand, from the data mining point of view, image mining has been proposed for knowledge discovery from data clustering and mining association rules [5]. It has been observed that automatic image analysis is in general very difficult, and much effort is required in finding an adequate feature scheme. Therefore most approaches remain domain-limited or require human expert interaction.

Previously we proposed to use CBIR techniques to tackle the problem of image collection profiling and comparison [6]. Feature maps were employed for self-organized profiling of image collections while in the meantime providing an effective graphical user interface for image or video collection navigation. Some distance measures were also proposed to quantitatively assess the similarity of these neural profiles.

In this paper, we extend this approach to investigating the plausibility of building a unified framework that can handle visual query and browsing of image/video contents, detect visual concepts from raw image data, or find interesting patterns or objects. We hope to use this framework to achieve data mining from images and videos on the semantics level, and leverage the semantic retrieval capability of image retrieval systems.

2   Computational Framework

Psychophysical findings have shown that high dimensional semantic structures can be effectively captured in low dimensions on the surface of a neural map [7]. This leads to our motivation of adopting a unified approach to achieve content-based retrieval as well as extraction of high-level semantic structures using labeled feature maps. Visual features are processed in two ways. Firstly clustering analysis of the feature maps can help to extract visual concepts shared by similar visual samples, and then effective classifiers can be built on these feature schemes to allow visual object extraction.

To enable low-level CBIR, global feature codes such as color histogram and texture energy histogram generated by Gabor filters are used. On the other hand, images are segmented into homogeneous regions using the technique in [8] and local feature codes are extracted by sampling the image regions. This not only enables image query using local visual clues, but also allows related visual concepts to be found through clustering analysis of regional visual features.

Upon satisfactory validation of the feature schemes, special objects such as 'grass', 'trees', and texts can then be detected and recognized by classifiers trained over the selected feature codes.

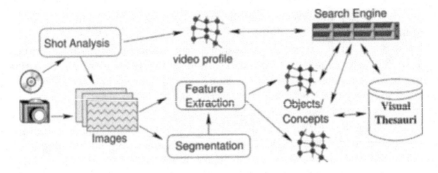

Fig. 1. The system diagram

The system diagram of the computational framework is shown in Fig.1. Three core components in the framework are explained as follows.

2.1 Shot Analysis

Video clips usually consist of a large number of image frames, and this huge volume of image data has to be reduced before further analysis is attempted. The solution is video segmentation and key frame extraction. Video shot boundary detection is largely based on the color histogram method used in image retrieval research. Color histograms of consecutive frames are compared. If the difference overflows a specified threshold, then a shot boundary is marked. Key frames can then be extracted as the representative image within each shot, and further image analysis is done on these key frames. Apart from key frame extraction, motion patterns of the video frames can also be analyzed and this has been found to be helpful for video summarization and retrieval especially for sports videos.

2.2 Feature Extraction

All feature schemes used in this study are based on the XM implementation of Core Experiments on the MPEG Video Group standard MPEG-7 [9], where a group of feature descriptors have been explicitly defined and rigorously tested. Due to the intensive research work in the field of CBIR, various descriptors on color and texture features based on global or local histograms have become mature. We briefly describe several feature descriptors used in our research as follows.

Color Layout Descriptor (CLD). CLD captures the spatial layout of the dominant colors on a grid superimposed on the image or the region of interest. This can be implemented as first dividing the image into 64 (8×8) blocks, and then deriving the average color of each block (or using dominant colors).

Color Structure Descriptor (CSD). CSD expresses local color structure in an image using an 8×8-structuring element. It is implemented as first scanning the image by an 8×8 pixel block, counting the number of blocks containing each color, and then generating a color histogram using the hue-min-max-difference (HMMD) color space. CSD has been found to be quite useful for the retrieval of natural images.

Homogeneous Texture Descriptor (HTD). HTD presents a quantitative characterization of texture for similarity-based image-to-image matching. It can also be used for object-based image retrieval. The computation process is as follows -

1. Partitioning the frequency domain into 30 channels (each modeled by a 2D-Gabor function);
2. Computing the energy and energy deviation for each channel;
3. Computing mean and standard variation of frequency coefficients, resulting a feature code of 62 dimensions:

$$F = \{f_{DC}, f_{SD}, e_1, ..., e_{30}, d_1, ..., d_{30}\}$$

Edge Histogram Descriptor (EHD). A given image is first sub-divided into 4×4 sub-images, and local edge histogram for each of these sub-images is computed. There are five categories of edges: horizontal, vertical, 45°, 135° diagonals, and isotropic. This will result in a descriptor of 80 bins. As commented in [9], unlike HTD, EHD is not appropriate for object based retrieval.

2.3   Features: Mapping and Classification

Among numerous clustering algorithms, SOM features the capability of carrying out vector quantization and multi-dimensional scaling simultaneously. It also has some attractive characteristics, such as readiness for visualization, probability density approximation of the data, and topology preserving. In [6] we proposed to use SOM for image collection navigation and also for collection profiling. For the later purpose some distance measures were introduced on top of the generated collection profiles trained by the SOM algorithm.

In this paper, the use of SOM is also two-fold: visual evaluation of visual feature schemes for conceptual clustering of image contents, as well as providing a user interface for semantic labeling. The visualization of the SOMs is generated from first carrying out two-dimensional principal component analysis (PCA) of the codebook and then using the projection from PCA as initial state for Sammon's mapping [10], which optimizes the low-dimensional visualization space by trying to preserve the distance order between prototypes through a gradient descent process.

We have found the use of k-Nearest Neighbor classifiers efficient in recognizing visual objects such as sky, grass, and pebbles etc. These classifiers work directly on the feature schemes validated in the previous clustering analysis phase.

3   Experiments and Results

Preliminary results have been obtained from experiments on several resources, including

- A digital image collection of the ISB Project at University of Otago, with site pictures taken over a two-year period. There are 154 images in total, including both indoor and outdoor scenes of various contents: construction sites, campus views, interior designs, and human close-ups;
- Video clips from the Roland Collection of Videos and Films on Art [11];
- Some CNN news video clips.

Algorithms for feature analysis, including SOM, PCA, Sammon's mapping and k-NN classification, are implemented in a Java-coded in-house Exodus package we developed for visual data mining purpose. Video processing and feature extraction utilities are coded in C and run on a FreeBSD system. Visual thesauri with sampled templates taken from image segments and all the feature maps generated are maintained using a PostgreSQL database system, based on which a search engine is to handle both content-based and semantic retrieval of images.

3.1   Video Processing

The UC Berkeley MPEG codec [12] is used and modified to decode and then analyze video shots in video clips. A simple global color histogram measured in the RGB space is employed to locate shot boundaries. The key frames are picked as the most stable shot frames (undergoing little change continuously) between the shot boundaries. As an example a CNN news clip 'Butler School' is tested with its key frames extracted.

We adopt a simplified 5-block CLD with average colors as key frame features, which then are used as input to train a SOM, so as to construct a 'snapshot' of the video clip. To preserve the timeline of the video stream, frame number is inserted into the feature code. By generating a one-dimensional map, the key frames can visualized over time while displaying some grouping of visual similarity, as shown in Fig.2. In Fig.3, a two-dimensional map is used instead. Although this profile lacks of indication of the timeline, the grouping on visual similarity is better displayed. There are, for example, clear indications of a cluster of human face close-ups on the lower left, and another cluster of maps on the upper right. Such a feature map will provide a useful interface for visual navigation, as well as for a guided process of concept exploration. On the other hand, by using some distance measure over the generated key frame based profiles, the search engine can compare different video clips quantitatively. This may provide an option for video clip retrieval by example.

3.2   Visual Concept Learning from Images

The major challenge to be met is however the mechanism of concept learning from visual contents. Our basic approach is to use feature maps to validate the effectiveness of feature scheme in clustering analysis, and then construct some classifier to carry out supervised learning and allow for object or concept detection. We have obtained some preliminary results from the experiments.

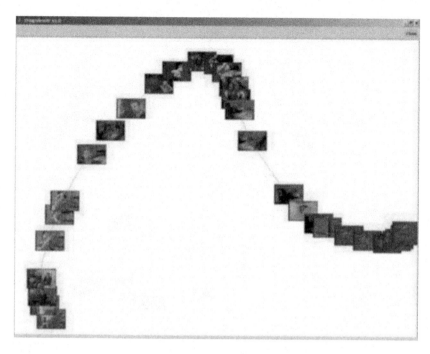

Fig. 2. Video summary of 'Butler School' constructed from a 1-D 'snake' map. Size of the map is 80

Artwork Versus Natural Scene. One experiment is done to distinguish images of artwork from those of natural scenes. By examining feature maps generated from key frames of two video clips from the Roland Collection, we find HTD features are quite promising to achieve the goal. Two Roland Collection videos are analyzed with key frames extracted and HTD features generated. Video clip No.13 is a short story on the artwork of a New Zealand artist, while No.603 is on prehistory sites with natural scenes. By training a SOM on HTD feature codes the frame images of artwork are clearly separated from those with natural scenes, as shown in Fig.4. The HTD features used are of 3 channels and 4 orientations, giving forth a HTD feature code of 14 dimensions (not including the energy gradients). Dimension reduction is then carried out using principal component analysis before generating the map.

Texture Thesaurus Mapping. In Fig.5 a feature map is trained for texture templates extracted from the Otago ISB image collection. A combined feature scheme consisting of both CLD and HTD is used to train the map. One can observe from the map that the sky templates are grouped on the lower right, and the grass templates grouped in the upper part. The pebbles template drifts to the lower left, while the tree templates mix either with grass or carpet templates in the middle. Upon visual assessment one may suggest the granularity of the texture is the major factor in setting forth such a layout. It can be seen from the

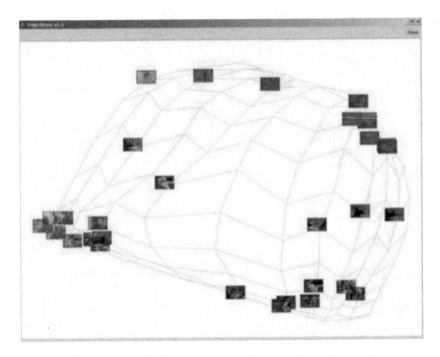

Fig. 3. Video summary visualized with PCA initialization. Size of the map is 12×12

figure that the granularity of these texture templates increases monotonously from upper right to the lower left of the map. The feature map can serve as a visual thesaurus for user to navigate through image collections with the help of a search engine operating on feature matching.

3.3   Classification

Once the feature scheme has been validated using a feature map, next thing one can do is to train some classifiers for concepts or objects in interest. The effectiveness of the feature scheme can then be further tested. If the outcome is satisfactory, an automatic process can then proceed to annotate image data with semantic contents.

To construct classifiers for the task, one needs to setup a database of templates with class labels. Because of the limited amount of labeled texture templates at the current stage we have only trained a simple k-nearest neighbor classifier for three classes, namely 'sky', 'grass', and 'others'. Table 1 gives the confusion matrix of the testing result on 30 templates extracted from the images.

The relatively poorer performance on grass recognition is mainly due to the lack of training templates. We hope to improve the segmentation quality and then automate the labeling process by flooding annotated templates across their corresponding segmented regions, so as to collect more training and testing image templates so that statistically sound validation results can be obtained and useful object detectors can be constructed using more robust classifiers.

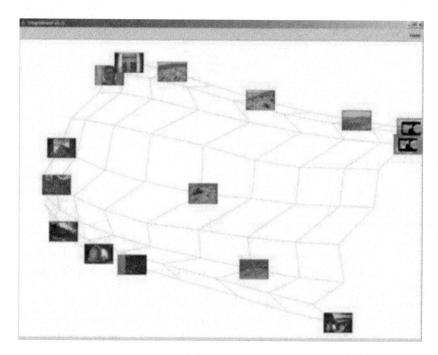

Fig. 4. Feature map trained on the HTD feature of RC video clip No.13 and No.603

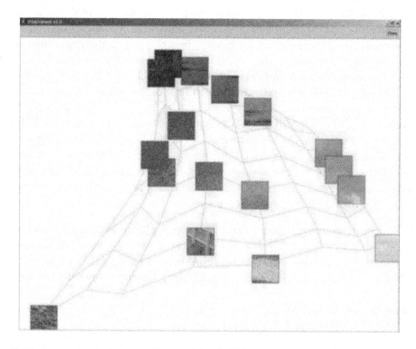

Fig. 5. Feature map trained on the combined CLD+HTD features of template images

Table 1. Confusion matrix of the classifier

Classes	Classified as		
	sky	grass	others
sky	85.5%	14.5%	0
grass	0	66.6%	33.3%
others	5%	0	95%

4   Discussion

In this paper, a computational approach is proposed to deal with the semantic gap acknowledged in image retrieval and data mining research. Self-organizing maps are used to produce profiles for video clips and to assist the exploration of various visual feature spaces proposed in the MPEG-7 core experiments. Semantic clusters related to some visual concepts or objects can emerge from the feature maps, whereupon classifiers can be constructed for accurate classification of visual concepts and objects.

Some preliminary results are reported in the paper, showing the capabilities of using the computational framework for image/video data navigation, as well as for visual discovery of concepts and objects. There are a number of unaddressed questions, such as

- How scalable is the current approach? This not only applies to the number of images or patterns being analyzed, but also the number of different objects or concepts that the current XM-based feature schemes can accommodate. For example, a simple task for human beings such as distinguishing indoor scenes from outdoor scenes [13] has found to be not easy to cope with. Further work needs to be done in improving the classification accuracy by examining their difference in lighting conditions combined with results from object detection.
- How to model the interrelationship between objects and concepts? When hierarchical feature maps are to be used for scalable feature clustering analysis, how does the map hierarchy guide concepts and objects related to the clusters formed on hierarchical maps to organize themselves into some semantic structure? Notably, there are some graphical representations of objects and concepts proposed, for instance, in [14].

We hope, in an incremental process our approach can lead to the construction of a mathematical framework for visual concepts and object extraction, as well as for the modeling of the interrelationship between these concepts, so that high-level multimedia data mining and semantic retrieval can eventually be achieved.

Acknowledgement. This work was supported by Otago Research Grant ORG 200200621, University of Otago, 2003.

References

1. Smeulders, A., Worring, M., Santini, S., Gupta, A., R., J.: Content-based image retrieval at the end of the early years. IEEE Transaction on Pattern Analysis and Machine Intelligence **22** (2000) 1349–1380
2. Carson, C., Thomas, M., Belongie, S., et al.: Blobworld: A system for region-based image indexing and retrieval. In: Proc. Int. Conf. Visual Inf. Sys. (1999) 509–516
3. Corridoni, J., Del Bimbo, A., Pala, P.: Image retrieval by color semantics. Multimedia Systems **7** (1999) 175–183
4. Wang, L., Manjunath, B.: A semantic representation for image retrieval. In: Proc. ICIP 2003, IEEE (2003) 523–526
5. Perner, P.: Image mining: issues, framework, a generic tool and its application to medical-image diagnosis. Eng. Appl. of Art. Intell. **15** (2002) 193–203
6. Deng, D.: Content-based comparison of image collections via distance measuring of self-organised maps. In: Proc. IEEE MMM 2004. (2004) 233–240
7. Edelman, S., Intrator, N.: Learning as formation of low dimensional representation spaces. In: Proc. 19th The Cognitive Science Meeting. (1997) 199–204
8. Deng, Y., Manjunath, B.: Unsupervised segmentation of color-texture regions in images and video. IEEE Trans. PAMI **23** (2001) 800–810
9. Manjunath, B., Ohm, J., Vinod, V., Yamada, A.: Color and texture descriptors. IEEE Trans. Circuits and Systems for Video Technology **2** (2001) 703–715
10. Sammon, W.: A nonlinear mapping for data analysis. IEEE Trans. on Computers **5** (1969) 401–409
11. RC: Rolland collection of videos and films for art (2004) http://www.roland-collection.com/
12. UCB: Berkeley mpeg tools (2004) http:bmrc.berkeley.edu/frame/research/mpeg/
13. Szummer, M., Picard, R.W.: Indoor-outdoor image classification. In: IEEE Intl. Workshop on Content-Based Access of Image and Video Databases, CAIVD, Bombay, India (1998) 42–51
14. Naphade, M., Kozintsev, I., Huang, T.: A factor graph framework for semantic video indexing. IEEE Trans. on Circuits and Systems for Video Tech. **12** (2002) 40–52

Mining Images to Find General Forms of Biological Objects

Petra Perner, Horst Perner, Angela Bühring, and Silke Jänichen

Institute of Computer Vision and applied Computer Sciences IBaI,
Körnerstr. 10, 04107 Leipzig
ibaiperner@aol.com
www.ibai-institut.de

Abstract. We propose and evaluate a method for the recognition of airborne fungi spores. We suggest a case-based object-recognition method to identify spores in a digital microscopic image. We do not use the gray values of the case, but the object edges instead. The similarity measure measures the average angle between the vectors of the template and the object. Case generation is done semi-automatically by manually tracing the object, automatic shape alignment, similarity calculation, clustering, and prototype calculation.

1 Introduction

Airborne microorganisms are ubiquitously present in the various fields of indoor and outdoor environments. The potential implication of fungal contaminants in bioaerosols in occupational health is recognized as a problem in several working environments. There is concern as regards the exposure of workers to bioaerosols especially in composting facilities, in agriculture and in municipal waste treatment. Despite this there is an increasing number of incidents of building-related sickness, especially in office and residential building. Some of these problems are attributed to biological agents, especially to airborne fungal spores. Besides the detection of parameters relevant to occupational and public health, in many controlled environments the number of airborne microorganisms has to be kept below the permissible or recommended values (e.g. in clean rooms, operating theaters, domains of the food and pharmaceutical industry). The continuous monitoring of airborne biological agents is consequently a necessity, as well for the detection of risks for human health as for the smooth sequence of technological processes. We describe our first results on the way to develop an automatic image-interpretation system for the detection and interpretation of airborne fungi spores. We describe the developed method for the case-based recognition of objects that are probably fungi spores in digital images. Future work will concentrate on classifying the objects. For our study we used six different fungi spores.

P. Perner (Ed.): ICDM 2004, LNAI 3275, pp. 60–68, 2004.

2   Image Acquisition and Sample Images

2.1   Fungal Cultures

Six fungal strains representing species with different spore types were used for the study (Table 1). The strains were obtained from the fungal stock collection of the Institute of Microbiology, University of Jena/ Germany and from the culture collection of JenaBios GmbH. All strains were cultured in Petri dishes on 2 % maltextract agar (Merck) at 24°C in an incubation chamber for at least 14 days. For microscopy fungal spores were scrapped off from the agar surface and placed on a microscopic slide in a drop of lactic acid. Naturally hyaline spores were additionally stained with lactophenol cotton blue (Merck). A database of images from the spores of these species was produced.

Table 1. Images of Fungal Strains

| Alternaria Alternata | Aspergillus Niger | Rhizopus Stolonifer |
| Scopulariopsis Brevicaulis | Ulocladium Botrytis | Wallenia Sebi |

2.2   Image Acquisition

Image acquisition was conducted using a Zeiss-Axiolab transmission light microscope equipped with a 100x lens and a NIKON Coolpix 4500 digital color camera. The magnification is 1000x, using a 100x objective. The resulting pixel size ranges from 0.1 to 0.025 μm. The average spore size of common airborne fungi varies between 2 to 40 μm. Some digitized sample images are presented in Table 1 for the different fungal spores. The objects in the images are good representatives of the different kinds of fungal spores cultured under optimal conditions and constant climate conditions.

3   Case-Based Object Recognition

The objects in the image are highly structured. Our study has shown that these images, represented in Table 1, cannot be segmented by thresholding. Biomedical applications have the special characteristic that one object can have a great variation in appearance. Therefore the appearance of this object cannot be generalized by one model as, is well known from model-based object recognition. Instead we decided to apply a case-based object recognition procedure for the detection of objects in the image. Case-based object recognition uses a set of cases (sometimes 50 cases or more) to represent the appearance of an object. It should be noted that the objects in the image can be occluded, touching, or overlapping. It can also happen that only parts of the objects appear in the image.

The case-based object recognition method uses templates that generalize the original objects and matches these templates against the objects in the image. During the match a score is calculated that describes the goodness of the fit between the object and the template. Well known similarity measures are the normalized cross correlation [1], the Hausdorff distance [2] and the chamfer matching [3]. We did not use the gray values of the case, but used the object edges instead [2]. For the score of the match between the case and the image we modified the normalized cross correlation in order to measure the average angle between the vectors of the template and the object.

The case can be an object case that describes the inner appearance of the object as well as a contour case. In our case the appearance of the whole objects can be very diverse. The shape seems to be the feature that generalizes the objects. Therefore we decided to use contour cases.

3.1 Similarity Measure

While we have to search for correspondences between case and image pixels when employing the Hausdorff distance, we evaluate the image pixels that coincide with the case pixels by using the cross correlation. Therefore the calculation of the Hausdorff distance is more costly than the calculation of the cross correlation. On the other hand we are interested in matching oriented edge pixels which Olson and Huttenlocher [2] described for the Hausdorff distance. Therefore we propose a similarity measure based on the cross correlation, using the direction vectors of an image. This approach requires the calculation of the dot product between each direction vector of the case $\vec{m}_k = (v_k, w_k)^T$, $k = 1, \hbar, n$ and the corresponding image vector $\vec{i}_k = (d_k, e_k)^T$:

$$s_1 = \frac{1}{n} \sum_{k=1}^{n} \vec{m}_k \cdot \vec{i}_k = \frac{1}{n} \sum_{k=1}^{n} \langle \vec{m}_k, \vec{i}_k \rangle = \frac{1}{n} \sum_{k=1}^{n} (v_k \cdot d_k + w_k \cdot e_k) \tag{1}$$

The similarity measure of Equation (1) is influenced by the length of the vector. That means that s_1 is influenced by the contrast in the image and the case. In order to remove the contrast, the direction vectors are normalized to the length one by dividing them through their gradient:

$$s_2 = \frac{1}{n} \sum_{k=1}^{n} \frac{\vec{m}_k \cdot \vec{i}_k}{\|\vec{m}_k\| \cdot \|\vec{i}_k\|} = \frac{1}{n} \sum_{k=1}^{n} \frac{v_k \cdot d_k + w_k \cdot e_k}{\sqrt{v_k^2 + w_k^2} \cdot \sqrt{d_{k_i}^2 + e_k^2}} \tag{2}$$

Note that the normalization of s_2 differs from the normalized cross correlation (NCC): The NCC normalizes each pixel value by the expected mean of all values of the considered pixels. Therefore it is sensitive to nonlinear contrast changes, whereas our method is not. The similarity measure in Equation (2) takes into account only the angle between the direction vectors, i.e. it is invariant against illumination changes. The value of $\arccos s_2$ indicates the mean angle between the case vectors and the image vectors.

The values of s_2 can range from 1 to 1. In the case of $s_2 = 1$ and $s_2 = -1$ the case and the image object are identical. If s_2 is equal to one, then all vectors in the case and the corresponding image vectors have the same direction. If s_2 is equal to "-1", then the vectors have exactly opposite directions, which means that only the contrast between the case and the image is changed.

Contrast changes can be ignored if the absolute value of the dot product is calculated:

$$s_3 = \frac{1}{n} \sum_{k=1}^{n} \frac{\left| \vec{m}_k \cdot \vec{i}_k \right|}{\left\| \vec{m}_k \right\| \cdot \left\| \vec{i}_k \right\|} \tag{3}$$

The aim is to store only one case for objects with similar shapes of different scale and rotation. Therefore a transformed case must be compared to the image at a particular location. A more detailed description of the similarity measure can be found in [4].

3.2 Template Generation

A detailed description of the case generation can be found in [5]. The acquisition of the templates is done semi-automatically. Prototypical images are displayed to an expert. The screenshot of our developed tool is shown in Fig. 1. The expert manually traces the contour of the object with the help of the cursor of the computer. Afterwards the number of the contour points is reduced for data-reduction purposes by interpolating the marked contour by a 1st order polynomial. The marked object shapes are then pair-wise aligned using Procrustes Algorithm [7]. From the set of shapes general groups of shapes are learnt by clustering. Single-linkage technique is used for clustering [6]. The prototype of each cluster is calculated by estimating the median shape [7] of the set of shapes in the cluster. Each of these prototypes is the representative of a group of similar shapes and will be used as an object template for the recognition process.

3.2.1 Shape Approximation
We are considering the labelled contour S of an object, defined by a set of n pixels $s_i(x, y)$, $i = 1, 2, \hbar, n$. An approximation of this contour might reduce the set of points to a sufficiently large set of pixels that will speed up the succeeding computation time of the alignment and clustering process. The numbers of pixels in this set will be influenced by the chosen order of the polygon and the allowed approximation error.

Our approach to the polygonal approximation is based on the area/length ratio according to Wall and Daniellson [8]. We use the first labeled point s_1 of the object shape S as the starting point p_1 for the first approximation. Next, we virtually draw a line segment from the starting point s_1 to the successor point in S. The area A between this line and the corresponding contour segment of the object S are measured. If the area divided by the length L of the line is smaller than a predefined threshold T, then the same process is repeated for the next successor point in the set S.

This procedure is repeated until the ratio exceeds the threshold T. In that case the current point of set S becomes the end point of the approximated line P and the starting point for the next approximation. The same process is then repeated until the last point in set S is reached. The result of the approximation is a subset of m points p_1, p_2, $\hbar$, p_m where $m < n$ and $p_i \in S$.

The ratio A/L controls the maximal error of the approximation, since A is the area and L the side length of a virtual rectangle. If the ratio is low, then the other side of the virtual rectangle is small and vice-versa.

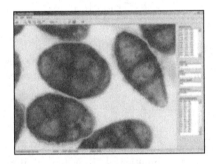

Fig. 1. Labeled and Approximated Shapes with Coordinates

3.2.2 Shape Alignment

The aim of the alignment process is to compare the shapes of two objects in order to define a measure of similarity between them. Consider two shape instances P and O defined by the point-sets $p_i \in R^2$, $i = 1,2,...N_1$ and $o_j \in R^2$, $j = 1,2,...N_2$, respectively. The basic task of aligning two shapes consists of transforming one of them (say P), so that it fits in some optimal way the other one (say O). Generally the shape instance $P = \{p_i(x, y)\}_{i=1...N}$ is said to be aligned with the shape instance $O = \{o_j(x, y)\}_{j=1...N}$ if a distance $d(P, O)$ between the two shapes can not be decreased by applying a transformation ψ to P. The differences between various alignment approaches is the group of allowed transformations (similarity, rigidity, affinity) on one side and the chosen distance function on the other side.

In our application we use the Procrustes distance, a least-squares type distance function. The alignment of shapes is limited to a similarity transformation in order to eliminate differences in the translation, the rotation and the scale of the two shapes P and O.

After computing a similarity transformation between P and O, the Procrustes distance is defined by:

$$D(P,O) = \sum_{i=1}^{N} \left\| \frac{(p_i - \mu_P)}{\sigma_P} - R(\theta) \frac{(o_i - \mu_O)}{\sigma_O} \right\|^2 \tag{4}$$

where θ is the rotation matrix, μ_P and μ_O are the centroids of the objects P and O, respectively and σ_P and σ_O are the sums of squared distances of each point-set from their centroids.

In the basic form, the Procrustes alignment centers and scales each set of points, so that the sum of squared distances of all points in each point-set is unity. Then a similarity transformation based on these centered pre-shapes is computed. Finally the Procrustes average shape and Procrustes residuals can be evaluated.

Figure 2 represents a screenshot of aligned shape instances of the fungal strain Ulocladium Botrytis with the calculated distances.

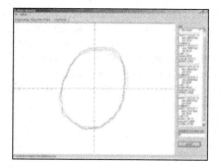

Fig. 2. Aligned Shapes of Fungal Strain Ulocladium Botrytis

3.2.3 Clustering

The alignment of every possible pair of objects in our database leads us to $N \times N$ pair-wise distances between N shape instances. These dissimilarity measures can be collected in a squared symmetric matrix with diagonal elements equal to value zero since the dissimilarity between an instance and itself is zero. This matrix is the input for the hierarchical cluster analysis [6]. It depends on the selected clustering method in which way the instances are merged together into groups. After having investigated different clustering methods we chose single linkage (nearest neighbour), where the linkage is done at the minimum distance between the two most similar instances of two different clusters.

The result of the hierarchical cluster analysis can be graphically represented by a dendogram. An example of the result for some instances of one species is shown in Fig. 3.

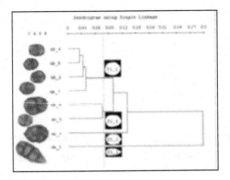

Fig. 3. Dendogram of Shapes of Strain Ulocladium Botrytis and the Calculated Prototypes

3.2.4 Prototype Calculation

We have divided our set of N shape instances $\{P_1, P_2, \hbar, P_N\}$ into k clusters $C_1, C_2, \hbar, C_k$. Each cluster C_i, $i = 1,2, \hbar, k$ consists of a subset of n_i shape instances. For each cluster we need to compute a prototype $\bar{\mu}$ that will be the representative of the cluster. This prototype can be calculated by computing the mean over all shapes in a cluster. As a result one will get an artificial prototype, a prototype that does not exist in reality. Therefore we decided to calculate the median of all shapes in a cluster. As the median shape of that cluster we chose the shape instance having the minimum distance to all other shape instances.

For the example shown in Fig. 3 we took four clusters. The resulting mean shape for each cluster is also shown in Fig. 3.

4 Results

We applied our method to six different airborne fungi spores (see Table 1). We labeled a total of 60 objects for each of the six fungal strains. These objects were taken for the case generation according to the procedure as described in Sec. 3. The result was a data base of cases. These cases were applied to images for the particular class which consist of unknown objects.

The threshold for the score was set to 0.8. The recognition rate is defined as the ratio of the number of correct recognized objects to the total number of objects in the image. The results of the matching process are shown in the Tables 2 and 3. The highest recognition rate can be achieved for the objects Rhizopus Stolonifer and Scopulariopsis Brevicaulis, since the variation of their shape is expressed well by the number of cases. For those classes where the variation of the shape of the objects is high, the number of the cases is also high. In the other cases the recognition rate shows that we do not have enough cases to recognize the classes with good recognition rate (see Alternaria Alternata and Ulocladium Botrytis). Therefore we need to increase the number of cases. For this task we should like to develop an incremental procedure for the case acquisition in our tool. Objects that have not been recognized well will be displayed automatically for tracing and then the similarity to all other shapes will be calculated and the clustering will be done in an incremental fashion as well. This procedure will ensure that we can learn the natural variation of the shape during the usage of the system.

The threshold for the similarity score needs to be very high. Otherwise too many cases will fire inside an object and in the background, since objects and background are highly structured. The next step will be to develop a hypothesis-test strategy to reduce the number of false alarms in this case.

Table 2. Recognized Objects in the Image

| Alternaria Alternata | Aspergillus Niger | Rhizopus Stolonifer |
| Scopulariopsis Brevicaulis | Ulocladium Botrytis | Wallenia Sebi |

Table 3. Results of Matching

Classes	Number of Cases	Recognition Rate
Alternaria Alternata	34	81.0
Aspergillus Niger	5	89.0
Rhizopus Stolonifer	22	96.2
Scopulariopsis Brevicaulis	8	98.2
Ulocladium Botrytis	30	85.0
Wallenia Sebi	10	78.8

5 Conclusions

We have described our method for the recognition of airborne fungi spores in digital microscopic images.

We used a case-based recognition method. The case is represented by edges and not by the gray-level itself. The similarity measure is based on the scalar product and is invariant against illumination changes and contrast changes. The case generation was done semi-automatically by manually tracing the contour of the object, automatic shape alignment, shape clustering, and prototype calculation. For future research we intend to develop an incremental case-acquisition procedure that should ensure that we can learn the natural shape variability over time.

Acknowledgement

The project "Development of methods and techniques for the image-acquisition and computer-aided analysis of biologically dangerous substances BIOGEFA" is sponsored by the German Ministry of Economy BMWI under the grant number 16IN0147.

References

1. L.G. Brown, A Survey of Image Registration Techniques, ACM Computer Surveys 24 (4), 1992, pp. 325-376
2. C.F. Olson, D.P. Huttenlocher, Automatic Target Recognition by Matching Oriented Edge Pixels, IEEE Transactions on Image Processing 6(1), 1997, p 103-113
3. G. Borgefors, Hierarchical Chamfer Matching: A Parametric Edge Detection Algorithm, IEEE Transactions on Pattern Analysis and Machine Intelligence 10(6), 1988, p. 848-865
4. P. Perner, A. Bühring, Case-Based Object Recognition, In: P. Funk, P. Gonzales, Proc. European Conference on Case-Based Reasoning, Springer LNCS, 2004, to be published.
5. S. Jähnichen, P. Perner, Case Acquisition and Case Mining for Case-Based Object Recognition, In: P. Funk, P. Gonzales, Proc. European Conference on Case-Based Reasoning, Springer LNCS, 2004, to be published.
6. P. Perner, Data Mining on Multimedia Data, Springer Verlag, lnai 2558, 2003
7. I.L. Dryden and K.V. Mardia, Statistical Shape Analysis, John Wiley&Sons, 1998
8. K. Wall, and P.-E. Daniellson, A Fast Sequential Method for Polygonal Approximation of Digitized Curves, Comput. Graph. Image Process. 28, pp. 220-227, 1984

The Main Steps to Data Quality

Joachim Schmid

FUZZY! Informatik AG, Eglosheimer Str. 40, 71636 Ludwigsburg, Germany
Joachim.Schmid@fazi.de

Abstract. To gain knowledge out of your data, your data has to be of high quality. Bad data quality becomes more and more the problem for companies, who start to exploit their data stocks. This article will show the main obstacles on the way to perfect data quality. It is based on our experience to improve data quality in large customer or business partner databases. The examples mentioned in this paper show data defects we have found during our daily work. There are also some notes how to improve data quality and avoid data defects.

1 Introduction

Companies, who want to be successful in their business have a strong demand on knowledge. Knowledge about their suppliers, the production processes, the market and their customers, about every part of their business. The good old days are gone, when small manufacturers had an all around knowledge, because they produced their goods at home, next door to their suppliers and customers. Today these companies are operating all around the globe having multiple suppliers, even for the same component or raw material. They are offering their goods and services to millions of customers in different markets. And still it is an requirement for success to have knowledge about the suppliers, the internal processes and the customers.

It is impossible to have a single person knowing all these things. No one can process the whole information, which is necessary to gain knowledge. That's the reason why the processing of the information has to be done by computers. There are a lot of advantages in this approach: computer networks can transfer the information from every point around the world to the business-intelligence system - just at the moment, when the information has been generated.

There is one big issue: data quality. Information arises from data. And data is very often erroneous. As a matter of fact, a lot of defective data records exist in our databases. In most cases these data defects are not obvious, because an error-tolerant human operator can work with such a defective data record, e.g. a call center agent will match a person calling in with the name "Peter Smith" to the record "Peter Smit" in the database.

Information is extracted from many data records by non-error-tolerant computer systems. The usage of data with bad data quality results in wrong information. Wrong information produces wrong knowledge inside the company. And with decisions based on wrong knowledge you will loose your way to success.

P. Perner (Ed.): ICDM 2004, LNAI 3275, pp. 69–77, 2004.

Good data is the basis for success. If you want knowledge you can trust in, you have to improve your data quality. This article will show the main obstacles on the way to perfect data quality. It is based on our experience to improve data quality in large customer or business partner databases. The examples show data defects we have found in name, address, bank account and other person-related information during our daily work.

Working on address information we mainly have to face the following problems:

- incomplete addresses due to missing data elements like building names.
- misspelling of city name, street name or building name
- transposition errors in post code or names
- outdated values due to merged cities, renamed or split streets,
- inconsistent data e.g. a building number does not match the number range associated to the given post code.

One consequence of these data defects is that without a correct address you can not reach your customer. You are not able to send him or her a single catalogue, ordered goods or an invoice. But also the analysis of such data is hindered by these data defects. Imagine a report showing the numbers of deliveries per postal region. Would you trust in this report, if there are more entries than postal regions or if the portion for postal region "-" is about 9%? Of course, no. Because it is obvious that there are two data defects in the data base: The portion for postal region "-" is equivalent to the portion of addresses without any post code. And the additional rows stem from invalid post codes.

All of our customers struggle with the mentioned data quality problems. The road to data quality starts with the determination of existing data defects. Then you have to choose an applicable solution.

2 Main Obstacles on the Road to Data Quality

2.1 More Entities Than Data Records

Improving data quality starts with the structure of the data. A good data structure means, that there is exactly one data record for one entity. In our business in almost every project "entity" defines a person, a household or a company.

Legacy systems in financial organizations often allow to have only one owner of a bank account. Therefore in a bank account record you have only one data field for the owner's first name, one for his last name, one for his or her address etc. A couple of years ago this data model met the real life very well. Today accounts are owned by more than one person, e.g. married couples or community of heirs. Because the bank clerk still has to use the old legacy system, he has to solve the problem to add a second owner. Fortunately the data fields for salutation and first name are long enough for a second salutation and a second first name. The solution for a bank account owned by a married couple could look like this:

Table 1. Record containing information about two persons

Account#	Salutation	First Name	Last Name	...
123456789	Mr. and Mrs.	Robert and Susan	Taylor	...

This solution works fine for creation and update of bank account information. But what happens if you want to use this data for other tasks like analyzing your customer database before you start a marketing campaign. If you analyze your data on person-level, your program won't work on such a data record containing more than one person. Just the determination of the number of persons in your database is no trivial task, due to the fact that it is not equal to a simple row count.

You must split the record into two records, one containing "Mrs. Taylor", one containing "Mr. Taylor".

Table 2. Two records each containing information about one person

Account#	Salutation	First Name	Last Name	...
123456789	Mrs.	Susan	Taylor	...
123456789	Mr.	Robert	Taylor	

Having one entity per data record it is much easier to work on the data. The number of records equals the number of persons in our database. You might count all records having a salutation = "Mrs." to get all female customers. But this will lead us to the next obstacle.

2.2 Multiple Data Elements in One Data Field

A good data structure also means in each record there is exactly one data field for one data element. A data field named first name containing "Mr. Frank M." is easily understood by a human operator. Now, if you want to know the number of male customers and you just count the records with salutation = "Mr.". Your program won't count this record, because "Mr." does not equal "Mr. Frank M.".

Before computer programs can sort, search and analyze this kind of data, it is necessary to parse the field contents, to identify the three data elements salutation, first name and middle initial, and store the new data elements in separate data fields.

Table 3. Records with one data field for each data element

Account#	Salutation	First Name	Middle Initial	Last Name	...
123456780	Mr.	Frank	M.	Summer	...

With a separate field for the data elements salutation, first name and middle initial you can easily write a program to search or sort by each of these data elements. Inside good structured data it is much easier to correct and match data, because it allows you to compare individual components, rather than long strings of data.

2.3 Watch Out for Hidden Information

In a very early data cleansing project it was obvious, that many postal codes were defective. These postal codes always ended with an asterisk. It seemed like the operator had inserted a wildcard character to indicate a missing digit. During cleansing of the data we did a postal validation and correction. Now all postal codes had correct values, especially including no asterisk. When our customers tested the cleansed data for the first time, they gave us a negative feedback: everything works fine, but they are not able to identify the so-called VIP-customers.

What happened? When the requirement to identify VIP-customers came up, there was no budget to add an additional data field to hold this indicator. Because there was at least one free character left inside the data field postal code, the operators decided to mark VIP-customers with an asterisk at the end of the postal code. This fact was completely transparent for the IT department and to us. There was hidden information in each data record.

Although this was a clever and cheap work-around, this caused problems for everyone working with this data not knowing the mystery. We solved the problems by adding a new data field and populating the field before postal validation.

2.4 National Standards Are Too Narrow for International Data

Many of our customers started with a national system for customer relationship management (CRM). As companies expand into new markets there is a need to deal with addresses from more than one country. As soon as you try to insert your first foreign contact into the CRM system you have to realize, that different countries have different addressing standards. The British postal code "W1U 7RT"does not fit into the five digits format of German postal code. And incompatible data types are not the only problem.

Nearly every European country has at least one specific address element. There are the Italian colors of the building numbers, the British building names, the Austrian backyards and stairs, the Swiss postal service areas (Botenbezirk) and so on.

Certainly you can solve these problems by setting up an extra data stock for each country. Then it is nearly impossible doing some analysis on this data with a global scope. Thus it is necessary to expand the data model. But be careful doing so. It is not useful to add any country-specific data field to the database. This would balloon your data model, and analysis would be complicated due to the fact, that every specific data field has to be handled by an extra condition.

You have to find the least common denominator of the country specific data fields. Therefore you have to identify those data fields, which are similar in semantics, and store them in the same data field. E.g. the British and the German postal code can be stored in one data field allowing entries made up from digits, characters and spaces with a maximum length of 8.

2.5 One Thing Represented by Different Values

Profiling the customer database of the UK-subsidiary of a German mail-order company we found the data field for gender populated with three values: m, f, w. Asking for the meaning of the values we found out: m stands for male, f for female and w for weiblich, the German word for female. One thing ("the customer is female") was represented by two values: f and w. Any selection on female customers, that is not based on the condition "gender = f or gender = w", will fail.

The solution is to standardize data. Standardization means the same thing is represented by the same value of a data element. Searching for your contacts at "Dr. Ing. h.c. F. Porsche AG" you may miss some entries. The missing ones are those with a variation in the company name, like "Dr. Ing. F. Porsche AG" or "Dr. Ing. h.c. Porsche AG". The differences are easily ignored by a human operator. But if your analysis program groups your contacts by company name, you will get an extra group for each variation. Standardizing your data is as important for good data quality as correcting your data.

2.6 Misspelled Data

Names are that kind of data you mostly have to deal with misspellings. Names of persons, cities, streets and buildings are created and changed by history and they are so diverse as humans and countries. There are no universal rules to decide whether a name is correctly spelled.

The only way to correct and standardize such names intelligently is to use software that compares to reliable reference data. National postal authorities are a good source of reliable address reference data. To get the correct spelling of a city name you have to do a look up in the city directory. Because you want to find the correct spelling matching to the misspelled name, this look-up has to be error-tolerant. This could be done by software based on fuzzy logic and some artificial-intelligence-algorithms.

2.7 Out-Dated Data

Once the data has been cleansed, one may think the job has finished. But anything changes and so does the customer information stored in the database. People get married or move. Villages are incorporated into cities. Streets are split and their names are changed. In Germany each quarter more than 100 city names disappear, more than 500 street names are changed. Thus in every month 1-3 % of the data records will go out of date.

Fortunately in some cases there is reference data available, which is reflecting the changes in the real world. E.g. directory of movers or so-called delta-files from the postal authorities. So some of these changes could easily be updated in the database. But how to find the affected records? Checking the whole data stock against these change-data - just to update a few percent of the records - is too much effort. Even if you want to be accurate and check it every month.

It is easy to update a data record, if you have a unique key like a customer ID or the postal code. It is more difficult, if you have to search for the record using a name like city name or street name. You will be in trouble, if you do not use the standardized form or if you combine two or more data elements in one data field. If the delta file tells you, that "Frankfurt am Main" has be changed to " Bad Frankfurt am Main", you will try to update all data records having city name = "Frankfurt am Main" and will not update those records with city names like "Frankfurt a. M." or "Frankfurt (Main)". If you always put street name and house number together in one data field, it would be very difficult to find all records affected by a change of the street name.

To solve the problems of out-dated data, you have to look for reference data reflecting the changes, set up a regular update process, use unique keys to identify the affected records (think of adding an extra field), standardize and structure data during cleanse process.

2.8 Inconsistent Data

If you have a good structure of the data records, standardized data and correct all misspellings and typos, you still have to deal with data defects.

The obstacles mentioned so far are more or less relevant to a single data field. In your database data fields are combined to a data record. But the combination of correct values will not automatically result in a correct data record. "B32 4AA" is a valid postal code in UK. "Birmingham" is a correct spelled post town. "Woodgate" is a correct spelled dependent locality, which belongs to "Birmingham". "Wood Lane" is a street in " Birmingham ", and 38 a house number existing in this road. "North Birmingham Busways" is a company sited in "38 Wood Lane". If you put all these correct and standardized data fields together, you will get an invalid address.

There are some inconsistencies inside the data record. If you send a letter to company "North Birmingham Busways" you have to use its assigned postal code "B24 9QL". And although "Wood Lane" is leading through "Woodgate", the company is situated in "Erdington".

A correct data record results not only in just putting some correct data fields together. After you have improved data quality on field level, you have also to improve it on entity level. To ensure consistency inside one data record is one of the main issues.

2.9 Duplicates

With structured, standardized and correct data you are more efficient to work on another kind of defects: duplicates. Duplicates are data records with different contents describing the same entity, e.g. a customer. If this customer is the one with the highest revenue, but his revenue is divided and spread among several duplicates, you will never identify him as an A-Level customer.

Looking at the sample data in the table you easily see the first two records describe the same person. Addresses are the same. Instead of the first name there is a matching initial. And there is a typo in the last name. What's about the third record? If you compare it to the first record, you will find an identical last name and city name. The first name could be matched by the nickname. Because the address of the third record

Table 4. Some duplicates

First Name	Last Name	Street Name	No.	City Name	Phone
Harry	Porter	Main Road	7	York	01977 683738
H.	Potter	Main Road	7	York	
Harold	Porter			York	01977 683738
Susan	Porter	Main Road	7	York	

is incomplete, we are not able to match the addresses. Therefore it is uncertain, whether the third record belongs to the same person as the first. Fortunately there is more information available: the phone numbers. Both phone numbers are the same. Now it is very reasonable, that the third record describes the same person as the first record. To eliminate duplicates you have to look at the data and decide, which are the matching rules to identify duplicates.

So far we have only looked for private duplicates. Looking at the last record you will see, that Susan lives at the same address as Harry and so it is very likely, that both live in the same household. This is important to know for mail-order companies, which want to send their catalogue only once to one household.

Eliminating duplicates and consolidating the information linked to each duplicate record to a single record gives you a unified view of this entity, e.g. of a customer.

3 How to Avoid Data Quality Problems

In the last ten years we helped all our customers to improve the data quality of their business partner database. Most of them struggle with some or all of the above mentioned data quality problems. The way to data quality starts with data profiling: a deep analysis of the current state to determine the existing data defects. Knowing which data defects occur, you can choose the applicable solution.

3.1 Data Model

As described above perfect data quality starts with the structure of the data. To ensure a good structure of your data you must have a good data model. Since years there are appropriate modeling techniques. First step is to start with an Entity-Relationship-Diagram [1] showing the conceptual model of your database. This model has to be transformed into a physical model, e.g. the tables of a relational database.

For an already existing database you have to check, whether the tables are in normalized form [2] and codd-conform. To check for normalization means to determine for each table in which normal form it is. Codd-conformity means to check for domain integrity, column integrity, entity integrity, referential integrity, and user-defined integrity. If the tables are in any normal form lower than the third normal form or if one or more integrity rules defined by Codd are violated, the design of the tables must be improved. Unfortunately changes of database tables will also cause changes to the programs working on these tables.

3.2 Tools

Since improvement of data quality is not a new issue there are several tools available to repair already existing and avoid new data defects. There are some tools available to analyze the data records looking for:

- data records containing more than one entity
- data fields containing more than one data element
- hidden information

These tools use some powerful algorithms: parsing algorithms. The parsing algorithms have been invented to build compiler for programming languages. These well-known and proofed algorithms are used to implement software to analyze and structure data records.

Tools using reliable reference data are very useful to

- standardize data elements
- correct misspellings and typos

and also partly for

- checking consistency
- and reflecting the changes in the real world.

These tools make a look-up in the reference data to get the correct value. The challenge is to find the correct entry even using an incorrect data element as the search criteria. This error-tolerant search can only be implemented using fuzzy logic and algorithms from artificial intelligence. These techniques are also used for a efficient duplicate detection.

3.3 Processes

A good data model is a good basis for good data quality. Tools can help to repair and avoid data defects. But the most important thing is to improve the processes, which produce and update the data [3]. You have to inspect the data flow inside your processes to identify the data sources and the data processing systems. Besides data quality problems inside the data sources and the systems the data transfer from one system to another is an important source of data defects.

It is also important to have a look on the persons involved in those processes. For each person or group of persons (e.g. department) you have to figure out whether they are data collectors, data custodians or data consumers. Make sure that every person is aware of his or her role and the specific tasks assigned to the role. The data consumer wants data, which is fit for use. Therefore it is necessary to adopt data-consumer perspective to find all the requirements on data quality [4]. Data quality or "fitness for use" is much more than only accuracy. There are many more aspects of data quality – so-called dimensions of data quality - as shown in [4] and [5].

Quality can never be added to a product by only testing it. Quality has to be build in during production. The same is with data quality. Therefore you have to find appropriate positions in the processes, where you can monitor data quality. At these points you have to check user-defined business rules and integrity rules. Defective data records found during these checks have to be sorted out. The even better way is to pass those records to a tool, which automatically repairs data defects. Those tools have also to be integrated into the processes.

4   Conclusion

Data Quality is the basis for success. Thus we help our customers to improve the data quality inside their business partner database. During many projects we found out, that the main obstacles on the road to data quality are:

- more entities than data records
- multiple data elements in one data field
- hidden information
- too narrow national standards
- non-standardized data
- misspelled data
- out-dated data
- inconsistent data
- duplicates

Fortunately the technology to correct data defects is available – provided by several tool vendors. The better way is to avoid the occurrence of new data defects. Good starting-points are to check the data model and the processes, which work on the data. If you find any structural defects causing the data defects, you will have to change the data model or the process.

These are the first steps on the way from data garbage to the road of success. More and more companies are beginning to wake up to the fact that the data they collect and manage should be viewed as a corporate asset. The quality of their data can be their competitive advantage.

References

1. Chen, P.P.: The entity-relationship model—toward a unified view of data. ACM Transactions on Database Systems, March 1976, 9-36.
2. Kent, W.: A simple guide to five normal forms in relational database theory. Communications of the ACM 26, 1983, 120-125.
3. Lee, Y.W. and Strong, D.M.: Knowing-Why About Data Processes and Data Quality. Journal of Management Information & Systems, Winter 2003-4, Volume 20, No.3, 13-39.
4. Strong, D.M., Lee, Y.W. and Wang, R.Y.: Data Quality in Context. Communications of the ACM, May 1997, 103-110.
5. Wang, R.Y. and Strong, D.M.: Beyond accuracy: what data quality means to data consumers. Journal of Management Information Systems 12, 4 (1996), 5–34.

Cost-Sensitive Design of Claim Fraud Screens

Stijn Viaene[12], Dirk Van Gheel[2], Mercedes Ayuso[3], and Montserrat Guillén[3]

[1] Vlerick Leuven Gent Management School, Reep 1, 9000 Gent, Belgium
[2] K.U.Leuven, Dept. of Applied Economics, Naamsestraat 69, 3000 Leuven, Belgium
{stijn.viaene;dirk.vangheel}@econ.kuleuven.ac.be
[3] Universitat de Barcelona, Dept. d'Econometria, Estadstica i Economia, Av.
Diagonal, 690 Barcelona 08034, Spain
{ayuso;guillen}@eco.ub.es

Abstract. In this paper we perform an exploratory study on the design of claim fraud detection for a typical property and casualty (P&C) insurance company using cost-sensitive classification. We contrast several cost incorporation scenarios based on different assumptions concerning the available cost information at claim screening time. Our empirical trials are based on a data set of real-life Spanish closed automobile insurance claims that were previously investigated for suspicion of fraud by domain experts and for which we obtained detailed cost information. The reported results show the added value of cost-sensitive claim fraud screening and provide guidance on how to operationalize this strategy.

1 Introduction

Classification techniques are aimed at algorithmically learning to allocate data objects, described as predictor vectors, to pre-defined object classes based on a training set of data objects with known class labels. Classification is one of the foremost learning tasks. This is no different for fraud detection. One of the complications that arise when applying these learning programs in practice, however, is to make them reduce the cost of (mis)classification rather than the error rate. This is not unimportant, since in many real-life decision making situations the assumption of equal (mis)classification costs, the default operating mode for many learners, is most likely violated. Medical diagnosis is a prototypical example. Here, a false negative prediction, i.e. failing to detect a disease, may well have fatal consequences, whereas a false positive prediction, i.e. diagnosing a disease for a patient that does not actually have it, may be less serious.

A similar situation arises for insurance claim fraud detection, where an early claim screening facility is to help decide upon the routing of incoming claims through alternative claims handling workflows [2]. Claims that pass the initial screening phase are settled swiftly and routinely, involving a minimum of transaction processing costs. Claims that are flagged as suspicious need to pass a costly state verification process, involving resource intensive investigation. Claim screening should thus be designed to take into account these cost asymmetries in order to make cost-benefit-wise optimal routing decisions.

P. Perner (Ed.): ICDM 2004, LNAI 3275, pp. 78–87, 2004.

Many practical situations are not unlike the ones above. They are typically characterized by a setting in which one of the predefined classes is a priori relatively rare, but also associated with a relatively high cost if not detected. Automated classification that is insensitive to this context is unlikely to be successful. For that reason Provost et al. [8, 9] argue against using the error rate (a.k.a. zero-one loss) as a performance assessment criterion, as it assumes equal (mis)classification costs and relatively balanced class distributions. Given a naturally very skewed class distribution and costly faulty predictions for the rare class, a model optimized on error rate alone may very well end up building a useless model, i.e. one that always predicts the most frequent class.

In this paper we aim at investigating the effect of making claim fraud screening sensitive to cost asymmetries. For this purpose we contrast six alternative scenarios that differ in terms of the cost information that claim screens have at their disposal. The data set that is used for this exploration consists of real-life Spanish closed automobile claims that were investigated for fraud by domain experts and for which we have detailed cost information. The rest of this paper is composed as follows. Section 2 describes the operational fraud control model for property and casualty (P&C) insurers. Section 3 tackles the mechanics of cost-sensitive classification and projects them onto the claim classification setting at hand. The data set that is used for the experimentation is described in Section 4, followed by a discussion of alternative cost incorporation scenarios based on different assumptions concerning the available cost information for classification at screening time. Section 5 closes off with a conclusion.

2   Fraud Control for the P&C Insurer

The operational fraud control is embedded in the insurer's claims handling process. Claims handling refers to the process that starts with a claim occurrence and report from the policyholder and ends with the payment, or denial of payment, for covered damages.

2.1   Operational Model

The generic operational claim fraud control model for insurers encompasses screening, investigation and negotiation/litigation phases.

(1) **Screening:** Early claim screening systems help decide upon the nature of incoming claims as either suspicious or not. This is the basis for routing claims through different claims handling workflows. Claims that pass the initial (automated) screening phase are settled swiftly and routinely, involving a minimum of transaction processing costs. Claims that are flagged as suspicious pass a costly state verification process, involving (human) resource intensive investigation.

(2) **Investigation:** Cases that raise enough questions during routine processing are referred to specialized investigators, whose task is to try to uncover the true nature of the situation and reach informed judgment through in-depth inquiry. Work here is mainly driven by the experience, the skill, the creativity

and situational empathy of the human investigator, which generally makes work proceed in a non-routine, ad hoc manner and take substantial time, effort and money.

(3) **Negotiation/Litigation:** With a strong enough case for fraud the insurer may decide to dismiss or reduce compensation or even decide to press charges. However, few fraud cases ever reach the courts. Litigation and prior special investigation typically involve lengthy and costly procedure. Insurers also are fearful of getting involved in lawsuits and loosing, which may compromise their reputation. Many an insurer's strategy is geared toward confronting the claimant with the gathered evidence and gently developing pressure to make him reduce or drop the claim. This also ought to deter the claimant from defrauding insurance again. The final decision on what action to undertake will typically not be made without explicit consultation with senior or qualified personnel (e.g. for balancing prudential against commercial arguments).

2.2   Economics of Fraud Detection

To illustrate the economics of a fraud detection system, suppose we dispose of a portfolio of 500,000 automobile insurance policies. At a yearly claim rate of 8% this would mean that on average one in every twelve policies generates a claim on a yearly basis, i.e. the portfolio gives rise to an average of 41,667 claims a year. At a fraud rate of 7.24%[1] this set of claims will on average contain 3,017 fraudulent ones. With this figure in mind it would make sense for us to allocate resources to fraud control that would allow us to audit 3,017 claims a year.

Let us now compare the economics of fraud control associated with alternative fraud screening models. The null model represents the decision not to invest in fraud control. Under this scenario every honest policyholder would see its yearly premium increase with 4.9 EUR to subsidize for fraud. In the ideal case early fraud screening is able to refer exactly those 3,017 claims that are fraudulent to the fraud auditors, who are able to build up a case for fraud and recommend no payment. In other words, of the 3,017 claims scheduled for audit, 100% are actual fraud cases. Thus, we termed this case the 100% model. In this case we would be able to decrease yearly premium rates up to 4.5 EUR. Note that we, on average, spent about 0.44 EUR per policy to cover the total audit costs. The 0% model is the other extreme that represents the case where all claims referred for auditing turn out to be honest, so only costs are incurred and no savings are realized. We can now simulate any model in between these two extremes. For example, even when our screening model isn't perfect, and works at let's say 70%, we still would be able to make a solid case for fraud detection. In this case 70% of the 3,017 cases referred to the auditors turn out to be actual frauds, i.e. we missed 905 actual frauds. On a yearly basis we would still save more than three quarters of a million EUR.

---

[1] This figure coincides with the fraud rate observed for the random sample of claims used for our analysis in Section 4.

3   Cost-Sensitive Claim Classification

Many classifiers are capable of producing Bayesian posterior probability estimates. These can then be used to classify data objects into the appropriatepredefined classes as follows. We restrict the discussion to the case of binary classification.

Optimal Bayes decision making dictates that a predictor vector $\mathbf{x} \in \mathbb{R}^n$ should be assigned to the class $t \in \{0, 1\}$ associated with the minimum expected cost [4]. Optimal Bayes assigns classes according to the following criterion:

$$\arg \min_{t \in \{0,1\}} \sum_{j=0}^{1} p(j|\mathbf{x})C_{t,j}(\mathbf{x}), \tag{1}$$

where $p(j|\mathbf{x})$ is the conditional probability of class j given predictor vector $\mathbf{x}$ (and therefore termed posterior probability), and $C_{t,j}(\mathbf{x})$ is the cost of classifying a data object with predictor vector $\mathbf{x}$ and actual class j as class t.

The available cost information is typically represented as a cost matrix $\mathbf{C}$ where each row represents a single predicted class and each column an actual class. The cost of a true positive is denoted as $C_{1,1}(\mathbf{x})$, the cost of a true negative is denoted as $C_{0,0}(\mathbf{x})$, the cost of a false positive is denoted as $C_{1,0}(\mathbf{x})$, and the cost of a false negative is denoted as $C_{0,1}(\mathbf{x})$. Note that if $C_{t,j}(\mathbf{x})$ is positive it represents an actual cost, whereas if $C_{t,j}(\mathbf{x})$ is negative it represents a benefit.

One often implicitly assumes that the cost matrix complies with the following two reasonableness conditions formulated by Elkan [5]. The first reasonableness condition implies that neither row dominates any other row. The second reasonableness condition implies that the cost of labelling a data instance incorrectly is always greater than the cost of labelling it correctly.

It can easily be verified that, under the above reasonableness conditions, the criterion for classification in (1) translates into the rule that assigns class 1 to a data object if

$$p(j = 1|\mathbf{x}) > \frac{C_{1,0}(\mathbf{x}) - C_{0,0}(\mathbf{x})}{C_{1,0}(\mathbf{x}) - C_{0,0}(\mathbf{x}) + C_{0,1}(\mathbf{x}) - C_{1,1}(\mathbf{x})} \tag{2}$$

and class 0 otherwise. In case the available cost information $C_{t,j}$ is independent of $\mathbf{x}$, i.e. there is a fixed cost associated with assigning a data object to class t when in fact it belongs to class j, the rule in (2) defines a fixed classification threshold in the interval $[0,1]$.

For our experiments we use a logistic regression model to estimate $p(j = 1|\mathbf{x})$. Logistic regression makes the assumption that the difference between the natural logarithms of the class-conditional data density functions is linear in the predictors:

$$\ln \left(\frac{p(\mathbf{x}|j = 1)}{p(\mathbf{x}|j = 0)} \right) = b + \mathbf{w}^T \mathbf{x}, \tag{3}$$

Table 1. Cost information for Spanish data

	Observed Honest	Observed Fraud
Predicted Honest	0	$claimed\_amount(\mathbf{x})$
Predicted Fraud	$audit\_cost(\mathbf{x})$	$audit\_cost(\mathbf{x}) - claimed\_amount(\mathbf{x})$

where $\mathbf{w} \in \mathbb{R}^n$ represents the coefficient vector and $b \in \mathbb{R}$ the intercept.[2] The class membership probability $p(j = 1|\mathbf{x})$ underlying classification in (2) can readily be obtained from the model in (3):

$$p(j = 1|\mathbf{x}) = \frac{\exp(b' + \mathbf{w}^T \mathbf{x})}{1 + \exp(b' + \mathbf{w}^T \mathbf{x})}, \tag{4}$$

where $b' = b + \ln\left(\frac{p(j=1)}{p(j=0)}\right)$, with $p(j = 1)$ and $p(j = 0)$ the class priors. We can use the class membership probability specification in (4) to obtain maximum likelihood estimates for $\mathbf{w}$ and b'. We assume that the class proportions in the training data are representative of the true class priors.

For our experiments on cost-sensitive claim screen design we hypothesize the following situation. Whenever a new claim arrives, our claim screening facility makes a prediction, specifically, either honest or fraudulent, costlessly. If the claim gets predicted as honest, then it is swiftly and routinely settled as stipulated by the obligations of the insurance contract. On the other hand, if predicted as fraudulent, then the claim gets audited, i.e. the prediction triggers a decision to acquire more information at a price. The claim investigation typically is costly, but has no (direct) effect on the claim amount. We make abstraction of any other strategic reasons to audit claims, either by targeting or at random. We furthermore assume that by auditing the claim we can exactly determine the true nature of the claim, i.e. either honest or fraudulent. Actual fraud is a reason for not paying the claimed amount. This yields the cost structure specified in Table 1 for the Spanish data at hand.

4   Scenario Evaluation

We analyze the effects of taking account of information on damages and audit costs at early screening time. We discuss several scenarios based on real-life data from a large Spanish insurance company.

4.1   Data Description

Our empirical trials are based on a data set of real-life Spanish closed automobile insurance claims that were previously investigated for suspicion of fraud by

---

[2] Besides the assumption in (3) logistic regression does not make any distributional assumptions for the predictors and has been shown to work well in practice for data that depart significantly from conventional normality assumptions (see e.g. [7]).

domain experts and for which we obtained detailed cost information. The data is a random sample of claims for automobile damages from accidents that occurred in Spain during 2000. The sample consists of 2,403 claims, 2,229 of which are honest and 174 of which are fraudulent. A claim record in the data set contains information on the insured, the claimant, the policy, the vehicle and the accident. The predictors are similar to those used by Artís et al. [1]. In addition, we had access to certain cost information. We included both the claimed amount, which is the final payment made by the insurer for automobile damages compensation, and the cost of the investigation needed to ascertain the true nature of the claim. Note that we do not consider fraud related to injuries or medical treatment. The identification of this kind of fraud may require different predictor information. A discussion on the kind of predictors that can be taken into account when looking for fraud in these cases is found in [3].

4.2   Results and Discussion

Six possible scenarios are studied. The scenarios differ in the assumptions concerning the available cost information at early claim screening time. The presentation sequence of scenarios follows a natural progression. We start with a first benchmark Scenario 1 where we assume that no cost information is available to the insurance company at screening time. Scenario 2 models the other extreme, where all claim-specific cost information is assumed to be known at the time of classification. Scenarios 3 and 4 pertain to cases in which average cost information is used to classify claims. Finally, in Scenarios 5 and 6 we assume that individual claim amounts are known to the insurance company at the time of early claim screening, but audit costs are estimated for each claim on the basis of the other available information.

Scenario 1: Cost-Insensitive Classification. This scenario assumes that no cost information is available to the insurance company at the time of claim classification. The company is left with no other option than to use an error-based classifier. A logistic regression model is used to predict the probability of claim fraud using all the predictors as inputs to the model except for the claim amount and the audit cost. An incoming claim is labelled as fraud, and will undergo further examination, if the predicted probability of fraud for the claim exceeds a classification threshold of 0.5, otherwise it is classified as honest and does not undergo further examination. For evaluation purposes, each claim in the data set is classified in this manner and the cost of classification of each claim is added to yield the total cost of classification for this scenario. This cost-insensitive scenario then corresponds to a total positive cost of +210,079.63 EUR. Closer examination reveals, however, that this model actually classifies all claims as honest claims and, thus, seems useless for fraud detection purposes. We may try to improve the probability estimation model by including claim amount among the predictors. Claim amount information could easily and accurately be obtained by adhering to a policy of each time sending an adjuster to the auto repair shop to assess the damages early in a claim's lifecycle. In this case, however, this did not have any effect on the total cost.

Heuristically fixing the classification threshold at 0.0724, i.e. the percentage of fraud cases in the random sample, an intuitive choice, yields better results. Using the probability estimation model without inclusion of the claim amount among its predictors then yields a percentage correctly classified of 65.5%, i.e. 54.0% and 66.4% for the subsamples of fraud and honest cases, respectively. This scenario corresponds to a total positive cost of +71,049.20 EUR. Including the claim amount among the predictors of the probability estimation model further improves the results to yield a total negative cost of -56,693.34 EUR, i.e. a benefit to the company.

Scenario 2: Full Costing. This scenario assumes that the insurance company has access to all individual cost information, i.e. claim amount and audit cost, at claim screening time. A logistic regression model is used to predict the probability of claim fraud using all the predictors as inputs to the model, i.e. with inclusion of the claim amount and audit cost. The threshold value for classification is then calculated according to the theory set out in Section 3, i.e. by taking into account the available information on the individual audit cost and claim amount for each claim. The model's performance is at a percentage correctly classified of 99.42%, 99.43% and 99.42% for the subsamples of fraud and honest cases, respectively. This scenario then corresponds to a total negative cost of -163,031.40 EUR. Note that this scenario is not of great practical value, since, typically, the exact cost of investigation for a particular claim is but known at the final stages of the investigation itself, and, typically, is directly related to the presence of fraud itself. This scenario does, however, constitute a benchmark or target for the following cost-sensitive claim screening scenarios.

Scenario 3: Average Costing. This scenario assumes that the insurance company has access to average claim amount and average audit cost information at claim screening time. For the Spanish automobile data at hand the average audit cost amounts to 72.26 EUR and the average claim amount is 818.14 EUR. To estimate the probability of fraud for a claim a logistic regression model is used that includes all the predictors except for the claim amount and audit cost. Since the available cost information is independent of the nature of the claim to be screened, the classification threshold above which a claim is labelled as fraud is fixed for this scenario (see Section 3); at 0.04 in this case. The results show a poor percentage correctly classified claims, only 23.51%, i.e. 89.66% and 18.35% for the subsamples of fraud and honest cases, respectively. We note that with a threshold fixed at a notably lower level than the one used in Scenarios 1, i.e. 0.0724, the number of cases mislabelled as fraud is notably higher. The total cost for this scenario then equals -38,533.48 EUR.

Scenario 4: Individual Claim Amount and Average Audit Cost. This scenario assumes that the insurance company disposes of individual claim amount information and average audit cost information for each incoming claim at screening time. A logistic regression model is used to predict the probability of claim fraud using all the predictors as inputs to the model except for the audit cost. The threshold value for classification is then calculated by taking into account the available information on the individual claim amount and average audit cost. This scenario yields a percentage correctly classification of 62.63%, i.e. 66.67% and 62.31% for the subsamples of fraud and honest cases, respectively. This scenario then corresponds to a total negative cost of -71,832.20 EUR. Comparing this result to the one obtained for Scenario 1, we observe that taking into account individual claim amount information for the determination of the classification threshold resorts a significant positive effect.

Scenario 5: Individual Claim Amount and Single-Model Predicted Audit Cost. This scenario differs from the previous one in that now, instead of simply assuming the audit cost to coincide with the average, the audit cost is predicted using a linear regression model based on the predictors excluding the audit cost. The fitted audit cost model, however, shows a low goodness-of-fit with an R^2 of 31.87%. Predicting audit costs with the variables at hand does not seem an easy task. Looking at the significance of the estimated coefficient parameters, we note a significant effect only for the type of coverage, the gender of the insured, the claim amount and the intercept. Including predictors relating to the employed investigation routines (see e.g. [10]) would probably be helpful, but this information isn't usually available early in the life of a claim. The probability of claim fraud is predicted as in Scenario 4. The threshold value for classification takes into account the available information on the individual claim amount and the predicted audit cost. With this threshold we obtain a percentage correctly classified of 58.18%, i.e. 71.26% and 57.16% for the subsamples of fraud and honest cases, respectively. This scenario then corresponds to a total negative cost of -70,659.41 EUR. This represents a slight worsening compared to the setup in Scenario 4. Improved audit cost prediction would probably improve the cost figure.

Scenario 6: Individual Claim Amount and Multiple-Model Predicted Audit Cost. This scenario tries to improve on the audit cost prediction by using two separate linear regression models, i.e. one for the subsample of fraud cases and another one for the subsample of honest cases. The rationale underlying this decision is that audit costs tend to show different behaviour depending on whether a claim is actually fraudulent or not. At screening time the expected audit cost $eac(\mathbf{x})$ for an incoming claim with predictor vector $\mathbf{x}$ is then calculated as follows:

$$eac(\mathbf{x}) = \hat{p}(\mathbf{x}) * acf(\mathbf{x}) + (1 - \hat{p}(\mathbf{x})) * ach(\mathbf{x}), \qquad (5)$$

with $\hat{p}(\mathbf{x})$ the estimated probability of fraud using the setup of Scenario 4, $acf(\mathbf{x})$ and $ach(\mathbf{x})$ the audit cost predictions according to the linear regression models for the subsamples of fraud and honest cases, respectively. The audit cost model fitted to the fraud cases shows a high goodness-of-fit with an R^2 of 84.58%. The R^2 for the model fitted to the honest cases is significantly worse with an R^2 of 36.62%. Once the expected audit cost for an incoming claim is calculated, it is used together with the individual claim amount information and the probability of claim fraud (predicted as in Scenario 4) for the calculation of the cost-sensitive classification threshold. This scenario yields a percentage correctly classification of 58.59%, i.e. 70.69% and 59.47% for the subsamples of fraud and honest cases, respectively. This scenario then corresponds to a total negative cost of -71,396.27 EUR. Thus, despite the audit cost models' improved goodness-of-fit vis-à-vis the situation in Scenario 5, the overall performance of classification in terms of the total cost is not improved.

It is clear that cost-sensitive classification, when compared to cost-insensitive classification, represents a serious improvement in terms of profitability of claim screening. For example, results for the 'purest' of cost-insensitive classifications, i.e. Scenario 1, even reveal a non-profitable fraud screening system. In defence of the latter, though, one must keep in mind the positive deterrence effect that has not been accounted for in this study. Our results certainly underline the principal conclusion of this study that cost sensitive decision making represents a clear improvement over error-based decision making. Still, the performance gap between the benchmark result for Scenario 2 and the best realistic alternative, i.e. Scenario 4, still amounts to 91,199.20 EUR, leaving significant room for further improvement. From the analysis of Scenario 5 we may hypothesize that extending the predictor set and/or using alternative (non-linear) modelling techniques are necessary to further improve the performance of audit cost prediction.

We end this discussion by pointing at the importance of the probability estimation exercise. A way to get some insight into its role is by looking at the Brier inaccuracy [6] for the three logistic regression models that figured in the above scenarios: 1) model 1 uses all the predictors as inputs to the model except for the claim amount and the audit cost; 2) model 2 extends the predictor set of model 1 with the claim amount; and 3) model 3 adds the audit cost to the predictor set of model 2. The Brier inaccuracy $(\overline{B})$ is derived from the Brier score $(\overline{BS})$, which is defined as follows for data $D = \{(\mathbf{x}_i, t_i)\}_{i=1}^{N}$ with predictor vectors $\mathbf{x} \in \mathbb{R}^n$ and class labels $t \in \{0, 1\}$:

$$\overline{BS} = \frac{1}{N} \sum_{i=1}^{N} \sum_{j=0}^{1} (\hat{p}(t = j \mid \mathbf{x}_i) - p(t = j \mid \mathbf{x}_i))^2. \tag{6}$$

This score coincides with the mean squared error of the probability estimates. However, since we do not have access to the true class membership probabilities and only the class labels are known, $p(t = j \mid \mathbf{x}_i)$ is replaced in (6) by $\delta(j, t_i)$, which equals 1 if both arguments match, 0 otherwise. This operation yields the Brier inaccuracy (range $[0,2]$; 0 is optimal), which equals 0.132, 0.129, 0.004 for models 1, 2 and 3, respectively; or, alternatively, 1.659, 1.600, 0.028 and 0.012, 0.014, 0.002 for, respectively, the fraud and honest subsamples. The gap between benchmark model 3 and the other models clearly leaves room for further improvement; improvement that, again, may come from extending the predictor set and/or using alternative (non-linear) modelling techniques. Moreover, the contrast in performance for the fraud and honest subsamples suggests that experimentation with models trained on data sets that do not reflect the natural data proportion among fraud and honest cases, i.e. data sets in which fraud cases are oversampled or receive a higher weight, may be beneficial.

5   Conclusion

We looked at the design of claim fraud screening for a typical P&C insurer using cost-sensitive classification. We started with a description of the problem and the available real-life Spanish automobile damages claims data. This was followed by a theoretical exposition on cost-sensitive claim classification. We then contrasted several claim screen cost incorporation scenarios, with the following conclusions: 1) The expected cost of implementing a cost-insensitive claim fraud screen can be positive, i.e. unprofitable (taking abstraction of any deterrence effect of fraud screening). 2) With claim amount information available at early screening time detection rules can be accommodated to increase expected profits. 3) The highest profits are obtained when one has perfect access to complete claim dependent cost information, i.e. claim amount and audit cost. This scenario is not realistic though, since the exact cost of investigation for a particular claim can only be known at the final stages of the investigation itself. 4) Average costing, i.e. using only information on average claim amount and average audit costs, proved to be the worst case among all benchmarked cost-sensitive scenarios. Still, even this scenario turned out as a profitable move. 5) An insurer that disposes of individual claim amount information and average audit cost information for each incoming claim at screening time may gain most from its fraud screening.

Acknowledgement. Thanks are given to Spanish grants FEDER, BBVA, SEC2001-3672 and SEC2001-2581-C02-02.

References

1. M. Artís, M. Ayuso, and M. Guillén. Detection of automobile insurance fraud with discrete choice models an misclassified claims. *Journal of Risk and Insurance*, 69 (3): 325–340, 2002.
2. R. Derrig. Insurance Fraud. *Journal of Risk and Insurance*, 69 (3): 271–87, 2002.
3. R. Derrig and H. Weisberg. AIB PIP claim screening experiment final report. Understanding and improving the claim investigation process. *AIB Filing on Fraudulent Claims Payment*, DOI Docket R98-41, Boston, 1998.
4. R. Duda, P. Hart, and D. Stork. *Pattern classification*. Wiley, 2000.
5. C. Elkan. The foundations of cost-sensitive learning. In *17th International Joint Conference on Artificial Intelligence*, Seattle, Washington, USA, August 2001.
6. D. Hand. Construction and assessment of classification rules. Wiley, 1997.
7. D. Michie, D. Spiegelhalter, and C. Taylor, eds. *Machine learning, neural and statistical classification*. Ellis Horwood, 1994.
8. F. Provost and T. Fawcett. Robust classification for imprecise environments. *Machine Learning*, 42 (3): 203–231, 2001.
9. F. Provost, T. Fawcett, and R. Kohavi. The case against accuracy estimation for comparing classifiers. In *15th International Conference on Machine Learning*, Madison, Wisconsin, USA, July 1998.
10. S. Tennyson and P. Salsas-Forn. Claims Auditing in Automobile Insurance: Fraud Detection and Deterrence Objectives. *Journal of Risk and Insurance*, 69 (3): 289–308, 2002.
11. S. Viaene and G. Dedene. Insurance fraud: issues and challenges. *Geneva Papers on Risk and Insurance (Issues and Practice)*, 29 (2): 313–333, 2004.

An Early Warning System for Vehicle Related Quality Data

Matthias Grabert[1], Markus Prechtel[1], Tomas Hrycej[1], and Winfried Günther[2]

[1] DaimlerChrysler AG, Research and Technology
[2] DaimlerChrysler AG, Global Services and Parts
Matthias.Grabert@DaimlerChrysler.com

Abstract. Vehicle production audit tests, warranty claims and car control unit data are stored in a central data warehouse for data mining analysis. Neural network based part failure rate estimations, adjusted for mileage and seasonality, are used for monitoring warranty claims. Association and sequence analysis connect production audit data, car control unit data and warranty claims for an early detection of quality changes both in production state and car field usage. Calculations are performed via grid computing.

1 Data Driven Quality Management

A major aspect of quality management is avoidance of quality defects. Nevertheless, 100% freedom from error in motor vehicle production and during their lifecycles cannot be achieved with these highly complex products. Therefore, a continuous quality monitoring at production time and during the lifecycle is mandatory to early address upcoming quality problems.

Vehicle service centers document repair cases with standardized codes, and all reports are later on transferred to the central claim database at least during the warranty period. Beside repair cases, protocols of car control units are read out during service center visits. Newest generation cars collect load spectrum data continuously and reports are later transferred at WLAN hotspots or via GSM to the carrier.

Data sources are of different kinds: While failure codes during warranty periods are completely documented and therefore available for all cars, only approximately 1% of manufactured motor vehicles are checked carefully directly before delivery. These production audits happen definitely earlier and allow thus a rapid identification and elimination of quality problems. Therefore, an early as well as detailed quality monitoring system optimally consists of different data sources in different lifecycle stages.

An ultimate goal of such a quality monitoring system is - beside a rapid detection of already existing problems – to give a reliable forecast of upcoming events or increasing failure numbers as early as possible.

"As early as possible" has to be seen in the context of structural conditions of each car component. Upcoming failures are mainly dependant on car age, mileage and – e.g. in commercial vehicles – usage profile.

P. Perner (Ed.): ICDM 2004, LNAI 3275, pp. 88–95, 2004.

The following data sources have been available at DaimlerChrysler for our early warning system:

- repair codes during warranty period (called in this paper "DB1")
- messages from control unit codes (called in this paper "DB2")
- results of production audits before delivery (called in this paper "DB3")

An overview of the software system as well as deployed data mining methods will be given in the rest of the article.

2 Models and Methods Overview

The early warning system is working on a two-steps base (Fig.1): First, the system is trained with data from the past (usually 24 months): complex mathematical distribution models are learned for warranty claims (DB1) taking into account seasonal changes of failure rate (e.g. air-condition fails usually during summer due to heavy usage). Models are adjusted for mileage and age of the vehicles. For vehicles without warranty entries, mileage has to be estimated since no information is then available in DB1. Furthermore, associations between warranty claims and control unit messages (DB2) as well as production audit results (DB3) are calculated in step one. In a second step, current DB1 data (usually last 12 months) are tested on a monthly base for significant changes against the calculated models of step one (Fig. 2). Grid computing is used for DB1 training and testing (~ 10,000 models are processed during testing only). Furthermore, the probability of a warranty case under the condition of a pre-occurring DB3 (audit result) or DB2 (control unit message)

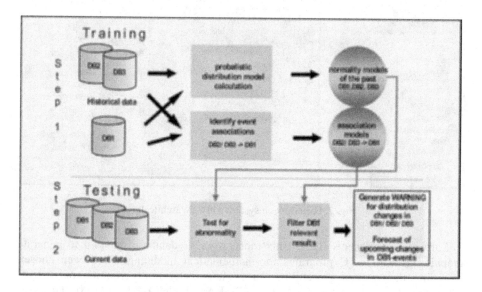

Fig. 1. Model related system architecture

event are calculated to quantify the association strengths. Significant associations are determined by a Chi-Square-Test. Warnings for the system user are then generated and displayed. Every warning is a candidate for a possible production weakness and has to be carefully evaluated for necessary consequences by a human expert.

2.1 Software Architecture and Implementation Details

Figure 2 displays the EWS software architecture. User and system administrator navigate through the password protected system via standard web browser within the DaimlerChrysler intranet. The system administrator configures the system and starts training or testing steps, when needed. Data is loaded via PERL::DBI from different data sources into a MySQL [1] based data warehouse. Motor vehicles with unreliable date of initial registration or repair date (e.g. before production date) are excluded from later analysis *(Data Cleansing)* [2]).

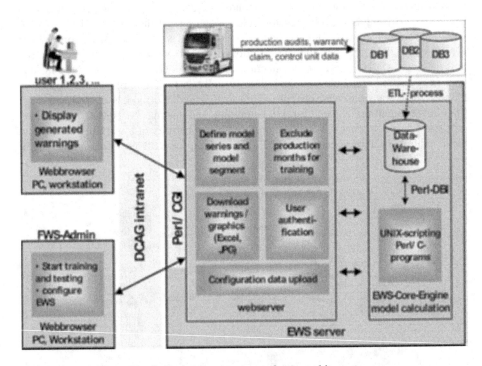

Fig. 2. Overview on system software architecture

Software components (Perl, Unix-tools, MySQL database, gnuplot to generate graphics as well as C programs for mathematical modeling) have been chosen regarding the ease of portability. The system is currently running on a two-processor HP A500 with 440MHz, 2 GB RAM under HP-UX 11.00. Time for porting to a different UNIX system (such as Solaris, Linux) is below one day.

2.2 Car Warranty Claims

Mercedes-Benz's warranty database (DB1) contains the complete repair history of every Mercedes vehicle during warranty time (at least first 12 months after initial registration, another 12 months depending on mileage). Currently data of 17 Mio. cars are collected in the database. Part failures are standardized documented during car repair using over 15,000 so called "damage codes".

The following part of the early warning system solely depends on DB1 data analysis using the above mentioned two-step architecture:

1. Calculate a mathematical model for the damage frequency of each damage code appearing in a specified model series for a given training period (typically 24 months of production).
2. Test the damage data of newly produced cars (e.g. last year of production) for significant distribution changes against the trained models (test period has to be different from training period!).

Tests are performed on a car group level. Vehicles in the group should be as similar as possible to guarantee a homogenous random sample for the stochastic modeling. Grouping criteria are:

- model series (e.g. E-Class, Sprinter, Actros)
- segments within the model series (e.g. Sprinter 2,8t or Sprinter with right hand drive)
- engine (power rating)
- model type (determined by the first 6 digits of the unique vehicle identification number)

Car groups can be defined in database tables by the system administrator, thus enabling the system to be easily adapted to new model series.

A distribution model is only built for a car group if enough failure cases are in the specified group for a specified damage code. The level of specialization is ascending for the describing criteria: After a calculation on model series level (lowest level of specialization), a calculation on segment level will be tried and so on. Specialization is aborted if no stochastic model can be calculated for a specific level (too few data).

Each stochastic model is finally evaluated by testing the model with the training data: If the trained model is not good enough to pass the test with data used for the learning phase, it will be discarded. Atypical production months (e.g. after production start of a new series) can be excluded from the training period on damage code level.

For the Sprinter model series, about 550 stochastic models are typically generated for about 90,000 cars and different damage codes during training. Training phase including data transfer from the central warranty database to the data warehouse (~100MB) takes about 6 days on a single machine. For a final model calculation, up to 600MB of prepared data have to be processed for each car group (estimation of missing mileage or date of initial registration, part failure rate for each month after registration). The parameters of the generated distribution model include no more than 500 bytes.

These long training periods could be reduced by 50% with the help of grid computing since calculation of each model is independent from another.

During test phase, typically the last 12 months of production will be tested against the trained models of the past. For each production month all available months after registration will be tested separately for a specific car group.

A warning is produced when the number of failures for a car group exceeds the model based significance level (figure 3) in a specific damage code. A 12-months test for the above mentioned Sprinter group takes about 1.5 days of computation time.

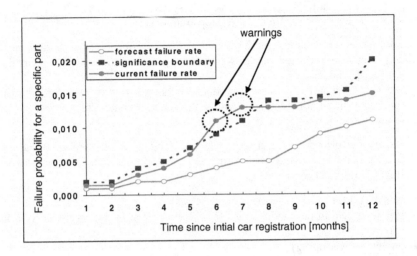

Fig. 3. The x-axis corresponds to months 1 ... 12 after initial registration. Car group, production month and damage code are fixed. The y-axis shows the cumulated failure probabilities (forecasted failure rate, current failure rate and calculated significance boundary). The current failure rate exceeds in two months the significance boundary (month 6 and 7). Thus, two warnings will be generated by the system for the specific car group and damage code

2.3 Production Quality Audit

Beside all quality monitoring performed during car manufacturing, approximately one percent of all cars are carefully audited directly before leaving the factory. Found quality issues are encoded according to the warranty damage codes and then entered into a database (DB3).

The early warning system for DB3 data should recognize significant changes in production quality and reveal a possible correlation between production failures and later on warranty cases (DB1).

An approach similar to the DB1-system is used to monitor production quality: Audit data are separated into training and testing set. Since neither time nor mileage is relevant for any failures directly after manufacturing, the failure probability can simply be estimated using the relative frequency of failures within the training period (usually several months of production). Warnings during the test phase are generated, if the observed number of failures exceeds the expected number of failures. To identify only significant changes in the failure rate, a hypothesis test based on the binomial distribution is applied.

The probability for a warranty failure under the condition of a preceding production failure is calculated to identify a possible correlation between both failure types. Significance of correlation is assured by a chi-square test [3].

2.4 Car Control Unit Messages

Modern motor vehicles like the Mercedes S-Class contain up to 60 control units to control important car functions such as the Anti-lock Brake System (ABS), Electronic Stability Program (ESP) and fuel economy. Beside the control task, these units monitor all connected devices (e.g. sensors) for correct functionality. Errors are internally stored and offer valuable diagnostic data at each garage visit. Since 1999, control unit messages are collected in a special central database (DB2) at DaimlerChrysler to early detect upcoming failures in specific morel series.

The early warning system for DB2 is built according to the second part of the production audit early warning system: The probability for a warranty failure under the condition of a preceding control unit error message is calculated and significant correlations are identified by a chi-square test. These correlations are valuable forecasts for potentially upcoming part failures and thus a further garage visit can be avoided for the client.

Unfortunately, not all Mercedes garages are connected to the DB2 databases. Therefore, not all control unit messages can be collected in the database which makes it impossible to identify changes in the error message distribution.

3 Details of Stochastic Models

Failure processes are stochastic processes and thus their appropriate representation is done with help of stochastic models.

The focus of interest is whether the frequency of newly occurred failures has increased in comparison with a reference time interval. Theoretically, comparisons with fixed reference values can be done, too. In practice, this fails because of the number of different failure types (about 15000), for which such reference values would have to be specified for each model series. Furthermore, the variability of the vehicle mission (described for example by the vehicle age, monthly mileage rate, or season of the year) would have to be taken into account. So a certain failure rate can be normal with a monthly rate of 20,000 kilometers while it is too high with a monthly rate of 2,000 kilometers. This makes the comparison with a reference time interval the only viable alternative.

In statistics, concepts for quantification of statements about the differences between two data sets have been elaborated. This quantification takes place in terms of probabilities. A typical instrument, frequently used in quality control, is the hypothesis test. In our case, it is hypothesized that the quality has not changed. In the statistical language, this corresponds to the assumption that the frequency of the newly occurred failures can be explained by the failure probability distribution observed in the reference interval.

To be able to do this, the reference probability distribution has to be represented by a model received directly from the data. For this, various distribution classes have been proposed (Weibull distribution, Gamma distribution, Fatigue Life distribution

[4]). Unfortunately, none of these standard distributions is flexible enough to capture the abundance of the really observed failure distributions, two examples of which are presented in Fig. 4.

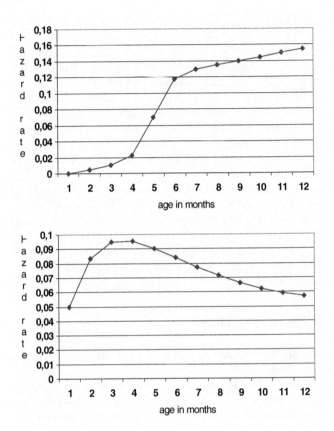

Fig. 4. Observed hazard rate, i.e., the failure probability at month T of vehicle age, conditional on this failure not having occurred until month T-1, for two hypothetical, but realistic failures types

The charts depict the curve of the observed hazard rate, that is, of the conditional probability that a failure occurs at month of age T if it had not occurred in the months 1 to T-1. The Weibull distribution can express only hazard rates proportional to gT^{g-1}, that is, depending from a power of T. The hazard rates of Gamma distribution are proportional to $T^{g-1} e^{-T}$. Furthermore, there is a scaling parameter. Also the Fatigue Life distribution has merely two free parameters. None of these distribution classes can reasonably approximate the two cases of Fig. 4.

It is important to point out that that the approximation of the failure distribution in the early warning system has to be considerably accurate. Otherwise, the test criterion might be violated merely through the approximation error even if applied to statistically "normal" data, launching a false alarm.

These high requirements are satisfied by no classical distribution family. This is why we adopted a numerical approach. The dependence of the hazard rate is directly approximated by the multi layer perceptron (a widespread type of neural net). In this way, we gained the generality not to be limited to a single dependence from time (as would be the case with standard distributions). Rather, multiple characteristics such as mileage rate and season of the year, whose effect on the failure rate can be expected, could be included. So a particularly accurate statistical representation of the normal failure process has been attained. The parameters of a multilayer perceptron are numerically estimated from the failure data minimizing the cross entropy of the observed and the theoretical distributions [5].

Beside this, the approach can be applied to monitor really occurring failures that had lead to warranty claims. But this framework is equally applicable to indirect quality indicators. For example, quality problems observed in the manufacturing outlet control can be tested for increased frequency. To quantify the relevance of these problems for warranty costs, a model of relationship between these indirect indicators and the warranty claims is needed. In the simplest case, such a model can consist of empirical conditional probabilities

$$P(failure | outlet\ problem)$$

To receive significant results, statistical tests such as the Chi square test for independence on the contingency table can be used.

If an outlet problem occurs with an abnormal frequency **and** this problem is statistically associated with a subsequent warranty claim, **then** a corrective action is required.

4 Conclusion

Through a joint analysis of the databases DB1, DB2 and DB3, the chain from manufacturing over online diagnostics to really occurring failures is closed. The product quality can be monitored simultaneously on several interconnected levels. The system has been in test operation since the end of 2003.

References

1. DuBois, P.: MySQL & Perl Developer's Guide: Webanwendungen programmieren mit Perl DBI, mod_perl und CGI, Markt&Technik Verlag, München, 2002.
2. Kimball, R. et al.: The Data Warehouse Lifecycle Toolkit. Wiley, 1998.
3. Hartung, J.: Statistik, R. Oldenbourg, München, 1987.
4. Stuart, A.; Ord, K.: Kendall's Advanced Theory of Statistics, Volume 1: Distribution Theory, Arnold, London, 1994.
5. Stützle, E.; Hrycej, T.: Forecasting of conditional distributions - an application to the spare parts demand forecast, Proc. 2001 IASTED Int. Conf. on Artificial Intelligence and Soft Computing, Cancun, 2001.

Shape-Invariant Cluster Validity Indices

Greet Frederix[1] and Eric J. Pauwels[2]

[1] Hogeschool Limburg,
Dept IWT, Universitaire Campus,
Gebouw H, B-3590 Diepenbeek, Belgium
greet.frederix@hogelimb.be
[2] Centre for Mathematics and Computer Science,
CWI Kruislaan 413, 1098SJ Amsterdam, The Netherlands
eric.pauwels@cwi.nl

Abstract. This paper discusses two cluster validity indices that quantify the quality of a putative clustering in terms of label-homogeneity and connectivity. Because the indices are defined in terms of local datadensity, they do not favour spherical or ellipsoidal clusters as other validity indices tend to do. A statistics-based decision framework is outlined that uses these indices to decide on the correct number of clusters.

1 Introduction and Notation

Clustering remains one of the mainstays in a large number of pattern recognition and machine learning applications. As a consequence there is no shortage of clustering algorithms and cluster validity indices (see e.g. [3, 4, 5] and references therein). Most of the latter measure various forms of within versus between variability and tend to favour clusters that are roughly spherical or ellipsoidal. In this paper we propose two simple geometric cluster validity indices that are completely free of such bias. Rather, they try to capture the basic geometric intuition that a cluster is a part of a point-set (in some metric space) which is relatively dense, as well as spatially isolated from the rest of the point-set. This point was also broached in [2, 7] although the solutions proposed in these papers are fundamentally different from the lines we pursue here. This work is an outgrowth of earlier work [6] in which we defined similar indices. However, in this paper we considerably improve on results obtained previously by introducing a methodology for estimating the statistical significance of the index-values.

At this point we should issue a disclaimer. When pursuing research on unsupervised learning, part of the difficulty is due to the fact that there is no clear-cut definition of what exactly a cluster is supposed to be. Our stance in this paper is pragmatic: the aim is to develop criteria that will yield the correct (or at least, an acceptable) clustering in those cases where the "correct" solution is obvious (see Fig. 7 for an example).

We end this section by introducing some notation for future reference. Consider a data set $\mathcal{D} = \{\mathbf{x}_1, \mathbf{x}_2, \ldots, \mathbf{x}_n\}$ of size n in p-dimensional space (i.e.

P. Permer (Eds.): ICDM 2004, LNAI 3275, pp. 96–105, 2004.

$\mathbf{x}_i \in \mathbb{R}^p$, which we assume equipped with the standard metric). An L-clustering is defined by a labelling function L which maps each point to its cluster label $g \in \mathcal{G} = \{1, 2, \ldots, K\}$: i.e. $L : \mathcal{D} \longrightarrow \mathcal{G} : \mathbf{x} \longmapsto g$. All points that are mapped to the same cluster label g will be called a L-cluster. To avoid confusion, we emphasize that in our notation, (geometric) clusters refer to the "real" clusters that are present in the dataset, while L-clusters are created through the (user-proposed) choice of an L-function. It goes without saying that the user's aim is to make sure that the L-clusters coincide with the geometric clusters, but attaining this goal is the essence of the problem.

Finally, we assume that there is (rough) estimate of the data density ϕ defined on $\mathcal{D}$; how this estimate is obtained is irrelevant for the discussion at hand. In fact, the methodology proposed in this paper is very robust with respect to estimate-induced variations of the density. For that reason, a quick-and-dirty density estimate based on nearest neighbours or a kernel estimate will do. We point out that such a rough estimate would not lend itself to clustering based on bump-hunting, as ϕ is likely to grossly under- or over-estimate the number of local extrema.

2 NN-Based Cluster Tension

2.1 Definition

The first cluster validity index captures the idea that clusters are locally homogeneous in that neighbouring points tend to have the same label. Put differently, lots of label-variation in the neighbourhood of a large number of points is indicative of poor clustering. To recast this straightforward intuition into a quantitative measure we investigate nearest neighbours. Denote by $N_k(\mathbf{x})$ the set of the k nearest neighbours of $\mathbf{x}$. By convention, the centre-point $\mathbf{x}$ does not belong to $N_k(\mathbf{x})$. We then define the local diversity (at $\mathbf{x}$) associated with labelling L by counting the number of neighbours that have a label different from the label at the centre point: $\delta_k(\mathbf{x}; L) = \#\{\mathbf{y} \in N_k(\mathbf{x}) \mid L(\mathbf{y}) \neq L(\mathbf{x})\}/k$. The (global) NN-tension (induced by the cluster labelling L) is then obtained by computing the weighted average over all data points:

$$T_k(L) = \frac{1}{n} \sum_{i=1}^{n} \delta_k(\mathbf{x}_i; L)\phi(\mathbf{x}_i). \tag{1}$$

The rationale for including the density as a weight-factor is that label diversity in high density regions is more significant as a contra-indication for good clustering. Notice that the number k of nearest neighbours is in fact a sort of scale-parameter, determining the size of the smallest clusters that can be picked up. In our experiments we took k to be equal to 5% of the dataset size.

The way this validity index can be used needs little explanation: Consider the case where a labelling L erroneously splits a single geometric cluster into two L-clusters (say A and B, see Fig. 1, top row). This will then give rise to a relatively high local NN-tension along the "faultline" separating A and B,

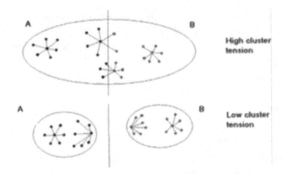

Fig. 1. *Top:* A single geometric cluster is erroneously split into two L-clusters A and B. This gives rise to relatively high NN-tension along the "faultline" separating A and B. *Bottom:* When the L-clusters A and B correspond to geometric clusters, the NN-tension is low or even zero

which is translated in a relatively high global NN-tension. Contrast this to the case where the L-clusters do in fact correspond to genuine geometric clusters (Fig. 1 bottom). Now NN-tension will be low throughout the dataset, keeping the global NN-tension low.

These simple considerations reinforce our original intuition: "high" tension is indicative of erroneous mergers, while "low" tension bolsters our confidence in the validity of the proposed labelling. However, in order to turn this qualitative appreciation into an operational decision criterion, we need some value for the typical value and expected variability of the NN-tension. Have another look at Fig. 1 where in both cases the putative clustering is indicated by a vertical line. Now, imagine that the proposed clustering was in fact generated by a horizontal line cutting both data-sets into two (approximately equal sized) groups. It is clear that for the top data-set the resulting tension would be comparable to the original one. For the second data-set (bottom) however, such a split would generate a tension which is significantly higher than the original one (which was probably close, or equal, to zero). This leads quite naturally to the following construction: To decide on the acceptability of the NN-tension $T^{(0)} \equiv T(L_0)$ associated with a putative cluster labelling L_0, we generate R random cluster labellings L_r ($r = 1, \ldots, R$) by separating the data using R random hyperplanes (i.e. hyperplane through a random data-point, and orthogonal to a random direction) and compute the corresponding tensions $T^{(r)} \equiv T(L_r)$. Next, estimate the p-value of $T^{(0)}$ with respect to the set $\{T^{(1)}, \ldots, T^{(R)}\}$, e.g. by computing the fraction of this set that is smaller than $T^{(0)}$, i.e. $p(T^{(0)}) = \#\{T^{(r)} \,|\, T^{(r)} \leq T^{(0)}/R$. We will now conclude that the proposed clustering is acceptable if this p-value is exceptionally small (e.g. $p < 0.05$, or even $p < 0.01$). We refer to Fig. 4 for a illustrative example.

2.2   Adjusting for Variations in Shape

Although definition (1) of global tension seems natural and straightforward to use, closer examination reveals a problem which is highlighted by the follow-

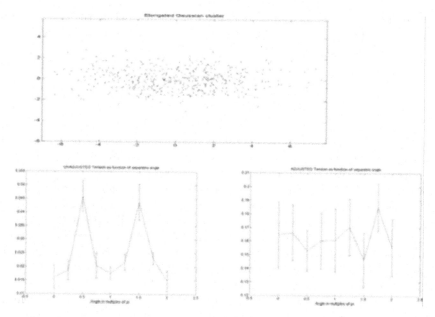

Fig. 2. *Top:* Elongated Gaussian cluster illustrating the dependency of the total tension on the split direction. *Bottom, left:* The unadjusted cluster tension (1) clearly shows a dependency on the angle of the separatrix, with low tension at angles where the separatrix is horizontal (i.e. angle $= 0, \pi, 2\pi$), and high tension when the separatrix is vertical (i.e. angle $= \pi/2$ and $3\pi/2$). For each angle, the curve shows the mean and standard deviation for 10 independent resamplings of the Gaussian cluster. This is also the reason why the results for 0, π and 2π are not identical! *Bottom, right:* The adjusted cluster tension (2) no longer exhibits such a systematic cyclic trend

ing simple example. Consider an elongated Gaussian 2-dim cluster, centered at the origin and positioned such that its long axis coincides with the x-axis (see Fig. 2). Now, suppose that this cluster has been split into two by using the k-means algorithm (for $k = 2$). A moment's thought will convince the reader that k-means will generate a separatrix (line separating the two groups) which is approximately vertical and passes through the origin (i.e. the cluster's centre of gravity). This entails that the "faultline" is relatively short, especially when compared to the separatrix that would result from a horizontal split (i.e. when this separatrix would coincide with the x-axis). As a consequence, a horizontal split will result in more points straddling the faultline and since eq.(1) averages over all points, this will result in higher average tension. This is detrimental to the computation of the p-value as proposed in the previous section, as it means that the original tension $T^{(0)}$ is systematically smaller than the ones that are obtained from random cuts that are not vertical. Phrased in statistical terminology, the original tension is biased towards small values, resulting in an artificially low p-value, even if the underlying cluster is compact (but elongated).

To remove this bias, we adjust definition (1) by restricting the averaging to all points that have non-vanishing local tension (we add one to the denominator to avoid potential division by zero problems):

$$T_k(L) = \frac{1}{N_p + 1} \sum_{i=1}^{n} \delta_k(\mathbf{x}_i; L)\phi(\mathbf{x}_i), \quad \text{where} \quad N_p = \#\{\mathbf{x}_i \mid \delta_k(\mathbf{x}_i; L) > 0\} \quad (2)$$

Since the denominator is now proportional to the number of points that effectively contribute to the total tension, this compensates for the shape bias, as illustrated in Fig.2 (bottom, right).

At first sight, this modification might seem to emasculate the criterion. Indeed, consider the extreme case where you have two 2-dimensional standard normal Gaussian cluster (labeled 1 and 2) which are well separated (e.g. by a distance of 10 say). Furthermore, assume there is a single point right in the middle between these two clusters. Clearly, because the Gaussians are well separated all points in these two clusters will only have neighbours with the same label (hence no tension). Whatever the label of the point in the middle is, it will have approximately half of its neighbours in the first Gaussian, and half of them in the second, resulting in a local diversity of approximately 0.5. Since eq. (2) now averages over a single point, one could get the impression that tension will be relatively high. However, remember that local tension is obtained by multiplying diversity and data-density. Clearly, the density at the isolated single point will be very low, resulting in a low value for the adjusted tension, as intended.

2.3   Experiments

The following experiments are meant to illustrate the potential of NN-based tension. In a first experiment, we generate two standard normal 5-dimensional Gaussian clusters (of 700 points each), such that the centra are a distance of 6 apart. To create two L-clusters we then generate a hyperplane orthogonal to the line connecting the two centra: points on either side of this hyperplane get different labels (say 1 and 2). The position of the hyperplane is then systematically shifted along the line: distance 0 means that it cuts through the centre of the first Gaussian, while distance 6 indicates that it cuts through the centre of the second Gaussian. Clearly, the optimal position corresponds to distance 3 when it cuts the connecting line exactly at the midpoint. For each configuration the associated tension is generate.

The results (shown in Fig. 3) confirm our intuition. The tension attains its highest values when the separatrix hyperplane slices straight through the cluster centres, whereas the minimum is obtained around the midpoint (as expected). It's also interesting to observe that these results are very robust with respect to the estimated density (ϕ in eq.(2)): In one case the density was estimated using the distance to the nearest neighbours, while the other result is based on the exact Gaussian density (from which the samples were drawn). Both graphs are almost identical, buttressing the point we made earlier.

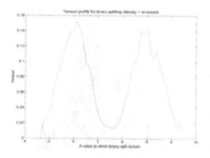 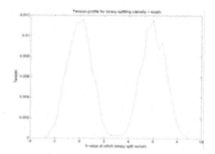

Fig. 3. Evolution of the NN-based tension T as a function of the position splitting hyperplane (creating the L-clustering: see main text for detailed description). *Left:* Tension based on the NN-based estimate for density ϕ. *Right:* Tension based on the exact version of density ϕ

In a second experiment, we tested the discriminatory power of the tension measure by comparing the tension (and the corresponding p-values) for cluster configurations for which the answer should be obvious. More precisely, we generated two (2-dimensional standard-normal) Gaussian clusters at a distance d apart. For small values of d (e.g. $d = 1$) the two Gaussians merge into a single geometric cluster (i.e. an independent observer who has no knowledge about the underlying generative process would judge it to be one cluster, see Fig. 4, top). Increasing the distance will progressively pry the Gaussians apart, up to a point (e.g. for $d = 5$) where two constituent clusters are clearly discernable (see Fig. 4, bottom). Typical results for the p-values of the original labelling relative to simulated labellings are shown in the right column of Fig. 4.

3 Connectivity Index

The second geometric cluster validity measure we discuss is the so-called connectivity index. This index captures the intuition that any two points in a cluster can be connected by a high density path, i.e. a path which at no point needs to traverse a "void". To fix ideas we will start with a simple setup (illustrated in Fig. 5). On the left, we have two geometric clusters (A and B) which we assume are recognized as such by the labelling. If we now pick random pairs of points in either cluster (yielding a and b, a' and b' respectively) and evaluate the cluster density ϕ at the midpoints m and m', we'll get a relatively high value as these points tend to be situated at high density locations. Contrast this to the situation on the right in Fig. 5 where we assume that the labelling L has erroneously lumped the two geometric clusters A and B in one big L-cluster. As a consequence, when we are drawing pairs of random points a and b (from the same L-cluster) there will be a significant fraction of pairs for which these points are part of different geometric clusters (illustrated by the points a' and b'; if A and B have comparable size this will occur with an approximate probability of

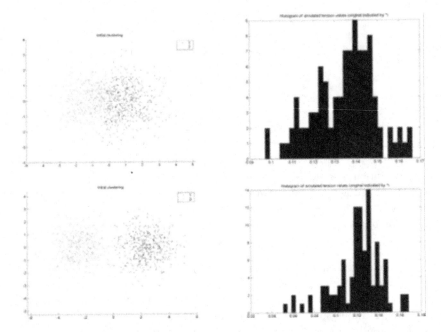

Fig. 4. *Top left:* Single geometric cluster erroneously split by vertical midline, resulting in an NN-tension $T_0 = 0.13$. *Top right:* Histogram for NN-tensions generated by 100 random clusterings. The p-value for T_0 equals 0.38 (large!), indicating that the putative split is erroneous. *Bottom left:* Two genuine geometric clusters for which $T_0 = 0.036$. *Bottom right:* Histogram for NN-tensions generated by 100 random clusterings. The p-value for T_0 now is less than 0.01 (small!), confirming the appropriateness of the proposed split

0.5). In such an event, the midpoint m' will likely fall in the void between the two clusters, and therefore register a low density $\phi(m')$.

We are now in a position to provide a formal definition for the connectivity index C associated with a labelling L:

1. Draw from the dataset K random pairs of points (a_k, b_k), making sure that the points in each pair belong to the same L-cluster, i.e. $\forall i : L(a_k) = L(b_k)$;
2. Construct for each pair the corresponding midpoint m_k and evaluate the data-density ϕ at that point. The connectivity index C is then defined to be the average over all random pairs:

$$C(L) = \frac{1}{K} \sum_k \phi(m_k). \tag{3}$$

To render this index really useful, we need to make it slightly more robust. The right panel in Fig. 5 shows what needs to be done: When confronted with a curved cluster, the chances are that the midpoint will fall in a "convexity void" and therefore return an underestimate for the density. If we allow m to hill-climb

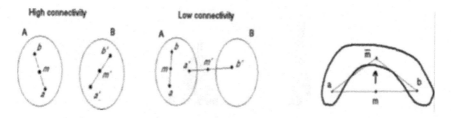

Fig. 5. Illustrating the definition of the connectivity index. *Left and middle:* Basic definition of connectivity index; see text for more details. *Right:* Better value for connectivity index is obtained by measuring the density along a high density ridge obtained by hill-climbing from m to $\bar{m}$ (constrained by the condition $d(a, \bar{m}) \approx d(b, \bar{m}))$)

towards the high density point $\bar{m}$, (keeping $\bar{m}$ approximately in the "middle" of the anchor points a and b by insisting that $d(a, \bar{m}) \approx d(b, \bar{m})$), we get a more representative density estimate. Sensitivity of this index can be further increased by repeating the procedure for the midpoints between a and $\bar{m}$, and $\bar{m}$ and b (which then contribute to the mean in eq.(5)). Basically, this means that we are estimating the density along a "snake" connecting a and b, which is attracted by the high density ridge.

To illustrate the validity of this concept, have another look at the data-sets in Fig. 4, but this time ignore the different labels, i.e. assume that each data-set is considered to be one L-cluster. In that case, the top dataset should have high connectivity, while the lower dataset should score a significantly lower value due to the gap between the two geometric clusters. This is borne out by the tests reported in Fig. 6 where the histogram shows the result for 200 computed connectivity indices, 100 for each dataset. They nicely cluster in two groups of 100 indices each: the left group corresponds to the low connectivity indices obtained for the lower dataset (consisting of two disconnected geometric clusters), while the right group comprises the higher connectivity indices obtained for the upper dataset in Fig. 4.

We conclude this section by indicating how the connectivity index is used in practice. To fix ideas, consider once again the case depicted in Fig. 5(top). Since there are indeed two geometric clusters, we expect the connectivity index to be significantly lower when we assume that both clusters are lumped together in a single L-cluster. To quantify what should be considered "significant", we proceed as follows. Recall that C as defined in eq. 3 is an average over a random sample of K paired anchor points. We can therefore easily resample and compute another instance of this parameter. Let $C_i^{(1)}$ denote the ith realisation of the C-index assuming that both clusters are lumped together in a single L-cluster, while $C_j^{(2)}$ denotes similar results under the assumption that the clusters are different. Allowing both i and j to run over r repeats, we subsequently compute the corresponding means ($M^{(1)}$ and $M^{(2)}$) and standard deviations ($S^{(1)}$ and $S^{(2)}$). To test whether $M^{(1)}$ is indeed much lower than $M^{(2)}$, we apply a standard T-test and evaluate whether the Student t-statistic

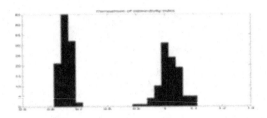

Fig. 6. Histograms for 200 connectivity indices; see main text for more details

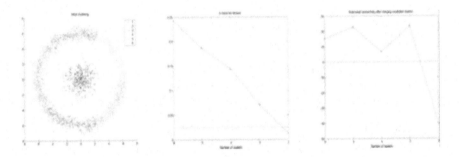

Fig. 7. Illustration of cluster selection based on both geometric cluster validity indices. *Left:* Complicated dataset initially divided up in 6 groups using k-means clustering. These groups are then systematically merged, such that each merger maximizes the reduction in NN-tension. The number of groups is thus stepwise reduced until finally two clusters remain: the ring and the central core. *Middle:* This graph charts the evolution of the p-value for the NN-tension during the evolution from 6 to 2 clusters. The final p-value (for 2 clusters) is exceptionally low ($p < 0.025$), indicating that the NN-tension for 2 clusters is exceptionally low. *Right:* This graph shows the evolution of the V-parameter (defined in section 3) for the connectivity index. Again, we see that this measure drops below the 0-threshold when two clusters remain. Both indices therefore agree on *two* being the correct number of clusters

$$t = \frac{M^{(1)} - M^{(2)}}{\sqrt{((S^{(1)})^2 + (S^{(2)})^2)/r}}$$

is less than -2 (which corresponds to an approximate p-value of 0.025). For convenience we introduce a new parameter $V = t + 2$, such that $V < 0$ flags that further mergers are contra-indicated.

A final illustration is provided in Fig. 7 were we applied **both** validity criteria on a challenging data-set in which points are distributed over a central cluster and a surrounding ring. An initial k-means clustering (with k=6) returns 6 groups, five of which are situated in the ring. Reducing the number of clusters in a stepwise fashion by merging the neighbouring clusters whose unification produces the largest reduction in NN-tension, finally yields two clusters (the ring and the central core). At this point, both validity indices indicate that further reduction of the number of clusters is contra-indicated, thus confirming that two is the correct number of clusters.

Acknowledgments. This work was partially supported by EC Project FOUNDIT (IST-2000-28427) and EC Network of Excellence MUSCLE (FP6-507752).

References

1. J.C. Bezdek, J. Keller, R. Krisnapuram, N.R. Pal: Fuzzy Models and Algorithms for Pattern Recognition in Image Processing, Kluwer Academic Publishers, 1999.
2. J.C. Dunn Well Separated Cluserds and Optimal Fuzzy Partitions, Journal of Cybernetics, **Vol. 4**, (1974), 95–104.
3. A.K. Jain, M.N. Murty, P.J. Flynn Data Clustering: A Review, ACM Computing Surveys, **Vol. 31**, No. 3, (Sept 1999), 264-323.
4. K. Jajuga, A. Sokolowski and H. Bock, Classification, Clustering and Data Analysis, IFCS Conference Poland, Springer, 2002.
5. L. Kaufman and P.J. Rousseeuw, Finding Groups in Data: An Introduction to Cluster Analysis, J. Wiley and Sons, 1990.
6. E.J. Pauwels and G. Frederix, Finding Salient Regions in Images, Computer Vision and Image Understanding, **Vol. 75**, No. 1/2, (July/August 1999), 73-85.
7. X.L. Xie and G. Beni: A Validity Measure for Fuzzy Clustering, IEEE Trans on Pattern Analysis and Machine Intelligence, **Vol. 13**, No. 8, (August 1991), 841-847

Mining Indirect Association Rules

Shinichi Hamano and Masako Sato

Department of Mathematics and Information Sciences,
College of Integrated Arts and Sciences,
Osaka Prefecture University, Sakai, Osaka 599-8531, Japan
shinchan0112@aol.com, sato@mi.cias.osakafu-u.ac.jp

Abstract. A large database, such as POS data, could give us many insights about customer behavior. Many techniques and measures have been proposed to extract interesting rules. As the study of Association rule mining has proceeded, the rules about items that are not bought together at the same transaction have been regarded as important. Although this concept, Negative Association rule mining, is quite useful, it is difficult for the user to analyze the interestingness of Negative Association rules because we would get them too many. To settle this issue, Indirect Association rule mining has proposed.

In this paper, we propose a new framework of Indirect Association rule via a mediator and a new measure μ based on measures P_A and P_D due to Zhang to mine Negative Association rules effectively without the domain knowledge. The μ measure has the advantage over the IS measure that is proposed with the first framework of Indirect Association rule mining, and satisfies all of the well-known properties for a good measure. Finally, we are going to analyze the retail data and present interpretations for derived Indirect Association rules.

1 Introduction

Past a decade, data mining techniques have attracted a lot of interest for obtaining the powerful insights that lead to benefits. Association rule mining[1], one of the famous data mining techniques, is now an important tool in CRM (*Customer Relationship Management*) for targeting consumers, enhancing cross-selling, and identifying trends and needs. Although many scholars have proposed the measures for understanding interestingness of derived rules[2, 4, 8, 10], the most fundamental measure, support, has been used to derive the frequent item-sets that have the support above a user-specified threshold, min-support. However, there exist many unconsidered item-sets (infrequent item-sets) that could give us great insights into business data. This concept derives the Negative Association rule mining [5]. A Negative Association rule such that there is a negative correlation between the item-sets X and Y enables us to figure out that customers who are going to buy X tend not to buy Y in the same transaction. It is impossible to analyze every single Negative Association rule in detail because the number of derived Negative Association rules could be large.

P. Perner (Ed.): ICDM 2004, LNAI 3275, pp. 106–116, 2004.
© Springer-Verlag Berlin Heidelberg 2004

In order to pick out the valid Negative Associations, Indirect Association rule mining was introduced by Tan et al.[6, 7, 8, 9]. Consider a pair of items $\{a, b\}$ with a low support value, i.e., they are rarely bought together at the same transaction. If there is an item-set M such that the presence of a and b are highly dependent on items in M, then the pair $\{a, b\}$ are said to be indirectly associated via M. Tan et al. have called such an item-set M a *mediator* for $\{a, b\}$, and adopted the IS measure[6, 7, 8, 9] to represent dependency between a mediator M and each item $x \in \{a, b\}$. Indirect association above, however, does not reflect correlations between a mediator and items in the pair, and moreover, the IS measure is a symmetric measure with no direction.

In this paper, we propose a new framework of Indirect Association rule via a mediator to enable us to analyze targeting consumers, competitors, potential consumers, and so on. For an item x, the notation $\neg x$ means the event that a transaction does not contain the item x. An Indirect Association rule in our framework is of the form $(M \Rightarrow \beta_a, M \Rightarrow \beta_b)$ for a rare item-pair $\{a, b\}$ and a mediator M, where $\beta_x \in \{x, \neg x\}$ for each $x \in \{a, b\}$. A rule $M \Rightarrow \beta_x$ implies a positive correlation between M and β_x, and thus $M \Rightarrow \neg x$ is a Negative Association rule such that there is a negative correlation between M and x. A mediator M is a common item-set for the consumers, i.e., M illustrates the similarity of behavioral patterns. The relations of M and each of items illustrate that the consumers who bought all items of a mediator take different actions of buying an item a or b. For example, if we discover an Indirect Association rule $(M \Rightarrow a, M \Rightarrow b)$, consumers that buy all items in M tend to buy either a or b but not both. It enables us to figure out that the items a and b are in choice-set of items, i.e., they are competitive products and could be alternative products. For another example, if we discover Indirect Association rule $(M \Rightarrow a, M \Rightarrow \neg b)$, consumers that buy all items in M tend to buy together with a but not with b. Let a be *Pepsi* and b be *Coca-cola*. The rules $M \Rightarrow Pepsi$ and $M \Rightarrow \neg$ *Coca-cola* are quite valuable to recognize the brand choice pattern. These consumers have brand loyalty for *Pepsi* and should be treated as superior consumers by *PepsiCo*.

As a measure for an implication rule $M \Rightarrow \beta_x$, we introduce a new measure μ with direction. The μ measure is based on measures P_A and P_D proposed by Zhang [10]. The measures P_A and P_D were presented for measure of association and disassociation (Negative Association) relationships between item-sets, respectively, and satisfied the all well-known properties for a good measure[10]. We are convinced that the μ measure is the most effective and accessible measure for marketers and the most powerful measure in the phase of interpreting derived rules.

In the next section, we present our framework of Indirect Association rule via a mediator. In section 3, we define the μ measure in more general form and investigate properties of the μ measure. Moreover, we compare it with various measures such as the IS measure, confidence and so on. Finally, we are going to experiment with the real retail data (POS data) and present some interesting interpretations for derived Indirect Association rules.

2   Indirect Association Rules

Let I be the finite set of items, and D be the set of customer transactions, called *database*, where each transaction T is a set of items such that $T \subseteq I$. We denote items of I by $a, b, c, \cdots$ and subsets of I, called *item-sets*, by X, Y, M and so on. In this paper, an item-set X means not only the subset of I but also the event that a transaction contains all items in the set X, and $P(X)$ denotes the probability that a transaction contains the set X. Moreover, by $\neg X$, we denote the negation of the event X, i.e., a transaction does not contain at least one item in X, and thus $\neg\neg X = X$ and $P(\neg X) = 1 - P(X)$.

Let us define the following sets:

$$I_f = \{a \in I \mid P(a) \geq t_f\}, \qquad RP = \{\{a, b\} \mid a, b \in I_f, \ P(a, b) \leq t_r\},$$

where t_f and t_r are a *frequent item threshold* and a *rare item-pair threshold* specified by the user, respectively, such that $t_r < t_f$. Note that if $t_r < t_f^2$, then there is a negative correlation between two events a and b because of $P(a, b) \leq t_r < t_f^2 \leq P(a)P(b)$ for $a, b \in I_f$. An item $a \in I_f$ is called a *frequent* item. Note that items in RP are always frequent items. A pair $\{a, b\} \in RP$, called a *rare item-pair*, is rarely presented together in the same transaction, and thus has been treated as uninteresting item-set because of the absence of statistical significance. However, we believe that rare item-pairs could give us great insights by deriving with a common item-sets mediator as shown below.

A *mediator* M for a rare item-pair $\{a, b\}$ is an item-set of I disjointed to $\{a, b\}$. If there is a mediator M that is highly dependent with both a and b, then such a pair is expected to relate to each other via M. The mediator helps to improve the interpretability of the extracted item-sets by identifying the context for which the Negative Association between a and b is interesting.

Let $x \in \{a, b\}$. We call a rule of the form $M \Rightarrow x$ a (positive) Association rule, and $M \Rightarrow \neg x$ a Negative Association rule. A positive (resp., Negative) Association rule represents that there is a positive (resp., negative) correlation between M and x. A Negative Association rule figures out that customers who are going to buy M tend not to buy x in the same transaction. Clearly there is a positive correlation between M and x iff $P(M \mid x) > P(M \mid \neg x)$ iff there is a negative correlation between M and $\neg x$.

Let the notation β_x denote x if $P(M \mid x) \geq P(M \mid \neg x)$, otherwise let β_x denote $\neg x$. Therefore, in either case, $P(M \mid \beta_x) \geq P(M \mid \neg \beta_x)$ holds. As a measure for an implication rule $M \Rightarrow \beta_x$, we define a new measure μ as follows:

$$\mu(M \Rightarrow \beta_x) = \frac{P(M \mid \beta_x) - P(M \mid \neg\beta_x)}{P(M \mid \beta_x)}$$

$$= \begin{cases} \dfrac{P(M \wedge x) - P(M)P(x)}{P(M \wedge x)(1 - P(x))}, & \text{if } \beta_x = x, \\[2ex] \dfrac{P(M)P(x) - P(M \mid \neg x)}{P(x)(P(M) - P(M \wedge x))}, & \text{if } \beta_x = \neg x. \end{cases} \qquad (1)$$

The numerator denotes a conditional measure of a relationship of M with β_x, and the denominator makes it normalized. Hence unlike confidence, the μ measure is normalized like the statistical notion of correlation. Furthermore, the μ measure is directional and it measures actual implication as opposed to co-occurrence.

Let us define a new framework of Indirect Association via a mediator.

Definition 1. *Let $\{a, b\} \in RP$ be a rare item-pair, and let M be a mediator of $\{a, b\}$, i.e., $M \cap \{a, b\} = \phi$. A pair of association rules $(M \Rightarrow \beta_a, M \Rightarrow \beta_b)$ is an Indirect Association rule via a mediator M, denoted by $(M; \{\beta_a, \beta_b\})$, if*
    (1) $P(M \wedge \beta_x) \geq t_m$,   *(Mediator Support Condition),*
    (2) $\mu(M \Rightarrow \beta_x) \geq t_\mu$, $x \in \{a, b\}$,   *(Mediator Dependence Condition).*
And the rare item-pair $\{a, b\}$ is indirectly associated via a mediator M.

Mediator Support Condition (1) is for the statistical significance between the mediator and the pair $\{\beta_a, \beta_b\}$. Marketers regard statistical significance as an important factor because they would like to know the common behavior of customers. That is, a mediator stands for the basic behavior of customers and relations between a mediator and each of rare item-pairs stand for characteristic behavior of customers. Therefore this condition is necessary as statistical significance. Mediator Dependence Condition (2) is for measuring the interestingness of the derived rules and for pruning the worthless rules. In order to derive both Association rule and Negative Association rule effectively, this condition is indispensable.

Let $\{a, b\} \in RP$ be a fixed rare item-pair and let M be a mediator for the pair. By the definition of the Indirect Association rule, a rule $(M; \{\beta_a, \beta_b\})$ is an Indirect Association rule if and only if, for each $x \in \{a, b\}$,

$$\mu(M \Rightarrow \beta_x) \geq t_\mu \quad \Longleftrightarrow \quad P(M) \leq t_{\mu,\beta_x} \times P(M \wedge \beta_x),$$

where

$$t_{\mu,\beta_x} = \frac{1 - t_\mu P(\neg \beta_x)}{P(\beta_x)}.$$

Theorem 1. *Let M_1 and M_2 be mediators for a rare item-pair $\{a, b\}$ such that $M_1 \subseteq M_2$.*
    (1) If $P(M_2) > t_{\mu,\beta_x} \times P(M_1 \wedge \beta_x)$, then $\mu(M \Rightarrow \beta_x) < t_\mu$ for any M with $M_1 \subseteq M \subseteq M_2$.
    (2) If $P(M_1) \leq t_{\mu,\beta_x} \times P(M_2 \wedge \beta_x)$, then $\mu(M \Rightarrow \beta_x) \geq t_\mu$ for any M with $M_1 \subseteq M \subseteq M_2$.

Corollary 1. *Let M be a mediator for a rare item-pair $\{a, b\}$ and let $c \in M$. If $P(M) > t_{\mu,\beta_x} \times P(c \wedge \beta_x)$, then there is no Indirect Association rule via a mediator including the item c.*

3   Measure μ

The support of an item-set X, denoted as $sup(X)$, is the ratio $|F(X)|/|D|$, where $F(X) = \{T \in D \mid T \text{ includes } X\}$ and $|\cdot|$ denotes the cardinality of a set. An association rule is an implication of the form $X \Rightarrow Y$, where X and Y are item-sets satisfying $X \cap Y = \phi$. The support of $X \Rightarrow Y$ is the support of $X \cup Y$, that is, $sup(X \cup Y)$. The famous measure confidence for $X \Rightarrow Y$, denoted as $conf(X \Rightarrow Y)$, is the ratio $sup(X \cup Y)/sup(X)$ and is often used for capturing the interestingness of the rule. When the number of transactions in database D is infinitely large, sup and $conf$ can be interpreted according to probability theory as:

$$sup(X \cup Y) = P(X \wedge Y), \quad conf(X \Rightarrow Y) = P(Y \mid X). \qquad (2)$$

On the other hand, a rule of the form $X \Rightarrow \neg Y$ is called a Negative Association rule, and represents a rule that customers who buy an item-set X are not likely to buy at least one item in an item-set Y. The support and confidence for a Negative rule $X \Rightarrow \neg Y$ are defined as follow [3]:

$$sup(X \Rightarrow \neg Y) = P(X) - P(X \wedge Y), \qquad (3)$$

$$conf(X \Rightarrow \neg Y) = P(\neg Y \mid X) = 1 - P(Y \mid X). \qquad (4)$$

The measure confidence has, however, the defect when there is a negative correlation between the item-sets. Brin [3] proposed the measure chi-squared test for capturing the correlation, especially negative correlation, between the item-sets to reinforce a weakness of the measure confidence. It is not good enough because the value of chi-squared test depends on the number of transactions. Therefore too many worthless rules could be derived from large database such as POS data. We define a new measure μ for $X \Rightarrow \beta_Y$, where $\beta_y \in \{y, \neg y\}$, as follows:

$$\mu(X \Rightarrow \beta_Y) = \frac{P(X \mid \beta_Y) - P(X \mid \neg\beta_Y)}{P(X \mid \beta_Y)} = \frac{P(X \wedge \beta_Y) - P(X)P(\beta_Y)}{P(X \wedge \beta_Y)(1 - P(\beta_Y))}. \qquad (5)$$

The numerator $P(X \mid \beta_Y) - P(X \mid \neg\beta_Y)$ denotes conditional measure of relationship of X associated with β_Y, and the denominator $P(X \mid \beta_Y)$ makes it normalized. Thus clearly $-\dfrac{P(\beta_Y)}{1 - P(\beta_Y)} \leq \mu(X \Rightarrow \beta_Y) \leq 1$ holds. Moreover, we have

$$\mu(X \Rightarrow \beta_Y) = 0 \iff \phi(X, \beta_Y) = 0, \quad \mu(X \Rightarrow \beta_Y) > 0 \iff \phi(X, \beta_Y) > 0,$$

where ϕ is a correlation function, that is,

$$\phi(X, Y) = \frac{P(X \wedge Y) - P(X)P(Y)}{\sqrt{P(X)P(\neg X)P(Y)P(\neg Y)}}. \qquad (6)$$

Zhang [10] presented new association rules for a measure of relationships between item-sets. He introduced two measures P_A and P_D to describe association and disassociation relationship between X and Y defined as follows:

$$P_A(X \Rightarrow Y) = \frac{P(X \wedge Y) - P(X)P(Y)}{P(X \wedge Y)(1 - P(Y))}, \text{ if } \phi(X, Y) \geq 0, \qquad (7)$$

$$P_D(X \Rightarrow Y) = \frac{P(X)P(Y) - P(X \wedge Y)}{(P(X) - P(X \wedge Y))P(Y)}, \text{ otherwise.} \qquad (8)$$

The μ measure defined above is essentially based on measures P_A and P_D which due to Zhang as seen in the following relations:

$$P_A(X \Rightarrow Y) = \mu(X \Rightarrow Y), \text{ if } \phi(X, Y) \geq 0, \tag{9}$$
$$P_D(X \Rightarrow Y) = -\mu(X \Rightarrow \neg Y), \text{ otherwise.} \tag{10}$$

The μ measure is identical with the measure P_A if there is nonnegative correlation between X and Y. Otherwise, μ and P_D have opposite signs although the absolute values are equal. In this paper, we adopt the μ measure to measure both positive and Negative Association rules instead of P_A and P_D. Of course, we are concerned with an association rule $X \Rightarrow \beta_Y$ with positive correlation for X and β_Y, and so confine ourselves to rules $X \Rightarrow \beta_Y$ with $\mu(X \Rightarrow \beta_Y) \geq 0$. If a rule $X \Rightarrow \neg Y$ is a valid rule with the μ measure, this indicates that there is a negative correlation between the item-sets X and Y. The set $\neg Y$ is equivalent to the set $X - X \cup Y$. In this paper, we are going to apply the μ measure to Indirect Association rule mining by judging from the point of view of properties for a good measure. By the definition of μ, it immediately follows that:

Theorem 2. *The μ measure satisfies the following five conditions:*
(1) $\mu(X \Rightarrow \beta_Y) = 0$ if X and Y are statistically independent, i.e., $P(X \wedge \beta_Y) = P(X)P(\beta_Y)$.
(2) $\mu(X \Rightarrow \beta_Y)$ monotonically increase with $P(X \wedge \beta_Y)$ when $P(X)$ and $P(\beta_Y)$ remain unchanged.
(3) $\mu(X \Rightarrow \beta_Y)$ monotonically decrease with $P(X)$ (or $P(Y)$) when the rest of parameters remain unchanged.
(4) $0 \leq \mu(X \Rightarrow \beta_Y) \leq 1$ if a correlation of X and β_Y is nonnegative.
(5) $\mu(X \Rightarrow \beta_Y) = 1$ if $P(X \wedge \beta_Y) = P(X)$.

The assertions $(1), (2)$ and (3) for $\beta_Y = Y$ are proposed by Piatesky-Shapiro for a good measure for association rule $X \Rightarrow Y$. By the assertions (4) and (5), values of μ attain one if and only if X completely associates with β_Y. We convinced that a good measure should satisfy the above five conditions to understand the interestingness of the rules easily. For example, chi-squared test does not satisfy the conditions (1) and (2). It is widely known that the value of the chi-squared test depends on the number of transactions. Consequently too many worthless rules could be derived from a large database such as POS data.

3.1   Comparisons with the Other Measures

The μ measure is an efficient measure because it reflects the correlation and confidence. The relations between μ and confidence or correlation are as follows:

Theorem 3. *The following two properties hold:*
(1) $\mu(X \Rightarrow \beta_Y)$ monotonically increases with $conf(X \Rightarrow \beta_Y)$ when $P(\beta_Y)$ remains unchanged.
(2) $\mu(X \Rightarrow \beta_Y)$ monotonically decreases with $P(\beta_Y)$ when $conf(X \Rightarrow Y)$ remains unchanged.

Next we investigate a relation between the μ measure and the IS measure. The IS measure has been proposed in [6, 7, 8] for the first model of Indirect Association rule mining to measure dependencies between the mediator and the rare item-pair. Tan et al. assert that the IS measure is efficient metric because it contains both statistical dependence and statistical significance as follows:

$$IS(X, Y) = \frac{P(X \wedge Y)}{\sqrt{P(X)P(Y)}} = \sqrt{I(X, Y) \times sup(X \cup Y)}, \qquad (11)$$

where $I(X, Y) = \dfrac{P(X \wedge Y)}{P(X)P(Y)}$ is the measure Interest proposed in [3]. The IS measure takes in $I(X, Y)$ for statistical dependence and $sup(X \cup Y)$ for statistical significance. The IS measure is unqualified for deriving Negative Association rules between a mediator and a rare item-pair because the value of the IS measure for the rule $X \Rightarrow Y$ is $\sqrt{P(X)P(Y)}$ when correlation is 0. Because $\sqrt{P(X)P(Y)}$ is according to the each of derived rules, we could have problems for deriving Negative Association rules. The first case, if the threshold of the IS measure is set too high above $\sqrt{P(X)P(Y)}$, we could not derive Negative Association rules at all. The second case, if the threshold of the IS measure is set too low, we could derive too many worthless rules. In this case, there would be many statistically insignificant rules, that is, the item-sets X and Y might be nearly independent statistically. As you have seen, the properties of the IS measure is unqualified to detect interesting Negative Association rules. Furthermore the IS measure does not satisfy the conditions 2 and 3 of Theorem 1. As you have seen, chi-squared test and the IS measure that are proposed as good measures do not satisfy all the properties for a good measure. Therefore we are going to propose the μ measure to derive Indirect Association rules effectively.

4   Experiments

4.1   Algorithm

The algorithm of mining Indirect Association rules can be composed into three phases.

(1) Generate the sets of frequent items I_f and rare item-pairs RP. In this phase, generate the sets of frequent items I_f first. If $sup(a)$ is greater than the frequent item threshold t_f, then (a) is appended into I_f. Next, generate the sets of rare item-pairs RP, (a, b) is appended into RP if $sup(a, b)$ is less than the rare item-pair threshold t_r.

(2) Generate the sets of mediators $\mathcal{M}$ for each item-pair in RP. Although we applied Apriori-gen in this paper to generate the set of mediators, we could also apply another existing algorithms to this phase for deriving the sets of mediators $\mathcal{M}$.

(3) Generate all Indirect Association rules and prune the redundant rules. If $\mu(M \Rightarrow \beta_a) \geq t_\mu$ and $\mu(M \Rightarrow \beta_b) \geq t_\mu$, output the item-pair and a mediator $(M; (\beta_a, \beta_b))$.

For given item-set and database, we can obtain all Indirect Association rules by the following algorithm.

Algorithm
Input: item-set I, database D, thresholds (t_f, t_r, t_m, t_μ);
Output: the set of Indirect Association rules;
begin
(1) $I_f = \{a \in I \mid sup(a) \geq t_f\}$;
   $RP = \{(a,b) \in I_f^2 \mid a \neq b, \; sup(a,b) \leq t_r\}$;
(2) **for each** item-pair $(a,b) \in RP$ **do begin**
       $\mathcal{M}_{a,b} = \phi$; $\mathcal{M}_1 = \{\{c\} \mid c \in I - \{a,b\}, \; sup(c) \geq t_m\}$; $k = 1$;
       while $\mathcal{M}_k \neq \emptyset$ **do begin**
           for each item-set $M \in \mathcal{M}_k$ **do**
               for each pair $(\beta_a, \beta_b) \in \{a, \neg a\} \times \{b, \neg b\}$ **do**
                   if $\mu(M \Rightarrow \beta_a) \geq t_\mu$ and $\mu(M \Rightarrow \beta_b) \geq t_\mu$ **then**
                       $\mathcal{M}_{a,b} = \mathcal{M}_{a,b} \cup \{(M;(\beta_a, \beta_b))\}$;
           $\mathcal{M}_{k+1} = $ apriori-gen$(\mathcal{M}_k)$; $k = k + 1$;
       end;
   end;
(3) Answer $= \bigcup_{\{a,b\} \in RP} \{(M;(\beta_a, \beta_b)) \mid M \in \mathcal{M}_{ab}\}$;
end.

4.2   Retail Data

We have performed some data sets of POS data distributed for the domestic workshop of DATA MINING OLYMPIC 2000 held in KYOTO. Our algorithm has been written in Visual C++ for Windows. This experiment was performed on a 2.6GHz Pentium 4 with 1GB of main memory. These data sets are POS data of drug stores from April 1999 to March 2000. There are 5,169,613 transactions with 8,476 items in database of 100 shops. In this experiment, thresholds are defined as follows:

$$t_r = 0.000001, t_m = 0.0001(t_r \times 100), t_f = 0.001(t_r \times 1000), t_\mu = 0.5.$$

For space constraint, we are going to show two figures illustrating some of the derived Indirect Association rules from POS data.

The first figure shows that some of the derived Indirect Association rules for a rare item-pair that were chosen at random. These rare items are not competitive products in our consideration because it seems that there is no relationship between lipstick and detergent at all. The items of mediators for the first two rules are the same kinds of products except the maker. We can get great insights that antiphlogistic and vitamin drink are tend to buy together and with lipstick but not with detergent. However customers who bought vitamin drink and any other item tend to buy detergent together, but not lipstick. So antiphlogistic could be regarded as key item for marketing.

Mediator	a		b	
Vitamin drink (A) Antiphlogistic (C)	$\Rightarrow a$	0.86	$\Rightarrow \neg b$	0.70
Vitamin drink (B) Antiphlogistic (D)	$\Rightarrow a$	0.80	$\Rightarrow \neg b$	0.73
Vitamin drink (A) Any other item	$\Rightarrow \neg a$		$\Rightarrow b$	
Vitamin drink (B) Any other item	$\Rightarrow \neg a$		$\Rightarrow b$	

COMPANY

A: TAIHO Pharmaceutical Co., Ltd.
B: TAISYO Pharmaceutical Co., Ltd.
C: KOBAYASHI Pharmaceutical Co., Ltd.
D: PIP-FUJIMOTO Co., Ltd.
E: ROHTO Pharmaceutical Co., Ltd.
F: P & G

rare item pair a: Lipstick (E) and b: Detergent (F)

Fig. 1. Derived Indirect Association rules for Lipstick and Detergent

Mediator	a		b	
Tissue paper (A) nepia Deodorant (C)	$\Rightarrow a$	0.80	$\Rightarrow \neg b$	0.67
Tissue paper (B) Deodorant (C)	$\Rightarrow a$	0.75	$\Rightarrow \neg b$	0.73
Tissue paper (A) hoxy Deodorant (C)	$\Rightarrow \neg a$	1	$\Rightarrow b$	0.92
Deodorant (C) Any other item	$\Rightarrow \neg a$	1	$\Rightarrow b$	

COMPANY

A: OUJINEPIA
B: DAIO-PAPER
C: CRECIA
D: KOBAYASHI Pharmaceutical Co., Ltd.

rare item pair a: Toilet paper (D) and b: Toilet paper (A)

Fig. 2. Derived Indirect Association rules for Toilet papers

The second figure shows that some of derived Indirect Association rules for a rare item-pair that we chose with arbitrariness in order to analyze competing situations. Many customers tend to buy a facial tissue and a toilet paper. OU-JINEPIA has two brands of facial tissue, hoxy and nepia. However customers who bought a facial tissue of nepia tend to buy a toilet paper of other competing maker. Customers who bought a facial tissue of hoxy tend to buy a toilet paper of the same brand. Furthermore customers who did not buy a facial tissue always tend not to buy a toilet paper of DAIOPAPER at all.

Without the domain knowledge, many useful Indirect Association rules that described the several interesting situations were derived. These interpretations of derived rules could not be the real behavioral characteristics because our model does not take in the representative explanatory variables, such as price and promotion. In our consideration, these rules are regarded as reliable from the point of view of underlying behavioral pattern. We can say that the first two rules in Figure 1 illustrate a co-essential behavioral pattern because each of items in the rules belongs to the same item category. Even though our model does not take in some information, we deem that these interpretations could be considered adequate and proper. We are convinced that our model enables the users to understand the behavioral pattern of customers and the competitor.

5   Conclusion

We have discussed our new framework of Indirect Association rule mining with the μ measure. Indirect Association rules enable us to form many interpretations about the competitors and the customer behaviors. We could find many valid Indirect Association rules from POS data even tough we did not take into the consideration of price. As a future work, we are going to extend this model cover the price and other informations.

Acknowledgements

We would like to thank Professor Satoru Miyano at University of Tokyo and Associate Professor Katsutoshi Yada at Kansai University for letting us use valuable business data and giving advice.

References

1. R. Agrawal, T. Imielinski and A. Swami: *Mining Association Rules between Sets of Items in Large Databases*, in Proceedings of the 1993 ACM SIGMOD International Conference on Management of Data, Washington, D.C., USA, May 26–28, 1993, pp. 207–216, 1993.
2. R.J. Bayardo Jr. and R. Agrawal: *Mining the Most Interesting Rules*, in Proceedings of the Fifth ACM SIGKDD International Conference on Knowledge Discovery and Data Mining, San Diego, CA, USA, August 15–18, 1999, pp. 145–154, 1999.
3. S. Brin, R. Motwani, and C. Silvertein: *Beyond market baskets: Generalizing association rules to correlations*, in Proceedings of 1997 ACM-SIGMOD International Conference on Management of Data, Tucson, AZ, 1997.
4. B. Liu, W. Hsu and Y. Ma: *Mining Association Rules with Multiple Minimum Supports*, in Proceedings of the Fifth ACM SIGKDD International Conference on Knowledge Discovery and Data Mining, San Diego, CA, USA, August 15–18, 1999, pp. 337–341, 1999.
5. A. Savasere, E. Omiecinski and S. Navathe: *Mining for Strong Negative Associations in a Large Database of Customer Transactions*, in Proceedings of the Fourteenth International Conference on Data Engineering, Orlando, Florida, USA, February 23–27, 1998, pp. 494–502, 1998.
6. P.N. Tan and V. Kumar: *Interestingness Measures for Association Patterns: A perspective*, Technical Report # TR00-036, Department of Computer Science, University of Minnesota, 2000.
7. P.N. Tan, V. Kumar and J. Srivastava: *Indirect Association: Mining Higher Order Dependencies in Data*, in Proceedings of the Fourth European Conference on Principles of Data Mining and Knowledge Discovery (PKDD-2000), Lyon, France, September 13–16, 2000, Lecture Notes in Computer Science **1910**, pp. 632–637, 2000.
8. P.N. Tan, and V. Kumar and J. Srivastava: *Selecting the Right Interestingness Measure for Association Patterns*, in Proceedings of the Eighth ACM SIGKDD International Conference on Knowledge Discovery and Data Mining, Edmonton, Alberta, Canada, July 23–26, 2002, pp. 32–41, 2002.

9. P.N. Tan: *Discovery of Indirect Association and Its Applications*, Dr. Thesis, UNIVERSITY OF MINNESOTA, July, 2002.

10. T. Zhang: *Association Rules*, in Proceedings of the Fourth Pacific-Asia Conference on Knowledge Discovery and Data Mining, Current Issues and New Applications (PAKDD-2000), Kyoto, Japan, April 18–20, 2000, Lecture Notes in Computer Science **1805**, pp. 245–256, 2000.

An Association Mining Method for Time Series and Its Application in the Stock Prices of TFT-LCD Industry

Chiung-Fen Huang, Yen-Chu Chen, and An-Pin Chen

Institute of Information Management, National Chiao Tung University, Hsinchu, Taiwan
No. 1001, Dashiue Rd., Hsinchu, Taiwan 300, R.O.C.
huangcf@ms60.url.com.tw; yunchu@ms6.hinet.net

Abstract. TFT-LCD is one of industries currently promoted by the "Two Trillion and Twin Star Industries Development Plan" in Taiwan. This study endeavors to find out the stock price associations between the suppliers and manufacturers in the value chain of the TFT-LCD industry by means of data mining techniques, and meanwhile, to improve the Apriori algorithm so that it can facilitate association mining of discrete data points in a time series. An efficient data mining method which consists of two phases is proposed. In the first phase, data are classified and preprocessed using the algorithm proposed by R. Agrawal et al. (1996), then Apriori algorithm is applied to extract the strong association rules. The second phase further improves the Apriori algorithm by breaking down the traditional limitation of relying on pattern matching of continuous data for disclosing stock market behavior. By mining the association rules from the discrete data points in a time series and testing the corresponding hypotheses, statistically significant outcomes can be obtained. The proposed data mining method was applied to some real time-series of the stock prices of companies in the supply chain of TFT-LCD industry in Taiwan. It is suggested that a positive correlation does not necessarily exist between the companies' stock prices in the supply chain of TFT-LCD industry. For instance the result shows that, if the stock price of Sintek Phonrotic Corp., a company in the up stream of the value chain, soars for more than 5% in a day, the stock price of Tatung, a company in the down stream of the same value chain, may not respond positively accordingly. If an investor can short the stock of Tatung on the 7th day and long it back on the 10th day after Sintek's stock price soaring for more than 5%, the annual return of investment is 199.88% with 95% confidence interval. In conclusion, the results may reveal helpful information for the investors to make leveraged arbitrage profit investing decisions, and it might be interesting to apply this proposed data mining method to the time series in other industries or problems and investigate the results further.

Keywords: Data Mining, Association rule, Apriori Algorithm, TFT-LCD, Time series analysis.

1 Introduction

While more and more data generated in the form of time-series, there are much more needs to find frequent patterns in time-series data. Time-series data mining becomes

P. Perner (Ed.): ICDM 2004, LNAI 3275, pp. 117–126, 2004.

more and more popular in recent research areas and has broad applications like analysis of customer purchase patterns, web traversal patterns, etc.

Take the example of stock price fluctuation of TWSE. There may be some implications that when the stock price of some companies in supply chain went upwards, the stock price of the other companies in the related industry might also be affected. It is interesting to find the relationships among the stock fluctuation patterns. Learning from the association rules within these patterns might help the investors making decisions more precisely.

In this study, we try to find out the stock price association for the entire value chain in the TFT-LCD industry by means of data mining techniques, and, at the same time, to improve the Apriori algorithm so that it could be applied to the cross-day discrete discontinuous data. Two-phase experiment associated with the industry was conducted. In the first phase, data were prepared using the algorithm proposed by R. Agrawal et (1996), then Apriori algorithm is used to compute the support and confidence value. The strong association rules among the data are found accordingly. The second phase is to improve the Apriori algorithm. The idea is to break down the traditional limitation of continuous pattern when considering the stock market behavior. The results of this study reveals that a positive relationship does not necessarily exist between the companies' stock price in the supply chain of TFT-LCD industry. By using the idea, investors may make leveraged arbitrage profit investing decisions more precisely.

2 About TFT-LCD

Taiwan's flat-panel display industry developed out of the TN/STN LCD industry and expanded to the production and processing of TFT-LCD (Thin Film Transistor-Liquid Crystal Display) and upstream components, such as color filters, polarizers, backlights, and glass products. With large demand from local notebook PC manufacturers and technical advantages borrowed from the semiconductor industry, Taiwan's TFT-LCD industry has achieved its current strong position in less than five years of development. In 2001, Taiwan's TFT-LCD production reached NT$123.4 billion (US$3.65 billion), ranking third in the world and accounting for 26.1 percent of the world's total output.

With the commencement of the "Two Trillion and Twin Star" program, measures are being taken to offer more incentives to businesses, resolve patent-related problems, and strengthen R&D and training of new talents. These actions will not only help free Taiwan's TFT-LCD industry from technological dependence and its current shortage of skilled staff, but also give it a more completely integrated structure. Through the cooperation of government and industry, the TFT-LCD industry is expected to achieve a value of NT$1.37 trillion (US$40.53 billion) by 2006, making Taiwan the largest TFT-LCD supplier in the world.

3 Data Mining

3.1 Data Preprocessing

The task of data preparation is to transform the transactions in the database into the format we need. For example, in order to find the association rules of the fluctuations for daily stock prices, we need to transform the daily data of stocks into daily fluctuation rates.

There are three steps in the phase of data preparation. First we compute the fluctuation for each attribute values, to get rid of noisy data. Second, we transform the attribute values in the transaction, in the form of fluctuation. Then, we classify the fluctuation rates into several classes and label them as defined before.

3.2 Modified Apriori Algorithm

The first algorithm of mining association rules, called Apriori algorithm, was proposed by Agrawal and Srikant in 1994[15]. The methodology is so important in frequent pattern mining that there are many approaches adapting from it.

The Apriori algorithm employs iterative, level-wise approach, where frequent k-itemsets are deduced from (k-1)-itemsets. Let Lk be the frequent k-items, and Ck bethe candidate k-itemsets. In the first pass, it counts the support of data items to determine the frequent 1-itemsets. Then, it uses frequent itemsets Lk-1 found in the (k-1)th pass to generate the candidate items Ck and then scan the database, D, to counts the supports of candidates in Ck, Let Lk be the itemsets in Ck with their supports no less then the minimum support.[12]. In order to fit our experimental model, we modify Apriori algorithm and it is described in Figure3.1.

```
Input: Database, D, of transactions; minimum support
threshold, min_sup.
Output: L, frequent itemsets in D.
Method:
  Dim array [x, y]
  For (day = 1; EOF; day ++) {
     Data_preprocess;
     Cₖ = apriori_gen(Lₖ₋₁, min_sup);
     Gen_report;
  }
  L₁= find_frequent_1-itemsets(D);
  For (k=2; Lₖ₋₁ ≠∅ ;k++) {
     Cₖ = apriori_gen(Lₖ₋₁, min_sup);
     For each transaction t ∈ D{//scan D for counts
        Cₜ = subset(Cₖ,t);
           //get the subsets of t that are candidates
        For each candidate c ∈ Cₜ
           c.count++;
     }
     Lₖ = {c ∈ Cₖ|c.count ≥  min_sup}
  }
return L= ∪ ₖL
Procedure apriori_gen (Lₖ₋₁:frequent(k-1)-items; min_sup:
minimum support threshold)
  For each itemset l₁ ∈ Lₖ₋₁
     For each itemset l₂ ∈ Lₖ₋₁
        If (l₁[1] = l₂[1] ) ∧ (l₁[2] = l₂[2] ) ∧...∧ (l₁[k-
2] = l₂[k-2] ) ∧ (l₁[k-1] < l₂[k-1] ) then {
```

```
            C=  l₁ ∪ l₂ ;//join step:generate candidates
            If has_infrequent_subset(c,L_{k-1}) then
                Delete c; // prune step:remove unfruitful
candidate
            Else add c to C_k;
          }
   return C_k;
Procedure has_infrequent_subset (d:candidate k-
itemset;Lk-1:frequent (k-1)-itemsets); //use prior
knowledge
   For each (k-1)-subset s of c
       If s ∉Lk-1 then
           Return TRUE;
   Return FALSE;
```

Fig. 3.1. Modified Apriori algorithm

3.3 Interested Measures

Although a data mining process may generate a large number of patterns, typically only a small fraction of these patterns will actually be of interest to the given user. Thus, users need to further confine the number of uninteresting patterns returned by the process. This can be achieved by specifying the interested measures that estimate the simplicity, certainty, utility, and novelty of patterns. In this paper, we use novelty to test the measures of pattern interest.

Novel patterns are those that contribute new information or increased performance to the given pattern set. For example, a data exception may be considered novel in that it differs from that expected based on a statistical model to user beliefs. Another strategy for detecting novelty is to remove redundant patterns. If a discovered rule can be implied by another rule that is already in the knowledge base or in the derived rule set, then either rule should be reexamined in order to remove the potential redundancy.

4 Experiment

4.1 Data Preparation

This research is base on the closing stock price of the TFT-LCD industry supply chain related corporations. Considering the date of Optimax Co.(3051)'s stock going public, this study use the stock closing price from Oct. 28th,2002 to Jan. 15th 2004 as the basis of the experimentation data.

Eight companies were selected for the experiment. These corporations are all possess a supply chain relationship with CPT(Chunghwa Picture Tubes, LTD) TFT manufacturing. There are three companies in the upstream and four in the downstream of the supply chain.

In order to have a macroscopic concept for the study, all the data are divided into two categories. One is the whole data of 8 corporations. The other is to select one corporation from each of the three stream levels in the TFT-LCD industry supply chain: the upstream - supplier level, midstream - manufacturing level, and downstream - client level, accordingly. There will be twelve different combinations. These combinations of data are classified further.

Data need to be partitioned in order to quantify the quantitative attributes [19]. Here, the stock price movement of an attribute value is equally parted into several classes, as shown in Table 4.1. Each item of the data is represented by 5 digits, the first four digits stand for the stock number, and the fifth digit, A to G, represents the class that the item's stock price movement falls to.

Table 4.1

	Class 3	Class 4	Class 5	Class 6	Class 7
A	7 ~ 2.33	7 ~ 3.5	7 ~ 4.2	7~ 4.67	7 ~ 5
B	2.3 ~ -2.3	3.5 ~ 0	4.2 ~ 1.4	4.6 ~ 2.3	5 ~ 3
C	-2.33 ~ -7	0~ -3.5	1.4 ~ -1.4	2.34 ~ 0	3~ 1
D		-3.5 ~ -7	-1.4 ~ -4.2	0 ~ -2.3	1~ -1
E			-4.2 ~ -7	-2.3 ~ -4.6	-1 ~ -3
F				-4.7 ~ -7	-3 ~ -5
G					> -7

(%)

4.2 Experiment Result

At the first phase of the experiment, seven strong association rules are found in the group   consisting of all the eight companies (Table 4.2), six of the rules are left after applying Novelty test. The result reveals that there exists a stronger association, more than 66%, between the midstream and downstream in the TFT-LCD industry supply chain. By contrast, in the group consisting of data from each supply chain layer, two association rules of each in class 6 and class 7 are found. The findings are quite interesting and worth a further study.

Table 4.2

strong association rules		
2301B <- 2442B 2475B	(42.7%, 85.2%)	3
2301C <- 2442C 2475C	(22.0%, 71.2%)	5
2301C <- 3034C 2475C	(20.3%, 70.5%)	5
2301D <- 2442D 2352D	(13.7%, 63.4%)	7
2301D <- 3049D	(33.3%, 56.0%)	6
2442B <- 2475B 2301B	(20.3%, 68.9%)	4
2442B <- 2475B 2371B	(21.7%, 66.2%)	4

In order to have a further study about these four strong association rules, and to find out a discontinuous relationship, we modify the Apriori algorithm so that it can be applied to time series data, and also to discover the strong association rules among the cross-day transactions.

Table 4.3

Class 7 strong Association Rules	
2352D <- 2475C	(14.3%, 53.5%)
2301D <- 3051E	(25.3%, 52.6%)
2301D <- 2475D	(30.0%, 50.0%)
2301D <- 3049A	(10.0%, 56.7%)
2301D <- 2475D 3034D	(11.7%, 54.3%)
2352D <- 3051A	(10.0%, 53.3%)

In the second phase experiment of this study, the modified Apriori algorithm is used to mine the transaction data from the next day to the eleventh day. The result reveals that there is less than 20% confidence level between itemsets 2442 and 2475, which are the midstream and downstream companies accordingly in the TFT-LCD industry supply chain, in the following ten transaction days. Yet, there are two interesting rules finding in class 7 after the cross-day mining. Table 4.4 an illustrate the outcome.

Table 4.4. 3049 A → 2301 D

Day	X < 1%	X < -1%
1	73.30%	23.30%
2	53%	30.00%
3	50.00%	23%
4	50.00%	10.00%
5	66.70%	40%
6	76.70%	20.00%
7	76.70%	37%
8	63.30%	23.30%
9	63%	23%
10	63.30%	50%

4.3 Investitive Application

The results from the above experiment could help the investors to make proper financial decisions and make leveraged arbitrage profit. By applying the strong association rules revealed in section 4.3, the investor could see the relationship of the stock prices between the upstream and downstream companies in the supply chain of TFT-LCD industry, and make the proper investment decisions. For example, if the investor uses the rule 3049A-> 2301D to invest on Taiwan stock market, he might watch the trend of the stock market, and take some actions as follows:

1. Wait for the stock price of Sintek Co.(3049), the upstream company in the TFT-LCD industry, raises for over 5%.
2. Short sell the stock of Tatung, the downstream company in the TFT-LCD industry, on the 6th or 7th day after Sintek's stock price soaring for more than 5%.

3. Long the stock of Tatung back on the 10th day. If the investors do take such action by applying the association rule, as described above, the return on investment will be significant.

Table 4.5 shows the average transaction return and annual return on investment of the investment example.

Table 4.5

invest launch day	Day 1st	Day 6th	Day 7th
Trans. return rate	3.07%	1.86%	1.64%
year return rate	112.13%	170.02%	199.88%

4.4 Statistical Test

Again, H_0 is rejected, meaning rule Day 7th is better than Day 6th.

By the result of statistical hypothesis test, rule Day 7th is the best association rule in the three rules found in the second phase of the experiment. Therefore, in TFT-LCD industry, if one short sells the stock of the target company on the 7th day and long it back on the 10th day after the stock price of the upstream of the company soaring for more than 5% in one day, he would gain the greatest return on investment.

Table 4.6

	Day 1st	Day 6th	Day 7th
Sample num.	29	29	29
average	3.07	1.86	1.64
Stdev	10.44	6.67	6.08
(%)			

$$H_0 : \mu_{6th} \le \mu_{1st}, \alpha = 0.05$$

$$Z^\circ = \frac{\overline{3.09 - 1.86}}{\sqrt{\dfrac{(10.44)^2}{29} + \dfrac{(6.67)^2}{29}}} = 5.25$$

$$H_0 : \mu_{6th} \le \mu_{1st}$$

So H0 is rejected, which implies that rule Day 6th is better than Day 1st.
Next, the same statistical test is performed to compare rule Day 6th and Day 7th.

$$H_0 : \mu_{7st} \le \mu_{6th}, \alpha = 0.05$$

$$Z° = \frac{\overline{1.86 - 1.64}}{\sqrt{\dfrac{(6.08)^2}{29} + \dfrac{(6.67)^2}{29}}} = 14.2229$$

Again, H0 is rejected, meaning rule Day 7th is better than Day 6th.

By the result of statistical hypothesis test, rule Day 7th is the best association rule in the three rules found in the second phase of the experiment. Therefore, in TFT-LCD industry, if one short sells the stock of the target company on the 7th day and long it back on the 10th day after the stock price of the upstream of the company soaring for more than 5% in one day, he would gain the greatest return on investment.

5   Conclusion and Future Work

Data mining is a process of uncovering relationships, patterns and trends among huge volumes of data and then transforming them to valuable information that can leverage business intelligence and improve the process of making decisions [24]. A fundamental problem in data mining is finding frequent patterns in large datasets. The Apriori algorithm is one of several different algorithms that have been proposed to find all frequent patterns in a dataset, yet it is usually used on datasets containing continuous data. In this study, a modified Apriori algorithm is proposed to mine the association rule in time series data, and furthermore, to apply it to the cross-day discrete stock market data to find out some valuable information. It presents a data mining methodology to analyze discontinuous cross-day time-series data. The findings of this study might be helpful when making financial investment decisions:

1. In the same industry, there exists a stronger association for stock prices in vertical companies (companies in different streams in the supply chain) than in horizontal ones (companies in the same stream level in the supply chain).
2. A positive correlation does not necessarily exist between the companies' stock prices in upstream and downstream in the supply chain.
3. The study breaks down the traditional limitation of relying on pattern matching of continuous data in the same period of time. For example, when upstream company Sintek Co. (3049) has a stock price raising in one day, the stock price of downstream company Tatung Co. (2301) would decline for more than 1% with 50% confidence interval, in the 10th day after.
4. Applying the association rules found in the experiment, if an investor can short sell the stock of Tatung on the 7th day and long it back on the 10th day after Sintek's stock price soaring for more than 5%, the annual return on investment is 199.88% with 95% confidence interval.

By means of data mining technology, the study is focused on finding the companies' stock price association in the supply chain of TFT-LCD industry. The proposed data mining method could be applied to the time series data in other industries or problems and investigate the results further. Besides data mining methodology, some artificial intelligence technology, such as fuzzy, genetic algorithm, or neural network, may facilitate revealing more helpful information for the investors to make leveraged arbitrage profit investing decisions. It is hoped that this study will call people's attention to this opportunity.

References

1. Dan Braha and Armin Shmilovici, "Data mining for improving a cleaning process in the semiconductor industry", IEEE transactions on semiconductor manufacturing, vol. 15, No. 1, Feb 2002, 91-102
2. Michael Goebel and Le Gruenwald, "A survey of data mining and knowledge discovery software tools", SIGKDD Explorations. ACM SIGKDD. June 1999, Vol. 1. Issue 1, 20-33.
3. U. Fayyad, G. Piatetsky-Shapiro, and P. Smyth, "From data mining to knowledge discovery: An overview" in Advances in Knowledge Discovey and Data Mining, MIT Press, 1996, 1-36.
4. M. J. Berry and G. Linoff, Data Mining Techniques. New York:Wiley, 1997.
5. T. M. Mitchell, Machine Learning. New York: McGraw-Hill,1997
6. D. Braha, Ed., Data Mining for design and Manufacturing: Methods and Applications. Boston, MA: Kluwer Academic, 2001.
7. Goebel, M., and Gruenwals, L. A Survey of Knowledge Discovery and Data Mining Tools. Technical Report, University of Oklahoma, School of Computer Science, Norman, OK, Feb 1998.
8. Pawlak, Z. "Rough Sets: Theoretical Aspects of Reasoning About Data." Kluwer, Boston, 1991
9. Ron Kohavi and Foster Provost, "Applications of Data Mining to Electronic Commerce", Data mining and Knowledge discovery, Vol. 5,2001, 5-10.
10. Kamber, M., Han, J., and Chiaung, J. Y. "Using Data Cubes for Metarule-Guided Mining of Multi-Dimensional Association Rules." Technical Report U-Sfraser-CMPT-TR, 1997-10, Simon Fraser University, Burnaby, May 1997.
11. Lippmann, R.P. "An Introduction to Computing with Neural Nets." IEEE ASSP Magazine, Apr 1987, 4-22.
12. Hui Ching Han, "Mining Association Rules among Time-series Database", University of Taiwan, 2002.
13. J. Han, H. Lu, L. Feng, "Beyond Intra-transactional Association Analysis:Mining Multi-dimensiional Inter- transaction Association Rule," ACM Transactions on Information Systems, Vol. 18, No. 4, Oct 2000, 423-454
14. R.Agrawal, T. Imielinski, and A. Swami, "Mining Association Rules between Sets of Items in Large Databases, " Proc. ACM Special Interest Group on Management of Data, May 1993, 207-216
15. R. Agrawal and R. Srikant, "Fast Algorithms for Mining Association Rules in Large Database," Proc. 20th Int'l Conf. On very Large Databases, Santiage, Chile, Sep 1994, 478-499
16. J. Han and M. Kamber, "Data Mining: Concepts and Techniques ", Morgan Kaufmann, San Francisco, 2000.
17. A. Savesere, E. Omiecinski, and S. Navathe, "An Efficient Algorithm for Mining Association in Large Database," Proc. 21st Int'L Conf. On Very Large Databases, Zurich, Swizerland, 1995.
18. J. Han, J.Pei, and Y.Yin, "Mining Frequent Patterns without Candidate Generation," Proc. ACM Special Interest Group on Management Of Data, May 2000, 1-12

19. R. Srikant and R. Agrawal, "Mining Quantitative Association Rules in Large Relational Tables," Proc. ACM Special Interest Group on Management Of Data, Vol. 25, No. 2, June 1996, 1-12
20. Sector review, "Global TFT-LCD Industry 2004-05: From tightness to excess, and back.", Semiconductor Devices, Asia Pacific / Taiwan, 3 March 2004.
21. Taiwan Stock Exchange Corporation, http://www.tse.com.tw, Jan 2004.
22. Industrial development bureau ministry of economic affairs, http://www.moeaidb.gov.tw/idy/index1.jsp
23. Kenneth Janda, "Univariate Statistics", Northwestern University, http://www.janda.org
24. T.M. Mitchell, Machine learning and data mining, Communications of the ACM 33 (1990), 296-310

Clustering of Web Sessions Using Levenshtein Metric

Andrei Scherbina and Sergey Kuznetsov

Institute for System Programming, RAS 109004,
Moscow, B. Kommunisticheskaya, 25
sa@techsell.ru, kuzloc@ispras.ru

Abstract. Various commercial and scientific applications require analysis of user behaviour in the Internet. For example, web marketing or network technical support can benefit from web users classification. This is achievable by tracking pages visited by the user during one session (one visit to the particular site). For automated user sessions classification we propose distance that compares sessions judging by the sequence of pages in them and by categories of these pages. Proposed distance is based on Levenshtein metric. Fuzzy C Medoids algorithm was used for clustering, since it has almost linear complexity. Davies-Bouldin, Entropy, and Bezdek validity indices were used to assess the qualities of proposed method. As testing shows, our distance outperforms in this domain both Euclidian and Edit distances.

1 Introduction

Recently Internet gained certain social and economical influence. Nowadays companies that conduct business in the Web are interested in as much information about its customers as possible. Web administrators also require efficient tools for server usage analysis. Demand for intellectual analysis of web usage lead to new researches in this domain. The method to automatically classify web users can improve marketing and technical support greatly. Clustering is a well known method to classify large amounts of data, and it is usable in this domain as well.

This paper aims to find a method of semantically correct web session comparison. The metric from the Coding theory was modified to correctly handle web sessions. Presented distance uses sequence of pages in session and their content. This distance is further used to cluster web sessions. In this paper we present method with good clustering results and nearly linear complexity. However, some possible improvements are noted as well. The technique of correct user behaviour classification is the ultimate goal of our research.

The paper is organized as follows. Section 2 reviews social and economical context of web mining. Definitions of web mining terms are provided. A summary of used technologies and their intersection with other scientific domains is given. Section 3 describes the goal of proposed work in detail. In section 4 method realisation is described. In section 5 performed tests and comparison with other distances are presented. Last section concludes the paper by evaluating achieved results and describing possible improvements of the method.

P. Perner (Ed.): ICDM 2004, LNAI 3275, pp. 127–133, 2004.

2 Internet and Data Mining

Last years showed the fast growth of electronic commerce. The main reasons for this success are simplicity and speed with which transactions over Internet could be carried out. Another reason is the possibility to track user behaviour, which drew customers and buyers, developers and users much closer. So the end user interaction itself took drastic change. A scientific project, in the past, Internet now developed into the greatest or at least the fastest growing cconomical field.

Serious commercial value of Internet together with great amounts data stored in it, lead to intensive research and development of tools for automated data analysis. Among other methods, data mining was applied to this field. *Data mining* is the non-trivial process of identifying valid, novel, potentially useful, and ultimately under-standable patterns in data. Term *knowledge discovery from data bases* is often used interchangeably with data mining. These definitions are clearly described in [1].

Data mining from Internet (web mining) is the discovery and analysis of useful in-formation from Internet. Traditionally two parts are distinguished in web mining:

Web content mining is the automated information retrieval from web documents. *Web usage mining* is the discovery and analysis of information related to user-server interaction.[2,3].

Web usage mining methods allow effective processing of technical data, which was gathered during past years of Internet use. Companies store vast amounts of data in log files, which are automatically created by servers. Other sources of data are: browser journals and personal information on users, received by server scripts. Se-quential pattern generation, association rule discovery, clustering, and other data min-ing methods are used for the automated analysis of user access patterns.

The main obstacles for web usage mining include: vast amounts of data flow, exis-tence of various mechanisms (proxy servers, caching), which obscure real data, and as with any information gathering - security issues. All these problems still lack optimal solutions. Also there are various technical problems in application of data mining techniques (such as clustering) to this field.

The main customers for web usage mining systems are companies, which trade or provide their services in the Internet. The main goals for them are personalisation of pages and web site optimization for easier navigation. Network providers and administrators also take interest in such systems because of possibilities for network optimisation, traffic reduction, and improvement of provided services (for example, intellectual caching [4]).

3 Clustering in Web Usage Mining

Client classification allows to develop and fulfil various marketing strategies and technological solutions. Clustering is widely used in web usage mining for pages per-sonalisation: at first users are divided into categories. Then the information that the user sees on the site is changed for him depending on to which category he belongs [5]. Clustering is also used for decision making support in providing network services [6]. For example, clustering results are useful to see bottlenecks in site performance.

Before analysis, data is split into logical parts (sessions or transactions). Session is a set of page links followed during one website visit. Transaction is a set of semantically close page visits of one user. A transaction can include visited pages from either one or many sessions. To extract transaction splitting and merging of sessions is used. Clustering methods are used either on transactions or on sessions. In this paper the term "session" is used, however, received results can be easily applied to transactions.

The main problem of clustering user sessions is the selection of metric. For session analysis it is important to know which pages were visited and in what sequence it was done. Metrics traditionally used for web usage mining do not take into account the order of pages in the session. Euclidian metric that work fine with structured data performs much worse in this domain. To apply Euclidian metric in this field some effort is required to transform data to form suitable for use with this metric. In section 5 application of Euclidian metric is shown and test results are compared to Levenshtein metric performance.

We aim to obtain a method of semantically correct user access sessions clustering. Two main properties of the method are: 1) It must take into account order of pages in sessions. 2) It must correctly handle sessions of various lengths. Also the method must be as efficient as possible.

4 Levenshtein Metric Application

Prior to analysis we assign a unique numerical identifier for each page. Then each session could be defined as a list of visited pages (string of numbers). Huge analytical experience is developed on optimal metric selection for string comparison. Keeping that in mind, selected representation for user session proves easy to use. We propose to use Levenshtein metric with some modifications for sessions clustering.

A number of pairwise character operations to transform one string to another can be defined. In this work the following edit operations are used: character insertion, deletion, and substitution. Cost is assigned for every edit operation. Levenshtein metric is the total cost of best sequence of edit operations that convert one string to another. Edit distance [7] is one of these metrics; it has unity cost assigned for addition and deletion, and cost two assigned for character substitution. For example, best sequence of operations to change "cat" into "part": change "c" into "p" (cost is 2), insert "r" between "a" and "t" (cost is 1). So edit distance between these strings is 3.

Hay et al[8] and Runkler and Bezdek [9] have also proposed to use edit distance for web sessions clustering. Edit distance was tested without modifications and results received were adequate but not too good. In [10] edit distance with some minor modifications was tested, but the results were still far from optimal.

In this paper we present edit distance modification, based on pages categories. Each page on the site has the URL, like "dir1/dir2/pagename.htm". We assume that two pages from the same directory on the server have similar content. And if two pages belong to different directories, but share the same first level directory, then they at least belong to the same knowledge domain.

We propose a new distance, based on Levenshtein metric. It is defined as follows. Insertion and deletion of a symbol has weight 15. Substitution has weight depending on closeness of two pages. If the pages belong to the same directory, then the weight is 16. If two pages share the same first directory in URL - then the weight is 21. And if two pages are from completely different directories, then the weight is 30. So if two sessions have pages from the same site category, then they are closer, then the ones from two different categories.

We used unmodified edit distance and Euclidian metric for comparison. For Euclidian metric all sessions were represented as N-dimensional vectors, where N is the total number of pages on site. Each vector had values as follows: $v_i(j)=1$ if page j was visited during session i and $v_i(j)=0$ otherwise.

For testing we have employed Fuzzy C-Medoids[11] clustering algorithm. It is a variation of Fuzzy C Means method.

Let $X = \{x_i | i = 1, 2, \ldots, N\}$ be a set of N objects. Let $r(x_i; x_j)$ denote the distance between object x_i and object x_j. Let $V = \{v_1, v_2, \ldots, v_c\}$, represent cluster medoids in X. At each step of the method, we minimize:

$$J_m(V;X) = \sum_{j=1}^{N} \sum_{i=1}^{C} u_{ij}^m r(x_j, v_i). \tag{1}$$

We used following membership model:

$$u_{ij}^m = \left(\frac{1}{r(x_j, v_i)} \right)^{1/(m-1)} / \sum_{k=1}^{c} \left(\frac{1}{r(x_j, v_k)} \right)^{1/(m-1)}. \tag{2}$$

We set m to 1.5 for our experiments.

The main difference of used method from Fuzzy C Means is that only selected objects from each cluster is used to recalculate medoids. Objects in X with highest membership values for the particular cluster, are used for medoids calculation. During our experiments we used top 60 objects for each cluster. This way very low time complexity of the method is achieved.

5   Test Results

For testing we used data from www.citforum.ru - one of the leading Russian IT resources in Internet. Main characteristics for this data are: around 92 000 visits per day, around 9000 user sessions per day and more then 10 000 pages available on site. Usually long sessions with 50 or more visits are generated by automated software so they do not show actual human behaviour. Very short sessions on the other hand are hard to analyze since no notable patterns are shown. We removed sessions with less then 4 and more then 50 visits to improve quality of data. Testing was performed on 5500 sessions from three days period.

To compare proposed distance with edit distance and Euclidian distance we used cluster validity indices. As you can see in the figures 1 and 2, either partition entropy or Bezdek [12] index showed better results for presented distance. We conclude that it separates sessions into crisper clusters then Euclidian or edit distances do.

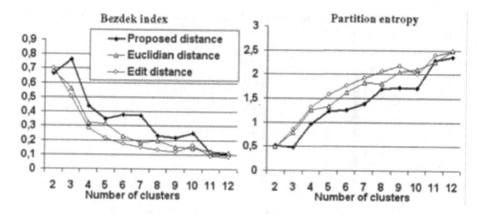

Fig. 1. Bezdek index and partition entropy

Davies-Bouldin index was used to evaluate the quality of clusters. Each object was strictly assigned to the cluster, at which it had highest membership. So we used this index on crisp clusters. We have tested our method on 2 to 10 clusters, and as you can see on the figure 2, seven clusters are optimal for the test data. Same tendency can be noted at figure 1.

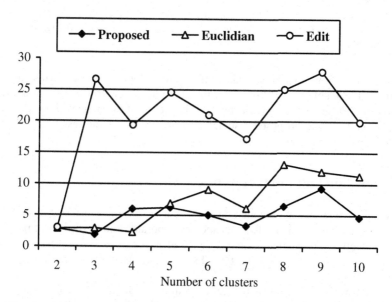

Fig. 2. Davies-Bouldin index. Clusters generated with proposed distance are more compact and have larger intercluster distance, then ones generated with other distances

Some of the sessions on test site were generated by search engine crawlers. These sessions show the same behaviour pattern. So semantically correct data classification places all of these sessions into the same cluster. It was possible to check how different distances behaved. Here we present the results for seven clusters, since it was found to be the optimal partition for the data.

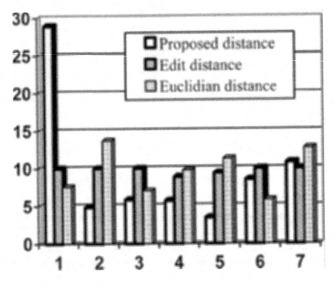

Fig. 3. Clustering of web crawlers sessions. We show here summation of membership functions for these sessions. As you can clearly see on this graph, proposed distance outperforms both other distances in clustering these sessions. All sessions were clustered with high probability to the same cluster

Test results show, that proposed method works better then other tried distances. The method was able to partition all of the automated web crawlers sessions into the same cluster. Partition Entropy, Bezdek and Davies-Bouldin indices showed that clusters received by using proposed distance are more compact and less fuzzy, then ones received with other distances.

6   Conclusion and Further Work

In this paper we proposed new method for web user sessions clustering. New edit distance modification was used. This distance incorporates knowledge about pages categories, as well as knowledge about sequence of pages in each web session. Fuzzy C Medoids method was used with this distance and nearly linear complexity was achieved.

Davies-Bouldin, Entropy and Bezdek validity indexes was used to assess our method. It compared favourably with both Euclidian distance and edit distance. We tracked how selected sessions of similar qualities (generated by automated crawlers) were clustered. Proposed method showed the best results.

Proposed distance could be further modified by coefficient varying. It is optimal to use self learning algorithm to handle this task. Also results of the clustering can be improved by using algorithm, which handles noise better then Fuzzy C Medoids method.

Evaluation of clustering results is still an interesting issue. It is nearly impossible to use expert to verify quality of web sessions clustering. Efficient validity index to automatically assess the quality of the partition is needed. Further research of various validity indices in domain of web sessions is planned. We intend to use association rules to judge cluster quality. The idea is simple: if for each cluster there is at least one association rule, unique for sessions of that cluster, then clustering is adequate for data semantics.

References

1. U.M. Fayyad, G. Piatetsky-Shapiro, P. Smyth, and R. Uthurusamy: Advances in Knowledge Discovery and Data Mining. AAAI Press/MIT Press, 1996.
2. Robert Cooley, Bamshad Mobasher, Jaideep Srivastava: Web Mining: Information and Pattern Discovery on the World Wide Web. Proceedings of the 9th IEEE International Conference on Tools with Artificial Intelligence (ICTAI'97), November 1997.
3. Daniela Florescu, Alon Levy, Alberto Mendelzon: Database Techniques for the World-Wide Web: A Survey. SIGMOD Record, vol 27, number 3, pp. 59-74, 1998.
4. Francesco Bonchi, Fosca Giannotti, Giuseppe Manco, Mirco Nanni, Dino Pedreschi, Chiara Renso, Salvatore Ruggieri: Data Mining for Intelligent Web Caching. In Proceedings of the International Conference on Information Technology (ITCC 2001), Las Vegas, NV, USA, 2001, pp. 599-603
5. B. Mobasher, H. Dai, T. Luo, Y. Sun, and J. Zhu: Combining web usage and content mining for more effective personalization. In Proc. of the International. Conference on ECommerce and Web Technologies (ECWeb), Greenwich, UK, 2000, pp. 165-176.
6. Chung-Min Chen, Munir Cochinwala, Claudio Petrone, Marc Pucci, Sunil Samtani, Patrizia Santa, Marco Mesiti: Internet traffic Warehouse. Proceedings of the 2000 ACM SIGMOD International Conference on Management of Data, Dallas, Texas, USA, 2000, pp. 550-558.
7. V. I. Levenshtein: Binary Codes Capable of Correcting Deletions, Insertions and Reversals. Soviet Physics Doklady 10(8), 1966, pp. 707-710 and Doklady Akademii Nauk SSSR 163(4), 1965, pp. 845-848.
8. T.A. Runkler and J.C. Bezdek: Web mining with relational clustering. International Journal of Approximate Reasoning, Vol. 32 (2-3), 2003, pp. 217-236
9. Hay B., Wets G. and Vanhoof K.: Segmentation of visiting patterns on websites using a Sequence Alignment Method. Journal of Retailing and Consumer Services, 2003, vol. 10, issue 3, pp. 145-153.
10. Scherbina A.: Application of Levenstein Metric to Web Usage Mining. in proceedings of 7th International Conference on Business Information Systems, Poznan, Poland, 2004, pp. 363-369
11. Raghu Krishnapuram, Anupam Joshi, Olfa Nasraoui, and Liyu Yi: Low-Complexity Fuzzy Relational Clustering Algorithms for Web Mining. IEEE Trans. Fuzzy Systems, Vol. 9, No. 4, August 2001, pp. 595-607.2
12. Maria Halkidi, Yannis Batistakis and Michalis Vazirgiannis: On Clustering Validation Techniques. "Journal of Intelligent Information Systems", vol. 17, number 2-3, 2001, pp. 107-145.
13. Xie, X. L, Beni, G.: A Validity measure for Fuzzy Clustering. IEEE Transactions on Pattern Analysis and machine Intelligence, Vol.13, No4, 1991.

A Data Mining Approach for Call Admission Control and Resource Reservation in Wireless Mobile Networks

Sherif Rashad, Mehmed Kantardzic, and Anup Kumar

CECS Department, JB Speed School of Engineering, University of Louisville,
Louisville, KY 40292, USA
{ssrash01, mmkant01, ak}@louisville.edu

Abstract. In this paper a mobility-based predictive scheme for call admission control (CAC) and resource reservation (RR) is proposed. The main goal is to reduce the call dropping probability and the call blocking probability and to maximize the bandwidth utilization. Mining the previous movements of the mobile users, generates local and global profiles, which are utilized effectively in prediction of the future path of the mobile user. This scheme is based on high level of prediction of the next base stations for the mobile user. The simulation is used to compare the performance of the proposed technique with other two techniques: FR-CAT2 and PR-CAT4. Simulation results show that the proposed scheme has a significantly better performance (in average about 25%) compared to the other two schemes.

1 Introduction

In the future mobile communications networks (such as 3G and 4G networks), it is important that they support a broad range of multimedia services which includes a real time applications with a quality of service (QoS) assurance [8, 9]. One of the important things to be considered in the wireless mobile environment is the scarcity of the available bandwidth and the mobility of the users. This makes the problem of QoS provisioning far more challenging in the wireless mobile networks than in the wireline networks [1, 9]. Call Admission control (CAC) and bandwidth reservation schemes are very important in providing the required QoS in the mobile networks.

Call (or connection) admission control refers to the task of deciding if a call should be admitted into and supported by the network [9]. CAC is considered as a provisioning strategy to limit the number of call connections into the network in order to reduce the network congestion and the call dropping [4]. The mobility of the users makes the dropping of the call a likely event in the mobile networks. Also, the new call may not be accepted if there is no available bandwidth to support this call. To ensure a guarantee QoS, the service providers have to maintain the ingoing calls when the mobile users move from one cell to another cell. Moreover, a cell has to accept as many new calls as possible taking into account that handoff calls will always have a priority over the new arriving calls. Because of user's mobility, bandwidth (or resource) reservation is used to reserve the bandwidth required for the handoff calls. This reservation is performed in the cells that will be visited by the user during the trip. This will help to complete an ongoing call without dropping.

P. Perner (Ed.): ICDM 2004, LNAI 3275, pp. 134–143, 2004.
© Springer-Verlag Berlin Heidelberg 2004

Call blocking probability (CBP), call dropping probability (CDP), and bandwidth utilization (BWU) are the important QoS parameters, which will be considered in this paper. When there is no enough bandwidth to serve the new arriving call, this call may be rejected (blocked). When there is no enough bandwidth to serve the handoff calls, this call may be dropped. Bandwidth utilization (BWU) is an important parameter that is used to measure the efficiency of using the reserved bandwidth. It is defined as the ratio between the amount of bandwidth used by various applications admitted into the network and either the total requested bandwidth or the total available bandwidth, whichever is the smaller [9,10,11].

Prediction of the mobile users' movements has been used to enhance the performance of the call admission control, resource reservation, location management and handover management in mobile networks. Recent publications, [1, 2, 3, 5, 6], proposed mobility-based schemes for CAC to enhance the performance of mobile networks in terms of QoS metrics. The schemes proposed in [1, 5] use the current mobility factors (velocity, direction, angle, or distance) to estimate the next cell. The movement history of the user over long period of time is not used in these schemes. The schemes proposed in [2, 3] are based on the movements' history of the user over a suitable period of time to predict the next base station.

In the next section, a general overview of the proposed technique is introduced. The details of extracting and building the local and global mobility profiles are explained in the third and fourth sections. The RR and PCAC schemes are explained in the fifth and sixth sections. The seventh section presents and discusses the simulation environment and the obtained results. At the end, we give a conclusion and the future work plan.

2 Overview of the Proposed PCAC-RR Methodology:

The basic idea of our research is to develop a mobility-based predictive call admission control and resource reservation technique (PCAC-PR) to enhance the performance of wireless mobile networks. The key here is how we can mine the previous behavior of the mobile users to generate the mobility profiles. These profiles contain the frequent paths and its associated probability. These frequent paths will be used effectively to predict the next movements. The generated profiles for each user will contain useful information related to the behavior of this user. This information includes the visited paths, the day period at which each path was visited, estimated time length of the path, and the probability of visiting that path. Data mining techniques are used to extract this information. Also, the proposed methodology provides a suitable QoS guarantee for mobile communications.

The proposed CAC and resource reservation schemes are mainly based on the generation of two types of users' mobility profiles. The first type is called the local mobility profile. This profile is generated locally for each user by his mobile host (MH). The MH will have the responsibility to collect the movement data of a user that uses this MH. This data is used to build the mobility profile of users and will continually updated based on users movements. The second type of the mobility profiles is called the global mobility profile. This profile is generated by each base station (BS). The BS will have the responsibility to collect the movements' data of the users passed through it. This global profile will be used if the local profile gives undesirable prediction accuracy (weak support).

Fig. 1 shows an overview of the system architecture. Every time the user enters a new BS, the MH will start to predict the next base stations according to the current local profile of this user. Once a conversation has started, this information about the next cells will be sent to the current BS (with additional information about the expected handoff time) before the handoff process. The current BS will use its own global profile if the MH couldn't predict the next cell (for the case of new visited base stations or rarely visited base stations). This methodology takes the benefits of both local and global profiles, where the combination enhances the accuracy of the prediction.

There are three main advantages of the proposed technique over the other techniques. First, the time of request is considered as an important factor in prediction technique. Second, this technique uses a hierarchical structure of local and global profiles, which improves the prediction accuracy. Third, this technique predicts the future path of the user (not only the next cell). These characteristics enhanced significantly the performance of the mobile network to provide better service. This will be shown later in results part.

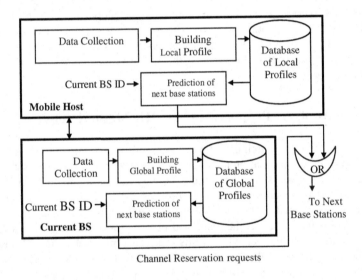

Fig. 1. The System architecture supported by the PCAC-PR technique

3 Local Mobility Profiles

The profiles will contain a set of sequences in the form of paths that are most likely to be visited. Each of these paths contains a sequence of cells IDs. For example, the profile $\{P_1, P_2, ..., P_n\}$ contains n paths each of them in the form $P_i = \{ BS_1, BS_2, ..., BS_m \}$, where BS_j is the ID of a base station in that path.

Local mobility profiles are generated separately for each mobile user. These local mobility profiles are built based on the data colleted by each mobile handset for a suitable period of time. The software in the mobile handset will have to collect the data and mine this data to generate the profiles.

Data collection and data mining are basic phases in forming local and global mobility profiles. In this part we will focus on the explanation of the local mobility profiles.

3.1 Local Paths

Data Collection. Data collection is performed during the navigation of the mobile user. Each time the mobile user enters a new cell, the data collection software records the ID of this new cell and the times at which the visit was started and ended.

Discovering of Local Paths. Data mining is an important task that is to be performed by the software inside the mobile handset. The main idea is to mine the collected data to generate the local profile for each user. We introduce hypothesis that user behaviors (and therefore user profiles) are not the same for different periods of the day. Therefore we propose dividing the day into several intervals. These intervals will be determined generally for the users according to the known rush hours, general work hours, etc. In our experiments, we have divided the day into the following intervals: T_1 (morning rush hours: [6:00 - 9:00]), T_2 (morning-noon: [9:00 12:00]), T_3 (after noon [12:00 - 5:00]), T_4 (evening rush hour: [5:00-6:00]), T_5 (evening: [6:00 - 12:00]), and T_6 (after midnight: [12:00 - 6:00]). The local profile contains the possible paths with associated probabilities for each time interval. This means that a path may have different probabilities for different intervals in a day. As we know, each path in the local profile is described by a sequence of base stations. Therefore it is necessary to transform the collected data in the MH into a sequence of symbols, where each symbol represents a base station. In our experiment, we have used a time slot of one minute ($\Delta t = 1$ min). Every continuous path can be transformed into a sequence of base stations ID for each recorded visit. Fig. 2 shows an example of using the time slots in the local profiles.

In this example, the mobile set started to visit base station BS_2 at time 1:01 pm and the visit ended at time 1:03 pm, then using $\Delta t = 1$ minute, we can say that this mobile user visited BS_2 for two consecutive time slots. The generated continuous path based on this time slot is as shown in Fig. 2. This type of path representation contains implicit information about speed of transition between the cells. This type of information will be very useful in predicting when the handoff will happen. Hence, we can enhance the overall performance by preventing unnecessary early bandwidth reservation. This is an important advantage of the proposed approach where we can predict not only the next base stations, but also the time at which the handoff will happen. In addition our approach can also predict, based on past history, how long a mobile user will stay in the next cells.

For each of the generated paths we calculate two types of probabilities. The first one is the overall probability for each path (during the whole day). This probability can be calculated from equation (1):

$$P(path_n, m_l) = \frac{\sum_{j=1}^{N_T} Num(path_n, T_j, m_l)}{\sum_{j=1}^{N_T} \sum_{i=1}^{N_p(m_l)} Num(path_i, T_j, m_l)} \quad (1)$$

where

- $P(path_n, m_l)$: is the probability of the mobile m_l to go through the path $path_n$,
- $Num(path_n, T_j, m_l)$ is the number of times for mobile m_l to go through $path_n$ during the time interval T_j
- N_T: is the number of time intervals
- $N_p(m_l)$: is number of stored paths for the mobile m_l.

The other type of probability is the probability of the path in a certain time interval, which could be expressed in terms of the probability of the path $path_n$ given the interval T_j which written as $P(path_n, m_l | T_j)$. This probability can be calculated from the equation:

$$P(path_n, m_l | T_j) = \frac{Num(path_n, T_j, m_l)}{\sum_{i=1}^{N_p(m_l)} Num(path_i, T_j, m_l)} \quad (2)$$

The generated paths and their probabilities for a single user will be used to build the local mobility profiles.

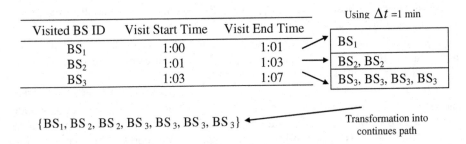

Fig. 2. An example of path generation

3.2 Building Local Mobility Profiles

In this section, we will explain how to analyze the discovered local and global paths to determine the frequent paths. The paths are tested according to the periodical and the overall probabilities to determine the set of paths to be considered as frequent paths for the given time interval and to assign a probability called *associated probability* to each frequent path. This probability determines the amount of the required bandwidth to be reserved in every cell belonging to that path. This following steps describe how to find the frequent paths:

1. For each time interval, we start to test probability of each path in the given time interval $P(path_n | T_i)$ with respect to a certain predetermined threshold LTH_1 (say 0.8).
2. If $P(path_n | T_i) > LTH_1$, then this path is considered frequent and *associated probability* of this path is equal to one ($P_{assoc}(path_n) = 1$)..
3. If the path probability is not high enough ($P(path_n | T_i) < LTH_1$), then the overall probability $P(path_n)$ is tested instead of $P(path_n | T_i)$.
4. If $P(path_n) > LTH_2$ (another certain predetermined threshold, say 0.6), then this path is considered frequent, and its associated probability will be $P_{assoc}(path_n)$ $=P(path_n)$.
5. Otherwise, the associated probability will be $P_{assoc}(path_n) = P(path_n | T_i)$ and the path is not frequent.

By the end of the algorithm, the paths are stored in a table called $LP(T_i)$ *(Local Profile at time interval T_i)* which will contain the predicted local paths as well as the corresponding associated probabilities.

The LP table corresponding to each time interval is stored locally in the mobile handset while. These paths with their associate probabilities will be used for the proposed resource reservation and CAC algorithms. An example of the generated local profile for a user is shown in Table 1.

Table 1. Example of the generated local profiles for a single user

Time Interval T_i	Visited Paths ($path_k$)	The Associated Probability $P_{assoc}(path_n)$
LP(T_1)	$Path_1=\{ BS_1, BS_2, ..., BS_m\}$	$P_{assoc}(path_n) = 1$
	$Path_2$	....
	...	...
	$Path_n$	...
...	...	...
	$Path_1$	...
LP(T_N)	...	...
	$Path_m$	...

4   Global Mobility Profiles

Global mobility profiles are generated and maintained by the base stations. The global mobility profiles will contain sequences of paths that are most likely to be visited by the users passing through the base station that maintains this global profile in its database. Each BS is responsible for collecting the mobility information of the subscribers passing through this base station. This information mainly includes the previous and the next BSs as well as the time at which these BSs were visited. This information is used to generate the global mobility profiles.

The data collection, discovering processes, and building the global mobility profiles will be similar to the process described before but from the point of view of the base stations. Also, here will have a table called GP(T_i) (*Global Profiles at time interval* T_i)) that will contain the global paths as well as the corresponding associated probabilities. The complete details of the global mobility profiles are described in [12].

5 Predictive Resource Reservation Scheme (RR)

In this paper, we assume that we have two types of calls: Class-I and Class-II. The calls form Class-I are the real time calls (such as video and audio). This means that these calls are sensitive to time variations. The calls from Class-II are the non-real time calls (such as text and Image). This means the time factor is not so significant for the call of Class-II.

The RR scheme will use the frequent paths computed earlier with their associated probabilities to reserve the suitable bandwidth, which will be used during the call handoff. Each cell will have a portion of the bandwidth reserved for handoff calls. In order to make a reservation for the bandwidth, the cells have to monitor the available bandwidth at any time, which will be used for reservation. For each cell C_i the available bandwidth at any T_j is denoted as $B_a(C_i, T_j)$. The available bandwidth could be calculated if we know the following:

- $B_t(C_i T_j)$: the total bandwidth of cell C_i at time T_j
- $B_u(C_i, T_j)$: the estimated bandwidth used by users in cell C_i at time T_j
- $B_r(C_i, T_j)$: the bandwidth reserved by cell C_i for handoff calls *at time* T_j

The available bandwidth in cell C_i at any time is calculated from equation (3):

$$B_a(C_i, T_j) = B_t(C_i T_j) - B_u(C_i, T_j) - B_r(C_i, T_j) \tag{3}$$

The service providers determine the total bandwidth assigned for each cell during the design phase. The bandwidth used by the users in cell C_i at the expected handoff time T_h can be estimated easily from the bandwidth used at the current time. If there is a call, the required amount of bandwidth to be reserved in the other cells have to be calculated to handle the handoff operation. The expected time at which the handoff will happen has to be taken into account also. Suppose that there is a call in cell C_i at time T_j, the proposed RR scheme will be as follows:

1. Starts to predict the future paths by looking at LP(T_j) (*the local profile*).
2. If there is at least a predicted frequent path in the local profile, then the bandwidth reservation is performed based on this local profile.
   i. For each cell C_k in the local paths, we start to estimate the handoff time (T_h) using the known time slot Δt.
   ii. Once we find T_h, we start to check the available bandwidth at T_h. The available bandwidth could be calculated from equation (3).
   iii. The required amount of bandwidth B_{req} to be reserved is determined as a portion from the actual required bandwidth B_{actual} according to the associated probability of the path using the following equation:

$$B_{req} = B_{actual} * P_a(path_n) \tag{4}$$

iv. If there is enough bandwidth available at time T_h , then the amount of bandwidth to be reserved will be B_{req} and the available and the reserved bandwidths are updated.

v. If there is no sufficient bandwidth available and the call is from Class-I, then this call can borrow some amount (B_{borrow}) form the Class-II calls in that cells.

vi. Otherwise the amount of bandwidth to be reserved will be the available bandwidth plus B_{borrow}.

3. If no local frequent paths could be predicted using $LP(T_j)$, then we have to access the global profile, $GP(T_j)$, and use the global paths in a way similar to the one described in the local profiles to reserve the required bandwidth.

6 Predictive Call Admission Control Scheme (PCAC)

The admitted call may be a new call or a handoff call. Each of these categories of calls will be handled in a different way taking into account that the handoff calls will have a priority over the new calls.

For new calls from Class-I, PCAC scheme will check the available BW in the current cell C_i (at which the admission is performed) as well as the available BWs in the next expected cells in the predicted frequent paths with high probabilities ($P_{assoc}(path_n)=1$). If each of these cells has available BW to cover this new call at the next time step, then the call is accepted and the required BW is allocated. Otherwise the call is blocked. For the new calls from Class-II, PCAC scheme checks only the available BW at the current cell. If there is an available BW, then the call is accepted and a BW is allocated ($B_{accepted}$).

Handoff calls can allocate BW from the reserved BW and from the available BW. Suppose that the admission for a handoff call is performed at the cell C_i and at the time interval T_j. The calls from Class-I will be accepted if the required BW $\leq [B_r(C_i ,T_j)+ B_a(C_i ,T_j)]$. Otherwise the call is dropped. For handoff calls from Class-II, The call will be accepted if there is BW available in the reserved or the available BWs.

This approach will maximize the probability of completing the call without dropping during the user navigation through the cells. More details about PCAC-RR scheme are provided in [12].

7 Simulation and Results

The simulation is conducted to compare performance of the proposed PCAC-RR scheme with PR-CAT4 and FR-CAT2 schemes that are described in [3, 7]. PR-CAT4 is a predictive scheme and it takes into account the movement to the next cell from the previous cell through the current cell. In FR-CAT2 scheme there is no prediction and a fixed portion of the total BW is reserved for the handoff calls.

The simulation details are provided in [12]. The experiments have been performed for the three schemes using call arrival rate ranging from 0.01 up to 0.1 calls/second for each cell. The results are shown in Fig. 3, Fig. 4 and Fig. 5.

Fig. 3 shows the resultant CBP for each algorithm. As we can see from Fig. 3, the PCAC-RR algorithm has the lowest CBP. This result is due to the fact that the improved prediction of the future movement(s) allows us to free more BW on the cells that are expected to be visited with low probabilities and this BW is available for the new calls. Also, we can see that the proposed PCAC-RR technique has a better performance than the PR-CAT4 technique because the prediction in the proposed technique is enhanced by using local and global profiles and by using the time of request as an important factor.

Fig. 4 and Fig. 5 show that the proposed PCAC-RR technique has the lowest CDP and the highest bandwidth utilization compared to the other techniques. This is because in the proposed algorithm, we predict a longer path (not only the next step as in PR-CAT4). This allows us to give advance notice of reservations for suitable amount of BW for the handoff calls in expected cells.

From all of these results, we can conclude that the proposed PCAC-RR technique enhances the performance of the cellular communications systems. This enhancement is in average about 25% compared to the other techniques.

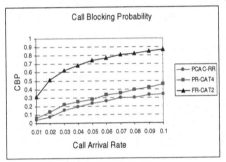

Fig. 3. Call blocking probability results

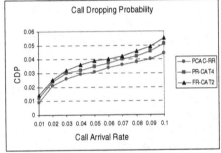

Fig. 4. Call dropping probability results

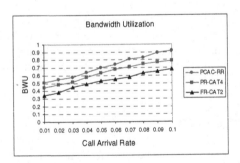

Fig. 5. Bandwidth utilization results

8   Conclusion and Future Work

In this paper, we proposed a predictive CAC and RR technique (PCAC-RR) which is based on the generation of local and global mobility profiles of mobile users. Data mining techniques are used to generate these profiles. The frequent paths at both profiles are utilized to predict the next path and the time at which the handoff will occur. The simulation results showed that the proposed PCAC-RR technique has a better performance compared to the two techniques.

In the future work, we are planning to apply the same predictive approach to the broadcasting problem in cellular systems.

Acknowledgment

This research is in-part supported by NSF grant #INF 7-001-006.

References

1. Mohammad Mahfuzul Islam, Manzur Murshed and Laurence S. Dooley.: New Mobility Based Call Admission Control with On-Demand Borrowing Scheme for Qos Provisioning. International Conference on Information Technology: Coding and Computing [Computers and Communications], ITCC (2003) 263–267.
2. F. Yu and V.C.M. Leung.: Mobility-based predictive call admission control and bandwidth reservation in wireless cellular networks. Computer Networks, Vol. 38, No. 5, (2002) 577-589.
3. Chang Ho Choi, Myung Il Kim, Sung-Jo Kim.: Call Admission Control Using the Moving Pattern of Mobile User for Mobile Multimedia Networks. 27th Annual IEEE Conference on Local Computer Networks, LCN (2002), 431-440.
4. Y. Fang and Y. Zhang.: Call admission control schemes and performance analysis in wireless mobile networks. IEEE Transactions on Vehicular Technology, Vol. 51, No.2, (2002) 371-382.
5. J. Hou and Y. Fang.: Mobility-based call admission control schemes for wireless mobile networks. Wireless Communications and Mobile Computing, Vol.1, No.3, (2001) 269-282.
6. Jon M. Peha, Arak Sutivong.: Admission control algorithms for cellular systems. Wireless Networks , Vol 7 , Issue 2 ,(2001) 117 – 125.
7. Yi-Bing Lin, A. NoerPel, and D. Harasty.: Non-Blocking Channel Assignment Strategy for Hand-Offs. IEEE ICUPC94, (1994) 558 – 562.
8. Ganguly, S. and Nath, B.: An Implicit QoS Provisioning Strategy in Multimedia Cellular Network. IEEE Wireless Communications and Networking Conference (WCNC), Vol. 1, (2002), 301-306
9. Kadi, M. E., Olariu, S. and Wahab, H. A.: A Rate-based Borrowing Schemes for QoS Provisioning in Multimedia Wireless Networks. IEEE Transactions on Parallel and Distributed Systems, vol. 13, no. 2, (2002) pp. 156-166.
10. Chen, H., Kumar, S. and Kuo, C. C. J.: Dynamic Call Admission Control Scheme for QoS Priority Handoff in Multimedia Cellular Systems. IEEE Wireless Communications and Networking Conference, (WCNC), Vol1 (2002) 17-21.
11. Levine, D. A., Akyildiz, I. F. and Naghshineh, M.: A Resource Estimation and Call Admission Algorithm for Wireless Multimedia Networks using the Shadow Cluster Concepts. IEEE/ACM Transactions on Networking, Vol. 5, No. 1 (1997) 1-12.
12. Sherif Rashad, Mehmed Kantardzic, Anup Kumar.: Technical Documentation of PCAC-RR Technique. Technical Report, CECS Department, University of Louisville, (2004) 1-36.

Mining of an Alarm Log to Improve the Discovery of Frequent Patterns

Françoise Fessant, Fabrice Clérot, and Christophe Dousson

France Télécom R&D, 2 avenue P. Marzin, 22307 Lannion, France
{francoise.fessant, fabrice.clerot, christophe.dousson}
@francetelecom.com
http://www.rd.francetelecom.com

Abstract. In this paper we propose a method to pre-process a telecommunication alarm log with the aim of discovering more accurately frequent patterns. In a first step, the alarm types which present the same temporal behavior are clustered with a self organizing map. Then, the log areas which are rich in alarms of the clusters are searched. The sublogs are built based on the selected areas. We will show the efficiency of our preprocessing method through experiments on an actual alarm log from an ATM network.

1 Introduction

Telecommunications networks are growing in size and complexity, which means that a constantly increasing volume of notifications must be handled by the management system. Most of this information is produced spontaneously by equipment (e.g. status change and dysfunction detection) and this message flow must be preprocessed to make an effective management possible.

Filters based on a per-notification basis fail to perform an adequate information pre-processing required by human operators or by management application softwares which are not able to process such amount of events. A pre-processing stage must "thin" this information stream by suppressing redundant notifications and/or by aggregating relevant ones. Numerical time constraints must also be taken into account since time information is *apropos* for the telecommunications alarm propagation. Many works deal with different approaches and propose more or less complex intelligent filtering: one can use some efficient rule-based languages [1], and/or object-based techniques [2]. More specific techniques are devoted to capture time constraints between alarms [3], [4]. In any case, the problem of expertise acquisition remains the same: how to feed the filtering system? Which aggregation rules are relevant?

A way to filter the information flow is to exploit the logs collected from telecommunications equipment. We have developed a tool called FACE (Frequency Analyzer for Chronicle Extraction) that performs a frequency-based analysis in order to extract "frequent patterns" from the logs. We only suppose that all the events are time-stamped. The searched patterns are sets of event patterns with time constraints between them (these sets are called "chronicle models") and the frequency criterion is defined as an user-defined minimal frequency threshold [5].

P. Perner (Ed.): ICDM 2004, LNAI 3275, pp. 144–152, 2004.

Identifying the most frequent chronicle models is relevant to reduce the number of alarms displayed to the operator: if a chronicle corresponds to a dysfunction, the corresponding set of alarms is aggregated before being displayed to the human operator; if not, the corresponding set of alarms is filtered. At the moment, we do not use any extra knowledge about the domain; the rule qualification (aggregation or filtering) is performed by an expert at the end of the discovering process.

Real experiments on telecommunications data show that most of the discovered chronicles are relevant and some of them have a real benefit for the experts. However, the chronicle process implemented in FACE, based on the exhaustive exploration of the chronicle instances in the alarm log, is very memory-space consuming and the main factor of this explosion is the size of the processed event logs.

To deal with that problem in the current implementation of FACE, the operational experts manually select some alarms types and/or some time periods in the alarms logs in order to extract a more manageable sublog to be processed by the tool. The purpose of this communication is to describe and to evaluate a pre-processing method to automatically extract relevant sublogs from an initial alarm log to simplify the use of the software and alleviate the memory saturation effect.

The pre-processing stage we propose can be decomposed in two main steps. Firstly we group together the alarm types which exhibit the same temporal behavior. Then we search for each group the areas of the log that are *rich* in alarms of the observed group. The sublogs are deduced from the alarms in these areas. The following sections describe our data pre-processing and the experimental results obtained on an actual alarm log from an ATM network.

2 Data Description and Representation

Previous experiments with FACE on alarm logs of various origins have revealed that the instances of chronicles tend to be distributed in a clustered way along time. This can be explained by the fact that most chronicles are indicative of faulty network states, which do not happen randomly in time but only happen for short periods of time before being corrected.

The data representation introduced below takes this into account, gives a great importance to the temporal behavior of the alarms and aims at grouping in sublogs alarms with similar temporal behaviors.

In the first data preparation phase the entire log is split in slices of fixed duration. Each slice, called *period,* can contain a variable number of alarms or can also be empty. The periods can be seen as unit elements of the log; they form a partition of it. The periods constitute the base on which the alarms will be described and from which the sublogs will be built.

The alarm types are then represented through their temporal evolution along the periods. The cumulative profile of an alarm type is computed by adding up its occurrences in successive periods and it is normalized in order to make it independent of the total number of occurrences. Such a description takes into account the time aspect present in alarm generation.

Our experiments are achieved with ATM (Asynchronous Transfer Mode) network data. We have about one-month alarms log with 46600 alarms dispatched through 12160 different types. An alarm type is characterized by an alarm message (a string) and a date and time of occurrence; 75% of the alarm types weight less than 3 occurrences. We fixed the duration of a period to 15 minutes and we obtained 2317 periods which contain about 16 alarms on the average. The figure 1 shows the occurrences of one alarm type of the log on all the periods and the figure 2 shows the corresponding normalized cumulative profile.

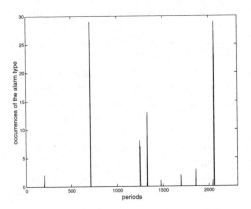

Fig. 1. Occurrence of an alarm type on all the log periods

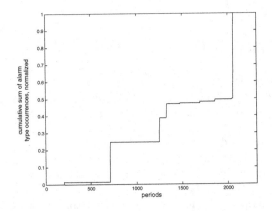

Fig. 2. Normalized cumulative profile of the alarm type of Figure 1 on all the log periods

The purpose of the next step of the method is to group together the alarm types which have the same temporal behavior.

3   Clustering of the Cumulative Profiles with a Self-Organizing Map

The alarms types are grouped together with a Self Organizing Map (SOM). A SOM is a useful tool for exploratory data analysis made up of a set of nodes organized into a

2-dimensional grid (the *map*). Each node has fixed coordinates in the map and adaptive coordinates (the *weights*) in the input space. The input space is relative to the variables setting up the observations. The self-organizing process slightly moves the nodes coordinates in the data definition space -i.e. adjusts weights according to the data distribution. This weight adjustment is performed while taking into account the neighboring relation between nodes in the map. The SOM has the well-known ability that the projection on the map preserves the proximities: close observations in the original multidimensional input space are associated with close nodes in the map. For a complete description of the SOM properties and some applications, see [6] and [7].

After learning has been completed, the map is segmented into clusters, each cluster being formed of nodes with similar behavior, with a hierarchical agglomerative clustering algorithm. This segmentation simplifies the quantitative analysis of the map [8].

We consider only the frequent alarm types -i.e. alarm types making at least 3 occurrences through the log: a chronicle being by definition characterized by instances with several occurrences in the log, infrequent alarm types cannot take part in the chronicle creation. We end up with a database of 3042 cumulative profiles (the observations) described on the space of the 2317 periods. We experiment with a 9x9 square map with hexagonal neighborhoods (experiments on SOM have been done with the SOM Toolbox package for Matlab [9]).

The clustering of the map has revealed 10 different groups of observations with similar behavior. Figure 3 details the characteristic behavior of the clusters. We plot the mean cumulative profile for each of the 10 clusters; each of the clusters being identified by a number. The mean cumulative profile of a cluster is computed by the mean of all the observations that have been classified by the nodes of the map belonging to the cluster.

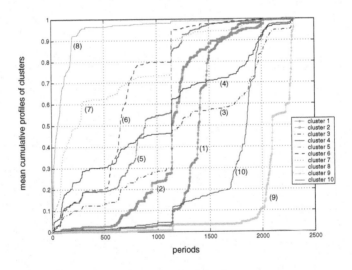

Fig. 3. Mean cumulative profiles of the clusters

The sharper the rise of a cumulative profile, the stronger the accumulation of the alarms. The visual inspection of the figure shows that the clusters indeed correspond to very different accumulation behaviors: some clusters correspond to accumulations on rather limited sets of periods (cluster 8, accumulating at the very beginning of the log, cluster 9 accumulating at the very end or cluster 1 accumulating in the middle, for instance); other clusters show a more even distribution in time (clusters 3 and 4, for instance).

At this stage we end up with a limited number of groups that characterize and summarize the whole alarm types: all the alarms types classified in a cluster accumulate in the same way through the log.

4 Sublogs Construction

Some periods of the log are more significant than others for a given cluster of alarm types. We define the importance of a period for a cluster by the number of alarms of the cluster included in the period, in proportion of all the alarms this period contains (with this definition, we tend to favor some periods producing few alarms but essentially alarms of the cluster).

We proceed as follows to select the most interesting periods for a cluster: we first order the periods according to their importance for the studied cluster; the periods which have the highest importance values are ranked first. The subset of periods corresponding to the cluster is simply built by adding the periods in order of decreasing importance until a given proportion of the alarms of the cluster are contained in the sublog.

The figure 4 illustrates the result of the period selection process for cluster 1. We arbitrarily fixed the stopping criterion to 90% (i.e. we retain the periods until the sublog

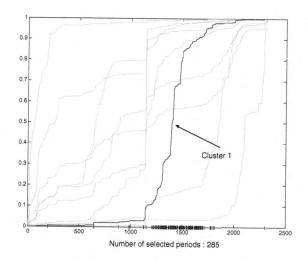

Fig. 4. Selected periods for an alarm type cluster

contains 90% of the alarms of the cluster). For the cluster given here as an example in the figure, we select 285 periods of the log and this corresponds to 7% of the whole alarms. A cross on the x-axis marks the selected periods. These selected periods clearly coincide with the accumulation areas of the cluster (essentially in the middle of the log for the cluster).

The figure 5 plots the location of the selected periods in the log for each cluster. The comparison with figure 3 shows that the selected periods for a given cluster correspond to the areas of alarm accumulation for this cluster.

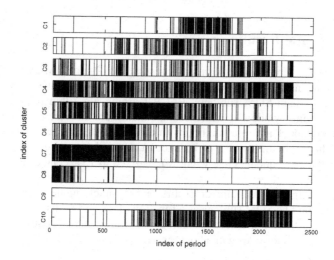

Fig. 5. Time location of the selected periods for the cluster

The number of periods which have to be taken into account to reach 90% of the alarms of a cluster vary a lot from a cluster to another, but whatever the observed cluster, the amount of selected periods never goes beyond 35% of the whole alarms.

Table 1. Number of periods and alarms in each sublog

Sublog index	Number of periods	Number of alarms
1	285	3079
2	287	9996
3	334	14204
4	783	16283
5	741	16083
6	361	11879
7	608	14725
8	136	4476
9	163	7043
10	658	10318
Total	4356	108086

At this step of the process, we have isolated as many subsets of periods as alarm type clusters. The sublog attached to a cluster of alarms is simply obtained by re-ordering in time the alarms of the corresponding subset. Note that we keep all the alarms belonging to the periods, including those of infrequent alarm types.

The Table 1 gives the number of periods in each subset and the corresponding number of alarms (recall that the entire log consists of 2317 periods and 46600 alarms).

Let us remark that our selection method considers each cluster independently of the others and, therefore, one period can be assigned to several subsets. The effect is that the sum of alarms over the all sublogs is about 2.5 the number of alarms of the initial log.

5   Experimental Results

In this section we report the experimental results we obtained when running FACE algorithm on the initial log and on the sublogs designed as previously explained (from now on we call them SOM sublogs). FACE learning algorithm requires two input parameters: the time window t_w which sets the maximum distance between the events of a chronicle model and the minimum threshold of the chronicle instances n_{qmin} which gives the minimum number of instances a chronicle model must have in the log to be considered as frequent. Time window t_w is fixed to 15 seconds and we choose to vary the value of n_{qmin}.

We report in figure 6 the number of different chronicle models discovered on the entire log and on the SOM sublogs as a function of n_{qmin}. We also plot this number for normal sublogs. To build normal sublogs we simply manually split the whole log into several successive slices with about the same number of alarms in each slice. We

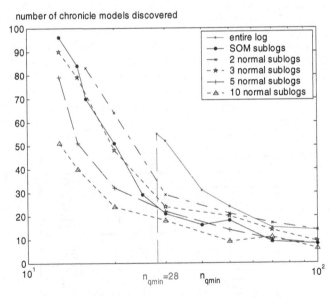

Fig. 6. Number of different chronicle models discovered

experiment with four different sets of sublogs (the log is successively split in 2, 3, 5 and 10 sublogs, we proceed as operational experts usually do to extract more manageable sublogs from an alarm log).

All experiments reported below have been run on the same computer (a Pentium 4 with 1.7 GHz of CPU and 1 Go of RAM) with no other application running than FACE.

We can observe that the entire log is impossible to process for n_{qmin} below 28; the reason is a lack of memory-space of the computer. The treatment remains possible on sublogs for much smaller values of n_{qmin} (the limit is reached for $n_{qmin}=16$ for the set of 2 sublogs and $n_{qmin}=13$ for the other sets of sublogs, and it is never possible to go below this value).

We are able to discover more chronicles with the sublogs than with the entire log (except for the set of 10 normal sublogs): for a given n_{qmin}, we discover more chronicles with the entire log than with the sublogs, but the exploration can be carried on sublogs for much lower n_{qmin}. Moreover, a detailed analysis of the discovered chronicles shows that we find from the sublogs all the chronicles we have found from the entire log and also many new chronicles: we do not loose any chronicle with SOM sublogs.

We now compare the number of discovered chronicle models for low values of n_{qmin}, with normal sublogs and with SOM sublogs. We can see that the highest number of chronicles discovered with normal sublogs is obtained for the set of 3 sublogs. SOM sublogs show a better performance. We found more chronicles with SOM sublogs. Therefore, the improvement obtained with the SOM sublogs cannot be attributed to the sequential processing of many smaller logs instead of the entire log and to the ability to reach low frequencies. This improvement has to be attributed to the data processing method adopted to build relevant sublogs.

Let us remark that the manual search of the good number of sublogs that will lead to the discovery of the maximum number of chronicles is a very time consuming process. The processing method we propose automatically extracts the relevant sublogs.

These experimental results validate our data processing method which takes into account the fact that chronicle instances do not happen randomly in time but in a rather clustered way; using this pre-processing we recover all the chronicle models discovered without pre-processing and we can analyze the log in a more accurate way and discover new chronicles. We also have observed that the total processing time of the SOM sublogs remains of the same order of magnitude as for the entire log.

6   Conclusion

The system FACE is very helpful for experts to discover monitoring knowledge from alarm logs. However, the chronicle discovery process implemented in FACE (based on the exploration of all the possibilities of chronicle instances) has the limitation to be very memory-space consuming; the main factor of this explosion being the size of the alarm log.

In this paper we have proposed a method to automatically extract relevant sublogs from an alarm log to simplify the use of the software and alleviate this memory saturation effect.

The method is decomposed in several steps. The first step consists in the description of the alarm types in a suitable representation that takes into account the temporal evolution of the alarm types through the log. Then the alarm types which have the same temporal behavior are grouped together with a self-organizing map. The result of the clustering is a description of the whole alarm types in few groups. Finally, the areas of the log that are the more relevant for the clusters of alarm types are isolated and the alarms in these areas are grouped in sublogs. The sublogs can be processed with FACE.

We presented experiments on an actual ATM log. The proposed data processing method turns out to be very effective: with the sublogs we have found the same chronicles that we were able to find while processing the whole log. Moreover we can carry the search on sublogs to a point that is impossible to reach with the entire log and obtain many new chronicles. We also have observed that the total duration process of the sublogs always remain moderate. Another interesting point is that the user can get intermediate results after the processing of each sublog and future research will consider the adaptation of the learning parameters of the tool independently for each sublog in order to discover the maximum number of chronicles.

References

1. Möller, M., Tretter, S., Fink, B.: Intelligent filtering in network-management systems. Proceedings of the 4th International Symposium on Integrated Network Management (1995) 304-315
2. Nygate, Y.A.: Event correlation using rule and object base techniques. Proceedings of the 4th International Symposium on Integrated Network Management (1995) 279-289
3. Dousson, C.: Extending and Unifying Chronicle Representation with Event Counters. Proceedings of the 15th ECAI (2002) 257-261
4. Jakobson, G., Weissman, M.: Real-time telecommunication network management: extending event correlation with temporal constraints. Proceedings of the 4th International Symposium on Integrated Network Management (1995) 290-301
5. Dousson, C., Vu Duong, T.: Discovering chronicles with numerical time constraints from alarm logs for monitoring dynamic systems. Proceedings of the 16th IJCAI (1999) 620-626
6. T. Kohonen. Self-Organizing Maps. 3rd edn. Springer-Verlag, Berlin Heidelberg New York (2001)
7. E. Oja. S. Kaski. Kohonen maps. Elsevier (1999)
8. Vesanto, J., Alhoniemi, E.: Clustering of the Self-Organizing Map. IEEE Transactions on Neural Networks. 11 (3) (2000) 586-600
9. Vesanto, J., Himberg, J., Alhoniemi, E., Parhankangas, J.: SOM Toolbox for Matlab, Report A57 Helsinki University of Technology, Neural Networks Research Centre, Espoo, Finland, (2000)

Feature Selection and Classification Model Construction on Type 2 Diabetic Patient's Data

Yue Huang[1], Paul McCullagh[1], Norman Black[1], and Roy Harper[2]

[1] School of Computing and Mathematics, Faculty of Engineering, University of Ulster,
Jordanstown, BT37 0QB Northern Ireland, UK
yhuang@infj.ulst.ac.uk, {PJ.McCullagh, ND.Black}@ulst.ac.uk
[2] The Ulster Hospital, Dundonald, Belfast, BT16 0RH, Northern Ireland, UK

Abstract. Diabetes is a disorder of the metabolism where the amount of glucose in the blood is too high because the body cannot produce or properly use insulin. In order to achieve more effective diabetes clinic management, data mining techniques have been applied to a patient database. In an attempt to improve the efficiency of data mining algorithms, a feature selection technique ReliefF is used with the data, which can rank the important attributes affecting Type 2 diabetes control. After selecting suitable attributes, classification techniques are applied to the data to predict how well the patients are controlling their condition. Preliminary results have been confirmed by the clinician and this provides optimism that data mining can be used to generate prediction models.

1 Introduction

Diabetes is a major global health problem, affecting around 194 million people worldwide, and that number is expected to increase to 300 million by 2025. In attempt to investigate a patient's prognosis, data mining techniques have been applied to a 'working' Type 2 diabetic database to generate information that can be verified by the clinician and possibly provide new knowledge. The data source is a secondary care database system [1]. Specifically, this research concentrates on:

1. Identifying significant factors influencing diabetes control;
2. Predicting individuals in the population with poor diabetes control status based on physiological and examination factors.

1.1 Data Mining

The role of data mining is to extract interesting (non-trivial, implicit, previously unknown and potentially useful) patterns or knowledge from large amounts of data. It comprises a variety of techniques used to identify nuggets of information or decision-making knowledge in data, and extracting these in such a way that they can be put to use in areas such as decision support, prediction and estimation. The data is often voluminous but, as it stands, is of low value as no direct use can be made of it; it is the

P. Perner (Ed.): ICDM 2004, LNAI 3275, pp. 153–162, 2004.

hidden information in the data that is useful. Data mining includes pre-processing, applying a data-mining algorithm, and post-processing the results.

1.2   Diabetes and HbA1c

According to a World Health Organisation, on a global scale, there are around 194 million people with diabetes in the adult population, 50% of which are undiagnosed [2]. Diabetes occurs when the body cannot produce enough insulin or the insulin produced is ineffective. There are two main types of diabetes: Type 1 and Type 2. The most common form is Type 2 diabetes, previously called non-insulin-dependent diabetes mellitus (NIDDM). Since its morbidity term can be up to 30 years depending on disease control, it greatly affects patient's quality of life and the prevention of its complications is very important. It has been shown that better blood glucose control will reduce the risk of complications significantly [3-6].

HbA1c is a laboratory test, which reveals average blood glucose over the previous 12 weeks. This test is recommended by the American Diabetes Association [7] to monitor long term glucose control. HbA1c is usually recorded every 3 months, but may be performed more often, if needed. Specifically, it measures the number of glucose molecules attached to haemoglobin, a substance in red blood cells. According to the investigation of UK Prospective Diabetes Study group (UKPDS), every 1% HbA1c reduction means 35% less complication risk, both for the micro- and macrovascular complications. Microvascular complications increase dramatically when the HbA1c measurement is over 10% [8].

1.3   Data Mining in Diabetes

Due to the greatly increased amount of data gathered in medical databases traditional manual analysis has become inadequate, and methods for efficient computer-based analysis are indispensable. To address this problem, knowledge discovery in databases (KDD) methods are being developed to identify patterns within the data that can be exploited. Data mining methods have been applied to a variety of medical domains in order to improve medical decision making; diagnostic and prognostic problems in oncology, liver pathology, neuropsychology, and gynaecology. Improved medical diagnosis and prognosis may be achieved through automatic analysis of patient data stored in medical records, i.e., by learning from past experiences [9].

Data analysis of diabetes has previously been reported. Breault et al.[10] examined a diabetic data warehouse using the Classification and Regression Tree (CART) system to deduce a series of association rules among different attributes. They emphasise that bad glycaemia control is primarily associated with a younger age, rather than the related complications or whether patients have related diseases. Their work shows that data mining can discover novel associations that are useful to clinicians and administrators. Although the classification accuracy achieved by CART was just 59.5%, the authors found it useful to derive rule sets.

Miyaki et al. [11] also adopted the CART algorithm to identify the factors that influence diabetic vascular complications. They used AnswerTree [12] to build the classification model, concluding that CART had the potential to rank predictors in order of importance and to assist in the prevention of diabetic vascular complications.

▪ Curt et al. [13] investigated the relationship between blood glucose and HbA1c among patients with Type 1 diabetes using linear regression analysis. Knowing this relationship can help patients with diabetes and their healthcare providers set day-to-day targets for blood glucose to achieve specific HbA1c goals. However, the reliability of this observation needs additional support from other researchers.

Richards et al. [14] describe the analysis of a database of diabetic patients' clinical records and death certificates. Simulated annealing was used for rule induction to find associations between observations made from patients at their first visit to the hospital and early mortality. Pre-processing methodology to account for missing clinical data was also described in this paper.

Rough Sets is another feature selection technique applied in the diabetes domain by Stepaniuk et al. [15]. Three methods (reduct stability, significance, and application of wrappers) were applied to choose the attributes which contribute most to the occurrence of Type 1 diabetes. The authors identified the most important condition attributes and discovered decision rules characterising the dependency between values of condition and decision attributes.

2 Data Preparation

It is estimated that 49,000 people in Northern Ireland (NI) have been diagnosed with diabetes and another 25,000 have the condition but don't know it. According to the investigation of National Health Service (NHS) in UK [16]:

- £1 in every £7 spent by the NHS in NI goes towards diabetes care;
- People with Type 2 diabetes have had the condition for between nine and 12 year before they are diagnosed;
- At least one third to as many as one half of the people diagnosed with diabetes   will have diabetes-related complications when initially diagnosed;
- Approximately three in every 100 people will develop diabetes.

These statistics are representation of most developed societies such as UKPDS.

2.1 Data Collection

The Ulster Community and Hospital Trust has collected diabetic patients' information from the year 2000 to the present in NI. The data was extracted from Diamond, which is a commercial diabetes clinical information system. The existing database contains 2,017 Type 2 diabetic patients' clinical information; 1,124 males and 893 females. The patients' age ranged from 20 to 96, with only 47 patients younger than 40. The mean value of the patients' age is 66. Therefore, the work concentrates on the older group. This is consistent with the fact that diabetes mainly affects the older age groups (>60) within the population.

A set of 425 features including patient characteristics, treatment, complication care, physical and laboratory findings were present in the database.

2.2 Pre-processing

As a 'real world' database, it is inevitable that there will be incomplete, noisy and inconsistent values. Therefore, pre-processing is a very important stage. The pre-processing work in this research consists of data integration, transformation and reduction.

Data integration combines data from multiple sources into a coherent database. This data is separated into six different databases, so the first step is to integrate meta-data from different sources, and then merge corresponding tables into one target table.

The main work in data transformation is discretization, which is to allow the application of data mining methods for discrete attribute values. In the study, the patients were divided into two groups: *better control* and *worse control*, based on their HbA1c test value. The method is to compare the patient's HbA1c test value and their target HbA1c value; if the Lab test value is higher than the target, the patient is partitioned to the worse control group; and vice versa. The target HbA1c value is generally 7, but varies according to individual condition. After discretization, the resulting data set had 30,330 records (34.33%: *Better than target*, 65.67%: *Worse than target*) of 2,017 patients' information.

The process of data reduction represents the selection of parameters that may influence blood glucose control. Preliminary data set inspection showed that for 37% of all attributes, data was missing for at least 50% of patients. These attributes were considered too sparsely collected and were not included in further analysis. Of the remaining parameters, forty-seven were suggested by the background knowledge of diabetic experts and international diabetes guideline [3]. The resulting data set had an average 10.3% of missing values. Among the initial 47 features, there are 6 attributes with 30-40% missing data, 3 with 20-30%, 3 with 10-20% and 11 with 1-10%.

3 Feature Selection

In an attempt to improve the efficiency of data mining algorithms, feature selection techniques are used with the data. Feature selection is the process of identifying and removing as much of the irrelevant and redundant information as possible. In the database, not all attributes available are actually useful. Hundreds of attributes are routinely collected but typically only a small number are used. Being a real world problem, a large number of noisy, irrelevant and redundant features are in the data. Clearly irrelevant variables have been removed with the help of the diabetic expert. The key factors influencing Type 2 diabetes control are expected to be detected by the feature selection. In the experiment, ReliefF [17] has been used for feature selection to investigate those important factors in the Type 2 diabetes data set.

3.1 ReliefF

Relief estimates attributes according to how well their values distinguish among instances based on Euclidian distance. For a given instance, Relief searches for its two nearest neighbours: one from the same class (called *nearest hit*) and the other from different class (called *nearest miss*). Relief's estimate $W[A]$ of attribute A is an approximation of the following difference of probabilities:

$$W[A]=P(\text{different value of } A \mid \text{nearest instance from different class})-P(\text{different} \quad (1)$$
$$\text{value of } A \mid \text{nearest from same class})$$

The rationale is that a good attribute should differentiate between instances from different classes and should have the same value for instances of the same class.

ReliefF extended Relief, solved the multi-class data sets problem, and can deal with noisy and incomplete data. ReliefF smoothes the influence of noise in the data by averaging the contribution of k nearest neighbours from the same and opposite class of each sampled instance, instead of the single nearest neighbour. Multi-class data sets are handled by finding nearest neighbours from each class, which is different from the current sampled instance, and weighting their contributions by the prior probability of each class [18].

Compared to other commonly used feature selection approaches such as Information Gain [17], ReliefF works well when given many highly relevant features mixed with largely irrelevant ones. However, it is sensitive to the definition of relevance that is used in its implementation, and is computationally expensive when handling a large data set.

3.2 Reduction of Input Parameters

Features were ranked using ReliefF, which measures the usefulness of a feature by observing the relation between its value and the patient's outcome. Intuitively, if there is a group of patients with similar attribute values, the observed feature is 'valuable' as a predictor if it has different values on pairs of patients with different outcomes, but the same value on pairs with the same outcome. Features with negative ReliefF estimate may be considered to be irrelevant. Features with the highest score are presumed to be the most sensitive and contributing most to the outcome prediction [19].

There are many possible measures for evaluating feature selection algorithms [20]. We use the criterion *Classification Accuracy* to evaluate the performance of ReliefF. In general, a classifier is expected to preserve the same accuracy with the reduced set of features as with all the available features or even to improve it due to the elimination of noisy and irrelevant features that may mislead the learning process.

Because it is difficult to estimate the correct number of predictors in feature mining applications [21], different sizes of attribute subsets were selected for each of three algorithms (*Naïve Bayes*, *IB1* and Decision Tree *C4.5* [22]) to find which set gave the best performance.

4 Prediction Model Construction

Classification is an active research topic in decision support. Classification in data mining aims to predict categorical class labels. It constructs a model based on the training set and the values in a classifying attribute and uses it in classifying new data [11].

The main work of this study is to distinguish bad blood glucose control patients from good blood glucose control patients based on physiological and examination factors. The intention is to improve the quality of treatment by automating the handling of routine situations, particularly blood glucose control, and ensuring a better quality of life by providing support from expert.

Algorithms in the WEKA [22] software package (*C4.5*, *IB1* and *Naïve Bayes*) were applied to analyse the data. Two sampling strategies were used strategy to evaluate the effect of each and determine the suitable size of attributes for model construction. In the split-sample method, two thirds of the dataset were selected randomly to be learned by the prediction models (training set: n=20,220). The remaining third was used to validate the models (testing set: n=10,110). Ten-fold cross-validation is another sampling method. It divides the data into 10 subsets of (approximately) equal size, and then train the data k times, each time leaving out one of the subsets from training, using it as the testing data set [23].

5 Results and Discussion

The attributes used for predicting the patient's diabetes control have been ranked by ReliefF. Each classifier presented above was applied to the data set with different numbers of variables. The top five predictors are *Age*, *Diagnosis Duration*, *Insulin Treatment*, *Smoking* and *Family History*, which have been additionally verified and confirmed by the diabetic expert.

The performance of all the models is listed in Table 1. Classification accuracy measures the proportion of correctly classified test examples, therefore, estimating the probability of the correct classification. From the table, we can find that before or after feature selection, *C4.5* always had the best performance for classification. This is in line with the acceptable clinical performance (over 75%) of prediction levels in other areas of medicine [24]. The results of *IB1* and *Naïve Bayes* were lower than *C4.5* before feature selection. There was no significant difference between two sampling strategies when applied to the classifiers for prediction.

Table 1. Classification accuracy (%) for Different Sizes Feature Subsets (10-CV/Training and Testing)

Attribute Number	Naïve Bayes	IB1	C4.5	Average
5	69.36/69.92	69.14/70.23	76.36/76.92	71.62/72.36
8	74.60/73.32	70.49/69.91	76.12/77.03	73.74/73.42
10	72.47/72.21	71.54/72.36	77.21/77.56	73.74/74.04
15	72.92/70.79	70.37/71.93	78.73/79.49	74.01/74.07
20	71.48/70.65	69.30/68.67	76.42/77.64	72.40/72.32
25	69.24/68.78	67.88/69.09	77.52/77.63	71.55/71.83
30	70.53/71.64	67.78/69.66	77.43/76.49	71.91/72.60
47	62.35/62.68	63.44/61.93	75.38/75.06	67.06/66.56
Average	70.37/70.00	68.74/69.22	76.90/77.23	----------------

Table 1 also presents the influence of different feature subsets to each classifier. On average, when the top 15 variables were selected for classification, the best prediction result can be achieved.

Fig 1 and 2 illustrate the influence of different numbers of features to classification accuracy. Generally, *C4.5* achieves the best performance for prediction, *Naïve Bayes* is the next, and *IB1* is last. The broken line shape of *IB1* is the most similar to the average. The trend of *C4.5* is comparably more stable and the position of the line is also higher than *Naïve Bayes* and *IB1*. For both sampling strategies, when the predictor number is 10, *IB1* can get the best result; *Naïve Bayes* can obtain the highest accuracy with 8 predictors; and *C4.5* carrys out best while 15 features are selected for analysis.

Compared with *IB1* and *Naïve Bayes*, the study indicates that feature mining did not affect the results of the decision tree *C4.5* significantly. The main reason is that decision tree schemes have inherent feature selection mechanism. During the procedure to construct a tree, they select the key predictor gradually. This is consistent with the research of Perner [21], which concluded that feature subset selection should improve the accuracy of the decision tree approach (but not significantly). *IB1* and *Naïve Bayes* did benefit from the reduction of the input parameters. Because *IB1* and *Naïve Bayes* cannot filter out the irrelevant or correlated information in the database, the representation and quality of data will affect their performance.

It is interesting that when all the available attributes are involved in the analysis, worse results are generated. This experiment shows that not all attributes are actually relevant in the database for diabetic control prediction. The performance of most practical classifiers (*C4.5*, *IB1* and *Naïve Bayes* in this study) improves when correlated and irrelevant features are removed. According to the decision tree constructed by *C4.5*, the variable "*Insulin Treatment*" was the best predictor for classifying patients' disease control. In the patients, "*Age*" was the second best predictor for classification. The attributes "*Family History*" and "*Diagnosis Duration*" are also key features for distinguishing the worse blood glucose control patients. The setting of the minimum instance number determines the size of the final tree. The key variables gained by the decision trees *C4.5* tallied with the parameters selected by the feature selection approach ReliefF.

It is well known from clinical studies that Type 2 diabetes is a progressive condition with overall blood sugar control deteriorating with time (UKPDS). Older patients and those who have been diagnosed with Type 2 diabetes for longer generally have the worst overall blood sugar control. It is therefore reassuring from the clinical standpoint (and affirms the validity of the data mining techniques used) that "*Age*" and "*Diagnosis Duration*" were the features selected as the principle factors in determining whether overall blood sugar control was good or bad.

Improving blood glucose control is a key aim in treating individuals with diabetes. Sustained good blood sugar control reduces the risk of long-term diabetes complications. Improved blood sugar control can be achieved with diet and regular physical activity, oral medications, insulin injections or by a combination of these approaches. In Type 2 diabetes, as time proceeds, patients generally move in a stepwise fashion through dietary treatment, then oral therapies and eventually end up needing insulin therapy to control their blood sugars. Despite all of these treatments blood sugar control continues to deteriorate with time – so it is likely that those on "*Insulin Treatment*" would have the worst overall blood sugar control. "*Insulin Treatment*" was selected as the best predictor for classifying blood sugar control. This again makes clinical sense.

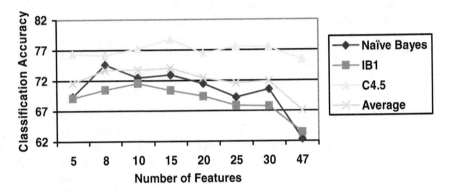

Fig. 1. Classification Accuracy of Different Data Mining Algorithms based on 10-CV

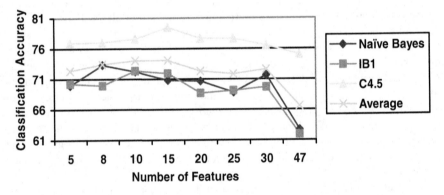

Fig. 2. Classification Accuracy of Different Data Mining Algorithms based on Testing Data

Overall there was high concordance between the features selected using data mining techniques and the factors anticipated as being important by the diabetes expert. The models' high best predictive performance and the clinical relevance of the features selected suggest that decision support and prediction will be achievable with further refinements.

6   Conclusion and Future Work

The paper reports on a study, which constructed outcome prediction models from a database of 2,017 Type 2 diabetic patients. The following conclusions can be drawn:

- Irrelevant features will reduce the performance (including efficiency and classification accuracy) of the practical classifiers under study;
- Feature selection enhances the performance of classification algorithms;
- "*Age*" is the most important attribute for both diabetic control;
- Younger patients (<60.37 years), with low LabRBG values (<10.75), diet treatment and short diagnosis duration (<4.54 years) tend to control disease better than other patient groups.

In the study, we applied the feature selection approach ReliefF and comparatively evaluated the performance of three machine learning methods *Naïve Bayes*, *IB1* and *C4.5* on the data set. *C4.5* provieded the best classification accuracy before and after feature selection because of its inherent feature selection mechanism.   The performance of *IB1* and *Naïve Bayes* were significantly improved after the application of ReliefF. This may be due to the elimination of noisy and irrelevant features that may mislead the learning process. The models provided a best predictive performance of 77%, which could assist decision making in individuals. The results are in accrodance with diabetes guidelines and the clinician's opinion. Future work will concentrate on enhancing the performance of ReliefF, as efficent and accurate feature selection is a prerequisite for generating predicitve models from large medical data sets. This will advance research into diabetes control.

References

1. Diamond, HICOM Technology, (2002) *http://www.hicom.co.uk/news.asp?NewsID=8*
2. IDF—International Diabetes Federation, Diabetes Atlas (Second Edition), (2003)
3. American Association, Medical Guidelines for the Management of Diabetes Mellitus. Endocrine Practice. Vol.8 (Suppl.1) (2002) 40-82.
4. Diabetes Control and Complications Trial Research Group: The effect of intensive treat ment of diabetes on the development and progression of long-term complications in insulin-dependent diabetes mellitus. N Engl J Med.329 (1993) 977-986.
5. UKPDS. Intensive blood-glucose control with sulphonylureas or insulin compared with conventional treatment and risk of complications in patients with type 2 diabetes. Lancet. 352 (1998) 837-853.
6. UKPDS. Effect of intensive blood-glucose control with metformin on complications in overweight patients with type 2 diabetes. Lancet. 352 (1998) 854-865.
7. American Diabetes Association, About us—American Diabetes Association, (2004), *http://www.diabetes.org/aboutus.jsp?WTLPromo=HEADER_aboutus&vms=142585600057*
8. Strattpm IM, Adler AI, Neil HAW., Association of Glycaemia with Macrovascular and Microvascular complications of Type 2 Diabetes., Br Med J. (2000); 321: pp.405-412.
9. Lavrac N. Selected Techniques for Data Mining in Medicine, AI Med. (2002 May), 16(1), 3-23
10. 10.Breault J, Goodall C, Fos P. Data mining a diabetic data warehouse, Artif Intell Med. (2002) Sep;26(1-2):37.
11. Miyaki K, Takei I, Watanabe K, Nakashima H, Watanabe K, Omae K.Novel statistical classification model of Type 2 diabetes mellitus patients for trailor-made prevention using data mining algorithm, J Epidemiol (2002 May);12(3):243-8

12. SPSS Inc, Target the right people more effectively— AnswerTree, *http://www.aspiresoftwareintl.com/html/spss_answer_tree.html*

13. Rohlfing C.L., Wiedmeyer H.M, Little R.R, Jack D.E., Tennill A., Goldstein D.E., Defining the Relationship between Plasma Glucose and HbA1c, Analysis of glucose profiles and HbA1c in the Diabetes Control and Complications Trial. Diabetes Care 25: (2002). 275-278

14. Richards G, Rayward-Smith VJ, Sonksen PH, Carey S, Weng C. Mining for indicators of early mortality in a database of clinical records. Artif Intell Med. (2001) Jun; 22(3):215-31.

15. Stepaniuk J, Rough set based data mining in diabetes mellitus data table. Proceedings of the Sixth European Congress on Intelligent Techniques and Soft Computing (EUFIT'98)2, Aachen, Germany, September 7-10, (1998), 980-984

16. Diabetes UK, Diabetes in Northern Ireland, (2004 Mar), *http://www.diabetes.org.uk/n.ireland/nireland.htm*

17. Kononenko I., Estimating attributes: Analysis and extensions of Relief, In Proceeding of the Seventh European Conference on Machine Learning, Springer-Verlag, (1994) 171-182

18. Hall M.A., Holmes G., Benchmarking Attribute Selection Techniques for Discrete Class Data Mining, IEEE Transactions on Knowledge and Data Engineering, IEEE, Vol. 15, No. 3, 2003, pp. 1437-1447

19. Demsar J., Zupan B., Aoki N., Wall M.J., Granchi T.H., Beck J.R., Feature Mining and Predictive Model Construction from Severe Trauma Patient's Data, Int J Med Inf, Elsevier Science, 63, (2001). 41-50.

20. Molina L., Belanche L., Nebot A., Feature Selection Algorithms: A Survey and Experimental Evaluation, Proceeding of IEEE International Conference on Data Mining, IEEE, 2002, pp. 306-313

21. Perner, P. Improving the Accuracy of Decision Tree Induction by Feature Pre-Selection, Applied Artificial Intelligence, Vol. 15, No. 8, (2001) 747-760

22. Witten I. H., Frank E., Data Mining: Practical Machine Learning Tools and Techniques with Java Implementations, Morgan Kaufmann, (1999)

23. 23.Turney P. Theoretical Analysis of Cross-Validation Error and Voting in Instance-Based Learning, J Experimental and Theoretical Artificial Intelligence, 6, (1994) 361-391

24. Colombet I, Ruelland A, Chatellier G, et al., Models to predict cardiovascular risk: comparison of CART, Multilayer perceptron and logistic regression, Proc AMIA Symp, (2000) 156-160

Knowledge Based Phylogenetic Classification Mining

Isabelle Bichindaritz [1], Stephen Potter[2], and Société Française de Systématique[3]

[1] University of Washington, 1900 Commerce Street, Tacoma, WA 98402, USA
ibichind@u.washington.edu
[2] University of Aberdeen, Aberdeen AB24 3UE, Scotland, UK
now at the University of Edinburgh, Edinburgh EH8 9LE, Scotland, UK
stephenp@inf.ed.ac.uk
[3] Museum National d'Histoire Naturelle, 61, rue Buffon, 75005 Paris, France

Abstract. Phylsyst is an intelligent system that mines phylogenetic classifications. Its idea stems from the work of phylogeneticists of the Société Française de Systématique and proposes to test an innovative method for inferring phylogenetic classifications. The main idea in Phylsyst is to represent the reasoning of an expert phylogeneticist constructing a cladogram following Hennig principles. Several methods of artificial intelligence concur to Phylsyst's efficient implementation of a phylogeneticist expert reasoning, the main one being data mining. Although phylogenetic tree mining has been little addressed in the data mining community, we hypothesize that this community has much to contribute to the worldwide efforts worldwide to Assemble the Tree Of Life. Phylsyst is such an attempt, and has been successfully distributed worldwide as a digital supplement to a special issue of Biosystema journal.

1 Introduction

Phylsyst is an intelligent system that mines phylogenetic classifications. Its idea stems from the work of phylogeneticists of the Société Française de Systématique (SFS) [11] and proposes to test an innovative method for inferring phylogenetic classifications. Phylogenetic classifications are trees whose leaves are taxa – generally species – and whose nodes are hypothetical common ancestors. These trees are called cladograms. The order of the tree follows the evolution of species, in a way similar to genealogical trees, except that taxa are groups of organisms. Most methods currently applied to the construction of such classifications have been statistical, and based on the principle of parsimony [11]. Some SFS phylogeneticists have found interesting to develop a method to construct phylogenetic classifications that is not based on statistics, but on a knowledge-based type of approach described in this paper. The result of this attempt is the Phylsyst system. The main idea in this system is to represent the reasoning of an expert phylogeneticist constructing a cladogram following Hennig principles [4]. Several methods of artificial intelligence concur to Phylsyst's efficient implementation of a phylogeneticist expert reasoning, the main one being data mining. Although phy-

P. Perner (Ed.): ICDM 2004, LNAI 3275, pp. 163–172, 2004.

logenetic trees are indeed a very specific kind of knowledge to mine, little addressed in the data mining community, we hypothesize that this community has much to contribute to the ongoing efforts worldwide to Assemble the Tree Of Life (ATOL). Phylsyst is such an attempt, and has been judged successful enough to be distributed worldwide as a digital supplement to a special issue of Biosystema journal [2].

2   Phylogenetic Classification Problem

The goal of phylogenetic classification is to construct cladograms (see Fig.1) following Hennig principles. Cladograms are rooted phylogenetic trees, where the root is the hypothetical common ancestor of the taxa in the tree.

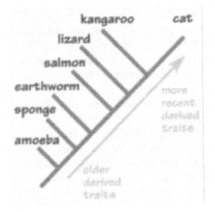

Fig. 1. A phylogenetic tree or cladogram

2.1   Taxon Matrix

The starting point of phylogenetic classification is a matrix describing taxa [13]. Taxa are groups of organisms such as classes, orders, families, genres, and species. A taxon is described as a list of character values, for instance ('1', '0', '1', '2', '1', '2', '0') are the values associated with seven different characters. A set of taxa is thus represented as a matrix, where columns are characters, and rows are corresponding values of these characters.

2.2   Character Value Types

The types of character values constrain the allowable evolutionary transitions because they represent evolutionary steps. There are mainly three types of values [13]:

Unordered Values carry no evolutionary information. For example, value '1' can precede or follow value '0' in evolution, and the same is true for the other values. Any switch between these values counts as one evolutionary step.

Undirected Ordered Values carry evolutionary information about the number of steps between them. This number is the absolute difference between two values, and is independent of the order. For instance, from '2' to '0', there are two evolutionary steps, and from '0' to '2' also.

Directed Ordered Values also carry evolutionary information about the number of steps between them, but in addition constrain the evolution order. Numerical order of the values follows the order of evolution: from '0' to '1' and to '2. Here also the number of evolutionary steps is the difference between two values.

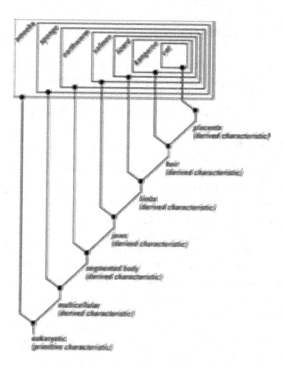

Fig. 2. Synapomorphic characters role in monophyletic groups

2.3 Hennig Principles

Cladistic analysis refers to the principles enunciated by Hennig [4]. There are four principles:

First Principle. Characters have states called plesiomorphic and apomorphic. A character is in plesiomorphic state if it is close to the initial state, for instance '0' would be a plesiomorphic state for directed ordered values. A character is in apomorphic state if it is far from the initial state. Synonyms for plesiomorphic are: primitive, ancestral. Synonyms for apomorphic are: modified, derived, and evolved.

Second Principle. A group is monophyletic if its taxa share apomorphies. These traits are synapomorphic. Monophyletic refers to a group that is descended from a single common ancestor (see Fig. 2). The sharing of plesiomorphic characters, called synplesiomorphic traits, defines a common ancestor more distant than synapomorphic ones, and thus this ancestor will not be exclusive.

Third Principle. The more a group shares synapomorphies, the more likely it is to be monophyletic.

Fourth Principle. The assumption by default is that each modified character shared by the members of a group has appeared only once in this group.

3 Methods in Phyloinformatics

Methods in phyloinformatics aim at constructing phylogenetic classifications based on Hennig principles. There have been many attempts at constructing computerized solutions to solve the phylogenetic classification problem. The most widely spread methods are parsimony-based [3]. Another important method is compatibility.

3.1 Parsimony Method

The parsimony method attempts to minimize the number of character state changes among the taxa (the simplest evolutionary hypothesis) [6, 12]. The system PAUP [12], for Phylogenetic Analysis Using Parsimony, is classically used by phylogeneticists to induce classifications. It implements a numerical parsimony to calculate the tree that totals the least number of evolutionary steps. [12] defines parsimony as the minimization of homoplasies. Homoplasies are evolutionary mistakes. Examples are parallelism - apparition of the same derived character independently between two groups -, convergence - state obtained by the independent transformation of two characters -, or reversion - evolution of one character from a more derived state to a more primitive one -. Homoplasy is most commonly due to multiple independent origins of indistinguishable evolutionary novelties. Following this general methodic goal of minimizing the number of homoplasies defined as parsimony, a family of mathematical and statistical methods has emerged over time, such as:

FITCH Method. For unordered characters.

WAGNER Method. For ordered undirected characters.

CAMIN-SOKAL Mmethod. For ordered undirected characters, it prevents reversion, but allows convergence and parallelism.

DOLLO Method. For ordered directed characters, it prevents convergence and parallelism, but not reversion.

POLYMORPHIC Method. In chromosome inversion, it allows hypothetical ancestors to have polymorphic characters, which means that they can have several values.

	C0	C1	C2	C3	C4	C5	C6	C7	C8	C9	C10	C11
T1	1	0	0	0	1	0	1	1	0	0	0	0
T2	1	0	0	0	1	1	1	0	1	0	0	0
T3	1	1	1	1	0	1	1	0	0	1	0	0
T4	1	1	1	1	0	0	0	0	0	0	1	0
T5	1	0	0	1	0	0	0	0	0	0	0	1

Fig. 3. Sample taxon matrix

All these methods are simplifications of Hennig principles, but have the advantage to lead to computationally tractable and efficient programs. The simplifications they are based on are that parsimony is equivalent to Hennig principles, and that numeric parsimony perfectly handles the complexity of parsimony.

3.2 Compatibility Method

Compatibility methods [7, 8] aim at maximizing the number of characters mutually compatible on a cladogram. Compatible characters are ones that present no homoplasy, neither reversion, nor parallelism, nor convergence. The phylogenetic classification problem is solved here by the method of finding the largest clique of compatible characters, a clique being a set of characters presenting no homoplasy. These methods present the same advantages, and the same disadvantages, as the parsimony methods. First, their goal is similar to parsimony, since maximizing the number of characters not presenting homoplasy, is a problem equivalent to minimizing homoplasies. Following, these methods are also a simplification of Hennig principles, they are also numeric methods, but they lead to computationally tractable and efficient

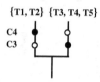

Fig. 4. Two monophyletic groups from two exclusive synapomorphies. A plain circle represents an apomorphic character (value '1'), an empty circle represents a plesiomorphic character (value '0')

4 Knowledge-Based Classification Method

[11] proposed a different method to build phylogenetic classifications, called PANUP. Phylogenetic Analysis Not Using Parsimony – PANUP – has for goal to mine taxon matrices for phylogenetic classifications based more closely on Hennig's principle. [11] transformed Hennig principles into a method for finding a network of synapomorphies as a basis to organize the taxa in monophyletic sub-trees. His method aims at systematizing the actual Hennig principles, and not some consequences of it like such methods as parsimony, maximum-likelihood, and compatibility.

This phylogeny expert also described an algorithm to build PANUP cladogram. He was capable of applying his principles to small matrices. Nevertheless, computerized methods had to model his solution to implement it into an efficient intelligent software capable of reproducing his reasoning process on a large scale – Phylsyst.

Phylsyst mines matrices of character values that are binary and directed ordered: '0' means plesiomorphic, and '1' means apomorphic. The original example for PANUP [11] is taken here (see Fig. 3). Phylsyst reasoning process is the following:

Find Reciprocal Synapomorphies. Reciprocal synapomorphies are those that are exclusive synapomorphies in a branch, and not present in a neighboring branch. One way of representing this is to search for so called doublons. A doublon is a pair of configurations of two characters. In Fig.3 for example, characters C0/C1 form the doublon {10, 01} because all taxa have either values C0=1 and C1=0, or C0=0 and C1=1. A reciprocal synapomorphy is a doublon {01, 10}, with an exclusive synapomorphy in each of the two branches for these characters. In the example given, C3 and C4 form this {10, 01} doublon, and thus an exclusive synapomorphy. And this is the only such doublon in this matrix. Thus, it constitutes two monophyletic groups: {T1, T2} sharing exclusive synapomorphy C4, and {T3, T4, T5} sharing exclusive synapomorphy C3 (see Fig. 4).

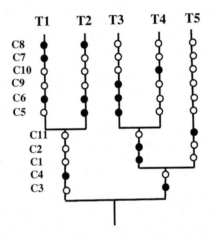

Fig. 5. Two monophyletic groups from two exclusive synapomorphies. Character representations follow the rules stated in Fig. 4

Taxon	1234567890123456789012345678901123
Berbera	01001101100001100001010101010010000
Mahona	01001001100001100001010101010010000
Ranzania	11001011110111000010111110010001
Caulophyl	11001011110111100110001000001011
Leontice	10011011110111100110000000001011
Gymnosp.	10011011110111100110000000001011
Bongardia	10110011100011110011000100000101101
Podophyl.	11001110100110011110111110011101
Dysosima	11001110100111010111011111001101
Diphylleia	11001110100111010001101110111011101
Achlys	11110011100011011010101101010001101
Epidem.	11010001110011100111110010101101
Vancouv.	11110001110111100101110010101101
Jefferson.	11110011000010110011111100100001101
Ptagiorheg	11110111000010110011111100100001101

Fig. 6. Input taxon/character matrix for Berberidac. '0' means plesiomorphic state, and '1' means apomorphic

The search for reciprocal synapomorphies goes on in the sub matrices obtained by removing characters C3 and C4, and can lead to straight forward partitioning as long as doublons are found.

Find Triplons That Do Not Lead to Parallelism. When no favorable doublon is available, PANUP proposes heuristics used by systematicians. For example, to choose triplons {00, 01, 10} or {00, 11, 10} over triplons {00, 11, 01} or {11, 01, 10} because these last two lead to parallelisms. Quadruplons all lead to more parallelism than triplons, and thus are chosen last. Fig. 5 shows the cladogram built following these principles.

5 The Phylsyst System

Phylsyst is an intelligent system modeling the expert systematicians reasoning to build phylogenetic classifications. It mines character matrices by reproducing how human phylogeneticists reason, representing their knowledge. Only when the mining process leads to several plausible trees does it use a scoring function to determine the best tree. This scoring function is an evaluation of how well the competing trees fit Hennig original principles. The algorithm proceeds through several steps:

1. **Search for {01, 10} Doublons.** This search is interpreted as searching for reciprocal synapomorphies. This step is reiterated on each sub-matrix corresponding respectively to taxa sharing 01, and to taxa sharing 10.
2. **Search for {00, 11} Doublons.** This doublon has the advantage of representing several evolved characters exclusively shared by one branch of the tree. Step 1 is then reiterated on each sub-matrix corresponding respectively to taxa sharing 00, and to taxa sharing 11.
3. **Hypothesize a {01, 10} Doublon.** In the case where it is possible to find a {01, 10} doublon by modifying less than a certain percentage of characters – for instance 25% - then hypothesize such a doublon and study the corresponding sub-matrices restarting the reasoning process in step1.
4. **Search for Triplons.** For each triplon {aa, bb, cc}, reiterate the reasoning process in step 1 for each sub-matrix corresponding to the taxa sharing aa, and bb, and cc.
5. **Search for Quadruplons.** For each quadruplon {aa, bb, cc, dd}, reiterate the reasoning process in step 1 for each sub-matrix corresponding to the taxa sharing aa, and bb, and cc, and dd.
6. **Evaluation of the Best Cladogram.** In particular in the case where a doublon is hypothesized, this process builds a family of possible cladograms. Three different scoring functions can be chosen by the user:
   a. Maximize the number of {01, 10} doublons.
   b. Maximize the number of synapomorphies closer to the root by minimizing score2:

$$score2 = \sum_{i=1}^{n}100*2^{-t_i} + \sum_{j=1}^{m}200*2^{-t_j} + \sum_{k=1}^{p}10$$

where t_i and t_j are the number of taxa in each doublon configuration, n represents the number of {01, 10} doublons, m represents the number of {00, 11} doublons, and p represents the number of hypothesized doublons

c. Maximize the branching nodes splitting the tree on large number of taxa:

$$score\ 3 = \sum_{i=1}^{n} 100 * (2^{-t_i} + 2^{-c_i}) + \sum_{j=1}^{m} 200 * (2^{-t_j} + 2^{-c_j}) + \sum_{k=1}^{p} 10$$

where t_i and t_j are the number of taxa in each doublon configuration, and c_i and c_j the number of characters for each doublon configuration.

An extract of a cladogram built by Phylsyst is provided in Fig. 7. It shows the doublons found, those hypothesized, the triplons or quadruplons found, and the taxa classified at different levels. It corresponds to the input matrix for Berberidac. family [8] on Fig. 6. The evaluation scores and some explanations are also provided.

```
clado1
    Level 1 01-10 Doublon split on characters: 8 12 27
    Level 1 values: 8(0) 12(1) 27(1)
        Level 2 01-10 Doublon split on characters: 18 29 25
        Level 2 values: 18(0) 29(1) 25(1)
        Taxon Diphylleia
        Level 2 values: 18(1) 29(0) 25(1)
            Level 3 01-10 Doublon split on characters: 14 17
            Level 3 values: 14(0) 17(1)
            Taxon: Dysosma
    Level 1 values: 8(1) 12(0) 27(0)
        Level 2 01-10 Doublon split on characters: 16 29 30 19
        Level 2 values: 16(0) 29(1) 30(0) 19(0)
            Level 3 00-11 Doublon split on characters: 1 7 33 25 23 13 11
            Level 3 values: 1(0) 7(0) 33(0) 25(0) 23(0) 13(0) 11(0) 10(0)
                Level 4 Agglom. Split
                Taxon: Berberis
                Taxon: Mahonia
            Level 3 values: 1(1) 7(1) 33(1) 25(1) 23(1) 13(1) 11(1) 10(1)
            Taxon: Ranzania
```

Fig. 7. Extract of a cladogram built by Phylsyst for Berberidac

In addition to the knowledge-based type of classification reasoning used for mining phylogenetic trees, Phylsyst combines several other methods of artificial intelligence:
Case-Based Reasoning is used in the system to store previously processed sub-trees. During the search process, it often happens that the system finds a sub-matrix identical or similar up to the percentage ratio accepted for doublon hypothesis to a matrix previously solved. The system stores the sub-matrices and corresponding sub-trees in its internal memory for future reuse. It uses case-based reasoning as a heuristic to speed up its classification process.
Conceptual Clustering is another method that is used in the system. When there is no doublon, nor acceptable hypothesized doublon, nor triplon, nor quadruplon, the system uses a classical similarity-based conceptual clustering algorithm to build its tree.

The algorithm clusters together taxa having maximum characters in common, and being as different as possible from other groups of taxa [1].

6 Discussion

The classification method and algorithms used to mine phylogenetic classifications in Phylsyst are original and resort to several artificial intelligence methods [10]. This system is an example of intelligent classification [1, 9] in the sense that it reproduces an expert's method for building classifications by hand. By representing algorithmically how the expert reasons, it can scale up the human method to large datasets.

In comparison with other phyloinformatics systems, PhylSyst is innovative because it tries to represent as closely as possible Hennig principles, closer than numeric methods. Numeric methods [3] assume that expert reasoning can be represented by numbers, often tend to loose capability for explanation, and puzzle the human user [11]. The contact with the actual biological domain is lost. On the contrary, Phylsyst attempts to reason as a human phylogeneticist.

The knowledge-based type of classification reasoning used for mining phylogenetic trees is related to data mining methods for decision tree induction, and for conceptual clustering. The difference with decision tree induction is that branching nodes can carry several characters, and that the branches do not represent the different values of these characters, but represent an evolutionary step, and thus a temporal dimension. The comparison with conceptual clustering is that the choice of the characters identifying a concept is based on a representation of expert phylogeneticists, thus the name of knowledge-based phylogenetic tree mining. Moreover, branches do not represent the traditional generalization relationship, but the relationship "is more evolved than". Few systems in data mining have studied tree mining for complex semantic relationships, but the wide dissemination of ontologies will foster tree mining for complex relationships. Phylsyst combines several other methods of artificial intelligence: *case-based reasoning* is used in the system to store and reuse previously processed subtrees. Classical *conceptual clustering* is used in the system when there is no doublon, nor acceptable hypothesized doublon, nor triplon, nor quadruplon. The algorithm clusters together taxa having maximum characters in common, and being as different as possible from other groups of taxa. It is a similarity-based conceptual clustering algorithm.

7 Conclusion

Phylsyst, although having been distributed and used worldwide for several years, is only a first version of a new generation of phyloinformatics systems [5, 14, 7]. Among the improvements planned, are a graphical tree representation and navigation, the extension of character values beyond binary states, and the explanation of the cladograms built, beyond the current level. Other planned developments are to expand the method to datasets combining genetic and morphologic characters. Finally, the ultimate goals are to represent more expert phylogeneticists' reasoning, in particular from Hennig, and to scale up the system to very large datasets.

References

1. Barthelemy, J.-P., Guenoche, A.: Les Arbres et les Représentations des Proximités. Masson, Paris (1988)
2. Bichindaritz I., Potter S.: PhylSyst: un Système d'Intelligence Artificielle pour l'Analyse Cladistique. Biosystema. 12 (1994) 17-55
3. Felsenstein, J.: The Troubled Growth of Statistical Phylogenetics. Systematic-Biology. 50(4) (2001) 465-467
4. Hennig, W.: Phylogenetic Systematics. University of Illinois Press, Urbana Chicago London (1966)
5. Lebbe, Vignes, J.R.: Modelling Taxonomic Description for Identification. In: Bridges, P., Jeffries, P., Morse, D.R., Scott, P.R. (eds.): Information Technology, Plant Pathology and Biodiversity. (1998) 37-46
6. Maddison, W.P., Maddison, D.R.: MacClade: Analysis of Phylogeny and Character Evolution. Version 3.0. Sinauer Associates, Sunderland Massachusetts (1992)
7. Martins, E.P., Diniz-Filho, J.A., Housworth, E.A.: Adaptation and the Comparative Method: A Computer Simulation Study. Evolution. 56 (2002) 1-13
8. Meacham, C.A.: A Manual Method for Character Compatibility Analysis. Taxon. 30(3) (1981) 591-600
9. Porter, B.W., Bareiss, R., Holte, R.C.: Concept Learning and Heuristic Classification in Weak-Theory Domains. Artificial Intelligence. 45 (1990) 229-263
10. Shapiro, S.C.: Encyclopedia of Artificial Intelligence. Wiley Interscience (1992)
11. Sigwalt, B.: Une Nouvelle Méthode d'Analyse Cladistique, PANUP: Phylogenetic Analysis Not Using Parcimony. Biosystema. 12 (1994) 5-16
12. Swofford, D.L.: PAUP: Phylogenetic Analysis Using Parcimony. Version 4. Sinauer Associates Inc. (2002)
13. d'Udekem-Gevers, M.: L'Analyse Cladistique. Problème et Solutions Heuristiques Informatisées. Biosystema. 4 (1990)
14. Vignes, R.: Caractérisation Automatique de Groupes Biologiques. Ph.D. Thesis, Université Paris VI, Paris (1991)

Author Index

Aiken, Jim 33
Ayuso, Mercedes 78

Bichindaritz, Isabelle 163
Black, Norman 153
Bobrowski, Leon 23
Borrajo, M. Lourdes 1
Bühring, Angela 60

Chen, An-Pin 117
Chen, Yen-Chu 117
Clérot, Fabrice 144
Corchado, Emilio S. 33, 42
Corchado, Juan M. 1, 33, 42

Deng, Da 50
de Systématique,Société Française 163
Dousson, Christophe 144

Fessant, Françoise 144
Frederix, Greet 96

Gheel, Dirk Van 78
Grabert, Matthias 88
Guillén, Montserrat 78
Günther, Winfried 88

Hamano, Shinichi 106
Harper, Roy 153
Hrycej, Tomas 88
Huang, Chiung-Fen 117
Huang, Yue 153

Jänichen, Silke 60

Kantardzic, Mehmed 134
Kenett, Ron 11
Kumar, Anup 134
Kuznetsov, Sergey 127

Lara, Ana 42

McCullagh, Paul 153

Pauwels, Eric J. 96
Pellicer, María A. 1
Perner, Horst 60
Perner, Petra 60
Potter, Stephen 163
Prechtel, Markus 88

Raphaeli, Orit 11
Rashad, Sherif 134

Sáiz, Lourdes 42
Sato, Masako 106
Scherbina, Andrei 127
Schmid, Joachim 69

Topczewska, Magdalena 23

Viaene, Stijn 78

Yáñez, J. Carlos 1

Zahavi, Jacob 11